PIRATE IMPERIALISM

PIRATE IMPERIALISM

Trade, Abolition, and Global Suppression of Maritime Raiding, 1825–1870

MANUEL BARCIA

Yale
UNIVERSITY PRESS
New Haven and London

Published with assistance from the foundation established
in memory of Philip Hamilton McMillan of the Class
of 1894, Yale College.

Yale University Press books may be purchased in quantity for educational, business, or promotional use. For information, please e-mail sales.press@yale.edu (U.S. office) or sales@yaleup.co.uk (U.K. office).

Set in Janson type by IDS Infotech, Ltd.
Printed in the United States of America.

Library of Congress Control Number: 2025936720
ISBN 978-0-300-26945-1 (hardcover)

A catalogue record for this book is available from the British Library.

Authorized Representative in the EU: Easy Access System Europe, Mustamäe tee 50, 10621 Tallinn, Estonia, gpsr.requests@easproject.com

10 9 8 7 6 5 4 3 2 1

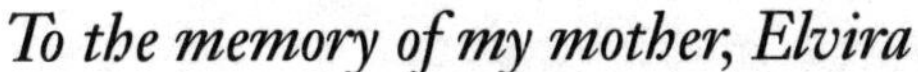

To the memory of my mother, Elvira

Pile on the brown man's burden,
   compel him to be free;
Let all your manifestoes
   Reek with philanthropy.
And if with heathen folly
   He dares your will dispute,
Then, in the name of freedom,
   Don't hesitate to shoot.

—HENRY LABOUCHÈRE, "The Brown Man's Burden," February 1899

Contents

Acknowledgments

THEY SAY IT TAKES A VILLAGE, and if that's true, this book owes its existence to the most brilliant and generous village anyone could wish for. Because of the breadth and scope of its content, it was only thanks to the kindness of an extraordinary circle of people, some of whom I had never met, that I was able to complete it. Each of them has left an indelible mark on its pages.

First of all, I would like to mention the many colleagues whose wisdom lit my path. Many of them took time to read parts of the book and commented extensively on its contents, while others shared their insights into themes and regions that were relatively new to me. Especial thanks to Rosanne Adderley, Gregorio Alonso, Richard Anderson, Nir Arielli, María del Carmen Barcia, Sanjoy Battacharya, Lloyd Belton, Fahad Bishara, David Blight, Richard Drayton, Bethan Fisk, Kristie Flannery, Bianca Gerlich, John Harris, David Head, Ananya Kabir, Valeria Mantilla, Jennifer Nelson, Marcus Rediker, Martin Rodrigo, Lou Roper, Jesús Sanjurjo, Randy Sparks, Danielle Terrazas Williams, Andrew Thompson, David Todd, Anita van Dissel, Kim Wagner, James Warren, and David Wilson. They all, in one way or another, reminded me that the best questions often lead to the longest journeys—thank you for urging me to take the scenic route.

I would not have been able to visit the archives that housed some of the documents used here had it not been for the Philip Leverhulme Prize I was awarded in 2014. The support of the Leverhulme Trust, even before this career-defining moment, was always there. My immense appreciation to them for having my back throughout the years. Colleagues, whom I now call friends, at the Gilder Lehrman Center for the Study of Slavery, Resistance, and Abolition at Yale University, were instrumental in the early stages of this book. I was a visiting fellow there as I was starting to develop the ideas presented here, and I gave my first ever talk on the topic at the center's headquarters on Prospect Street in New Haven.

I owe a debt of gratitude to my friends, who stuck with me through thick and thin (and through far too many unsolicited monologues), as I rambled on about obscure historical characters and events over far too many cups of espresso. Among those who endured these conversations over the years, I should not forget mentioning Amanda Bassra, Emily Berquist, David Brathwaite, Finn Brennan, Vincent Brown, Simone Buitendijk, Vanja Celebicic, Matt Childs, Emma Christopher, Ada Ferrer, Rocío Davis, Leida Fernandez, Frank Finlay, Dorothea Fischer-Hornung, Helen Foster, Bruna Freitas-Aïech, Henry Louis Gates Jr., Jeff Grabill, Katrina Keefer, Tilly Kirk, Marial Iglesias, David Lambert, Jennifer Lofkrantz, Addi Manolopolou, Claire Mulholland, Diana Paton, Aymée Robaina, Jasjit Singh, Annie Sun, Thomas Thurston, William Van Norman Jr., Eline van Ommen, Claudia Varella, Julia Wang, Michelle Zacks, Michael Zeuske, and everyone who commented on my Facebook and BlueSky posts about this book.

When the restrictions of COVID-19 were placed on archives and libraries worldwide, I was lucky to get the assistance of a number of collaborators in faraway places. Some, like Arda Akıncı and Turac Hakalmaz, facilitated access to repositories, and others, like Joanna Allan and Martin Seeger, found and copied documents that I could not have accessed otherwise. Especial thanks here to Fitria Sis Nariwari, Brendan Yeo Shun Yeo, Loong Dien Min, and Crispin Bates for working miracles to reproduce documents in Southeast Asia during the worst days of the pandemic. My colleagues at the School of History at the University of Leeds helped me troubleshoot everything, from copyright payments to travel advice. Particular thanks to Joanna Phillips, Meghan Innes, Lisa Grant, and Olivia Barnes for always taking the time to help and for sharing their chocolate bars.

When I began my research, I had no idea of how to create a useful map. By the time I finished, I was skilled enough to create each of the ones included in this book. I cannot thank Bruno Marshall Shirley enough for tweeting a thread on why and how historians should take advantage of free online tools online to create their own maps. Not only was he kind enough to share his knowledge, but every time I got stuck—and there were many—he was at hand to answer my many questions.

This book has not been my first rodeo with my editor at Yale University Press, Adina Popescu. She has never failed to impress me with her insights, compassion, and endless ways to offer encouragement at every turn, especially when these turns have been tricky to navigate. As I say thanks here, I am hoping there will be rodeos to come in the future. Thanks also to Eva Skewes, with whom I have got to work again, and to Eliza Childs and Erica Hanson for seeing the book through its final stages.

My golden retriever, Ahsoka, has been a constant companion since she came into our lives at the end of 2021. Our daily walks in the forest have been more than just breaks—they have been moments of clarity, inspiration, and peace, as she often reminds me to pause, breathe, and find joy in the simplest things. My son Kenny, who is just starting high school, has taught me the value of questions and the importance of pursuing their answers, even when the road seems endless. His humor and wisdom have constantly reminded me to keep my feet on the ground. My wife, Effie Kesidou, my true north, has been at my side for the late-night epiphanies, the early morning doubts, and the rollercoaster rides in between. This book is as much yours as it is mine.

As I was finalizing this manuscript for submission, I experienced the profound loss of my mother. I was fortunate to have her presence and love for fifty-two years. As I reflect on those she left behind—my father, sister, and nephews—it feels only right to dedicate this book to her memory. Adiós mami, fuiste la mejor madre que podría haber deseado.

Introduction

I spread the whole earth out as a map before me.
On no one spot of its surface could I put my finger and say,
here is safety.

—MARY SHELLEY, *The Last Man*

ON THE MORNING OF OCTOBER 26, 1840, Malay prince Tunku Mohamed Saad walked into a courtroom in the British colony of Penang to face accusations of piracy. Saad and his crew had been captured by British gunships in early July near the Langkawi Islands, from where they had been attacking British, Malay, and Siamese ships for almost two years. After a week of hearings, Saad and his crew were found not guilty, as the jurors and judge deemed their reasons for such attacks to be lawful. Given that they had been fighting against the Siamese occupation of Kedah, which had been legitimized and supported by the British through the unpopular Anglo-Siamese Treaty of 1826, accusations of piracy against them had to be dismissed, to the dismay of their main instigator, George Bonham, governor of the Straits Settlements.[1]

In 1838, Saad, alongside Tunku Mohamed Saib, another prince and nephew of the deposed sultan of Kedah, had led a successful attack on the Siamese garrisons at Kuala Kedah and Alor Setar, retaking the entire country and holding it for a few months, until a large Siamese force, commanded by Chao Phraya Nakhon Noi and Phraya Aphaithibet and supported by a British blockade by sea, forced them to run away and resort to what the British prosecutor referred to as actions that "were not in the nature of open warfare but of Piracy."[2] Once Saad's trial concluded with a non-guilty verdict, his crew and supporters were freed but he was not. Saad was remanded in custody following the direct intervention of Governor Bonham, and subsequently he was exiled to Calcutta and Allahabad, where he spent most of his remaining years. He returned to Penang for only a brief period shortly before his death in 1845.[3]

Saad's actions and the criminal case against him are illustrative of the main issues that I will discuss in this book. They highlight the many ways the suppression of "piracy" in the nineteenth century served as a proxy for formal and informal imperialist efforts by a number of Western and non-Western powers of the time. They also help to bring attention to how supposed efforts to "civilize" non-Western peoples, to abolish slave-trading practices, and to protect commercial interests were habitually used as pretexts to bolster imperial incursions in various parts of the world. Lastly, Saad's case also helps to shed light on the ways the suppression of "piracy" impacted inter-imperial relations, occasionally leading to alliances and other times contributing to conflict.

During the week-long trial, Saad and his crew were charged with multiple offenses. For example, they were accused of attacking Kedah, in violation of the 1826 Anglo-Siamese treaty; of damaging trade in the region by ransacking British, Malay, and Siamese vessels; of engaging in kidnapping and enslaving activities; and generally of being "felonious pirates."[4] Shortly after the trial concluded, Governor Bonham lamented that Saad had been absolved of all his crimes just because he had declared himself to be what we would call today a freedom fighter. To the jury, it was clear that Saad had been driven to retaliate against the Siamese who had occupied his country and enslaved his people, and against the British who had sacrificed Kedah to placate the Siamese and to consolidate their recent colonial territorial gains in Burma and Patani.[5]

During the trial, Saad's cause was deemed lawful, a circumstance that left the British authorities in the Straits Settlements and Calcutta scrambling to justify not only his ongoing detention and forced exile, but also their involvement in the prior surrender of Kedah to the Siamese Empire. Additionally, Bonham and his superiors in Calcutta had to grapple with the backlash associated with their continued and unpopular support for Siamese troops, who were frequently accused of engaging in brutal actions and of participating in extensive overland slave-trading activities involving Malay and Burmese populations. To the inhabitants of Penang and Singapore, Saad and his amphibious community of followers had turned to maritime raiding only after being forced out of their homes by the Siamese and being let down by their supposed allies, the British.

I use the term "amphibious" to refer to communities located near oceans, seas, and rivers—by bodies of water that imperialist agents, ships, and troops found easier to reach. The concept of "amphibious cultures," coined by scholar Orlando Fals Borda in his discussion of communities settled along the river Magdalena in Colombia, can be straightforwardly applied to the human populations that inhabited the regions discussed in the pages of this book.[6] These amphibious communities, which relied on hunting and fishing, and to a lesser extent on agriculture and maritime predatory activities, stood in the way of Western and non-Western imperialist endeavors during the period studied here. As such, they were subjected to invasions, raids, kidnappings, and even massacres under the guise of suppressing their real or imagined predatory activities.

The double-sided dimension of "piracy" suppression efforts at the time can be seen in elements of Saad's story that were repeated across the world during this time. In this book I tell a transnational, global story, not confined to one empire or region. It is also a story that offers plenty of documentary evidence to reveal the many ways in which what Lauren Benton has called a "new global regime of armed peace," marked by "widespread, chronic violence," unfolded across the world in the middle decades of the nineteenth century.[7] The acts commonly labeled as "piracy," which are referred to as maritime raiding within this book, posed a recurrent nuisance that hindered or delayed Western expansionism and the consolidation of empires during the nineteenth century. The vast reach of the British Empire positions it as a central figure in this narrative, but the British were not alone in their endeavors to assert control over amphibious peoples. These communities often found themselves with no other remedy but to resist and, on occasion, to resort to maritime raiding—encompassing activities such as kidnapping and slave trading—in order to adapt to the emerging sociopolitical conditions imposed upon them by men who had come from faraway lands.

The French, the Portuguese, the Dutch, the Spanish, and the Americans were equally involved in imperial endeavors, as were such non-Western powers as the Ottoman, the Siamese, the Russian, and the Chinese. Maritime raiding in the Atlantic, which was intrinsically connected with slave-trading activities, provides a peculiar case for comparison, as most of those involved in maritime raiding activities during this period were white westerners, whose treatment by these same imperial powers was frequently much more lenient, in spite of the singular violence associated with their human trafficking and piratical activities.

The global history of the suppression of maritime raiding carried out by Western and non-Western states, roughly between the mid-1820s and the late 1860s, is at the center of this book. My discussions focus on five wide, often interlinked, regions of the world, namely, the Atlantic basin, the Mediterranean Sea, the Persian Gulf, Southeast Asia, and the South China Sea. Ultimately, building on primary and secondary sources overwhelmingly produced by Western and non-Western states, I contend that suppression activities provided these empires a backdoor for territorial expansionism. Equally, they allowed them to enforce their own trading policies, not just regionally but globally, while simultaneously justifying their efforts under the banners of spreading civilization and abolishing slavery and slave trade.

Moreover, during this period maritime raiding became a critical flashpoint for both conflict and cooperation between Western and non-Western empires, as its rise and proliferation posed a threat to the ambitions of individual states. In more than one way, these suppression activities were often supported by cloudy arguments based on the Law of Nations, and by a distorted a priori understanding of

Western rights over non-Western peoples, what Peter Earle has referred to as "piratical imperialism."[8] In this book, essentially for simplifying reasons, I have chosen instead to use the phrase "pirate imperialism" in my discussion of Western and non-Western imperial suppression actions carried out against amphibious communities worldwide in the middle decades of the nineteenth century—actions that often resorted to the same type of piratical violence they accused amphibious peoples of. In doing so, I offer a reflexive, critical approach that acknowledges and dissects the power dynamics inherent to the global expansion of pirate imperialism.[9]

It is worth also noting here that in this book I deliberately avoid offering the argument that there were "very fine people on both sides." Rather, it is a story of imperialist overpowering and overkilling, which, following the lead of Richard Drayton, purposedly avoids downplaying the role played by coercion and violence.[10] It does so while also acknowledging that although there were multiple acts of intense violence carried out by those who were targeted by pirate imperialism, their actions were by no means comparable in magnitude, frequency, or impact to those carried out by pirate empires.

Maritime raiding, or piracy, has been a well-known and much-recorded phenomenon since ancient times. Already in the fourteenth century BCE, piratical actions were reported in the Aegean Sea, and over the next few hundred years such predatory activities seem to have only increased, not only in Europe but also in the Indian Ocean and in the seas of China.[11] More to the point, existing links between the abduction and enslavement of peoples and maritime raiding in the ancient Mediterranean world began a trend that continued for millennia. Up until the late fifteenth century, when the Europeans began their conquest and colonization of the Americas, maritime raiding and enslaving were widely recorded, often linked to each other, throughout the world in an ever-expansive way.[12]

With the arrival of the Age of European Exploration, previously disconnected regions of the world slowly but steadily began interacting more with each other. The extraction of natural resources like gold and silver, undertaken by the Spanish on their conquered

American lands, gave rise to a new kind of Atlantic buccaneer. Spanish ships and cities, especially those located in the Caribbean Sea, became the target of these daring raiders. For example, in 1554, French pirate François Le Clerk, better known in Hispanic America at the time as "Pata de Palo" or "Pegleg," attacked and occupied Santiago de Cuba. Only a few months later, in 1555, his compatriot Jacques de Sores ransacked Havana, burning to the ground the emergent city's most important buildings. The frequency of these attacks led the Spanish crown to establish annual transatlantic convoys to carry the gold and silver mined in their American possessions to Spain. This system, which came to be known as the Spanish Treasure Fleet, lasted until well into the late eighteenth century.[13]

In the sixteenth century maritime raiding also developed in other parts of the planet, and a number of famous pirates and their exploits were recorded throughout the world. In the Mediterranean, the names of Ottoman pirates Salah Reis and Uluj Ali, among others, were well known.[14] Turgut Reis, another Ottoman sea raider, became even more notorious after attacking the island of Gozo and enslaving its entire population in 1551.[15] In the Far East, Wang Zhi, the Xu brothers, and a multinational cast of pirates known as the Wokou terrorized the Chinese seaboard in the middle part of the century, notably leading to the legendary Jiajing Wokou raids, which caused extensive damage to Chinese coastal cities and towns.[16]

In the annals of maritime raiding, however, perhaps no other time and place has become so well known as the Atlantic world during the so-called Golden Age of Piracy, encompassing roughly the decades between the 1650s and the 1730s. Countless books, articles, and films have, over the years, made the public familiar with these Atlantic buccaneers and their adventures. Some of the best-known pirates of all times, including Henry Morgan, Anne Bonny, François l'Olonnais, Nicholas de la Concepción, Mary Read, and Edward Teach, better known as Blackbeard, gave this period a historical flair that has never been attained elsewhere before or after.[17] The flurry of studies on the Golden Age of Piracy has led to a popular image of pirates that is deeply associated with this period and region. Not surprisingly, the most famous pirates in the history of literature and film, including the likes of Captain Hook, the Black

Corsair, Captain Blood, and more recently, Jack Sparrow, are based on real buccaneers who lived during the Golden Age of Piracy.

Although many of these works have continued a tradition started in the nineteenth century or arguably even earlier, which presented pirates as romantic heroes, in more recent years groundbreaking scholarship has begun to examine all aspects of the lives and actions of these historical figures, shedding light on their role in the birth of modern capitalism.[18] Perhaps the most notable work in this vein is *The Many-Headed Hydra: Sailors, Slaves, Commoners, and the Hidden History of the Revolutionary Atlantic*, co-written by Peter Linebaugh and Marcus Rediker and published in 2000, in which the authors present pirates as a cast of outlaws who had the agency and the self-consciousness to challenge emerging capitalist structures of domination at sea.[19] Linebaugh and Rediker introduced the concept of "hydrarchy," in order to understand oceanic social struggles, both from above and from below.

Maritime raiding, however, did not disappear with the advent of the nineteenth century. As the Age of Revolutions unfolded, predatory activities at sea, often linked to the ongoing wars of independence taking place on both sides of the Atlantic, increased. Privateering in particular became a widespread phenomenon throughout the Atlantic world until the mid-1820s. Newly independent nations, along with their former colonial powers, continued the eighteenth-century practice of employing willing adventurers and seasoned slave traders to raid enemy cities and towns and capture their vessels.[20]

There is little doubt that privateers were frequently engaged in trafficking humans across the Atlantic. Some of the most notorious Atlantic pirates of the 1820s and early 1830s had been involved in privateering expeditions in previous years. In fact, their reputation preceded them wherever they went. In 1822, for example, an American merchant at St. Barts, Charles James Fitzmorris, complained profusely to his consul about the privateers that used the Caribbean island as a rendezvous point. In his words, they were "the worst of pirates" as, in the wake of the suppression activities by various navies in the region, they had begun attacking everyone, with little regards for previous alliances or ongoing wars.[21] Fitzmorris also accused many individuals living in St. Barts, "who, at different times,

[had] acted as the agents of privateers, both in the sale of merchandise and slaves."[22]

On the other side of the Atlantic, the situation was not dissimilar. American privateers made their way to African and European waters and, combined with Ottoman corsairs sailing from northern African ports, kept merchant ship captains in check. One example is the Russian ship *Helsingfors*, captured by a Tripolitan corsair in July 1829 off Cape St. Vincent, near the entrance of the Mediterranean Sea. The ship was plundered and sunk, and its captain, Salomon Sundman, and a number of the ship's sailors were abducted and taken to one of the Ottoman northern African provinces. The action led to a formal protest by the Russian chargé d'affaires before the Sublime Porte and to a demand from Sultan Mahmud II to issue imperial orders for the release of the captives.[23]

The early nineteenth century also saw a renaissance of maritime raiding in other parts of the world. A combination of factors, which included an economic stagnation that turned into "a full economic recession by the 1820s and 1830s," led to an increase in maritime raiding activities along the Chinese and Vietnamese coasts.[24] As Robert Antony has stressed, during this period "many areas of China witnessed the weakening of the traditional family system" with consequent "massive unemployment and underemployment, and the concomitant development of a huge floating population of itinerant wage laborers, porters, peddlers, and vagabonds."[25] Not surprisingly, then, sea raiders like Zheng Yi Sao and the Guangdong Pirate Confederation became prominent players in the region during the early years of the century.[26]

Something similar happened in the so-called Eastern Archipelago. Historians Nicholas Tarling, James F. Warren, J. L. Anderson, Joseph N. F. M. à Campo, and, more recently, Stefan Eklöf Amirell, Sandy J. C. Liu, Kristie Flannery, and Simon Layton, among others, have pointed out how Southeast Asia became a hotbed for raiding activities from the late eighteenth century onward.[27] In Sugata Bose's words, when European intrusion into the Indian Ocean increased, "piracy acquired a new connotation as a category of subversive Asian activity," leading to more instances of confrontation.[28] In particular, the seasonal incursions of Taosūg-sponsored raiders sailing from the Sulu Sea augmented when the needs for enslaved labor became more pressing, as Southeast Asian peoples struggled to supply Chinese and European needs for exotic products, such as birds' nests, trepang, and pearls.[29] These seasonal raids, as Kristie Flannery has recently shown, intensified in the eighteenth century, capitalizing on favorable winds associated with the monsoon cycles. Europeans operating in the region began referring to these winds as the Pirate Wind.[30]

Westward, in the Persian Gulf, in what it was perhaps the first European systematized campaign against non-white commerce disruptors at the time, naval operations along the coast of the Arabian Peninsula between Khasab and Bahrain cemented British supremacy in the region. This campaign constitutes an early case study for gunboat diplomacy deployment in order to protect European trade, one that would be replicated elsewhere in years to come. The heavy bombardment of Sharjah and Ras Al-Khaimah in 1809, and of Ras Al-Khaimah a second time in 1819, led to the signing of the General Treaty of Peace of 1820, that turned the so-called Pirate Coast into the "Trucial Coast."[31]

Pirate-related toponyms were in fact part and parcel of the descriptions often used by westerners to reassert their claims to exotic and distant places. The Pirate Coast in the Persian Gulf was but one case among many others. For instance, there was a Pirate Beach in Galveston, Texas; a Pirate Bay in Tasmania; Pirate Islands in various corners of the world, including the Philippines, the Cochin China (Vietnam), and off the coast of Cameroon; and of course the previously mentioned Pirate Wind in Southeast Asia. As Simon Layton has pointed out, the development of such toponyms "accompanied much maritime expansion . . . and was continually reinforced in late-nineteenth and twentieth-century historiography."[32] Although Layton's focus was on the Indian Ocean, his point holds for virtually every other maritime region of the world.

From the mid-1820s onward, a series of near-simultaneous events occurring in different corners of the globe led to a qualitative and quantitative change on maritime predatory practices. In the Atlantic and the Mediterranean, the disavowal and persecution of privateers obliged many of them to carry on as before but deprived from the support of any nation, as letters of marquee became harder and harder to obtain. In the Atlantic, many privateers transitioned from being part-time to full-time slave traders, while still engaging in high seas robberies, often attacking fellow slave trade ships.[33] In the Eastern Mediterranean, they became experts at crossing state maritime borders to evade persecution and capture.[34] In the Persian Gulf and the Western Indian Ocean, maritime raiding continued unabated in spite of the treaty of 1820 and the treaties that followed in the 1840s and 1850s.[35]

In Southeast Asia, with the realignment of imperial powers that followed the Anglo-Dutch Treaty of London in 1824, predatory activity at sea accelerated, in significant part fueled by renewed imperial expansionist moves by the British, the Siamese, the Dutch, the Spanish, and eventually the French.[36] In the South China Sea and the Western Mediterranean, these developments came slightly later, in the wake of the Opium War and the French and Spanish imperialist incursions and, ultimately, invasions of Algeria and Morocco. All in all, these hastened concomitant processes peaked almost everywhere in the 1840s and 1850s, creating a truly global problem for the ever more expansionist policies of European and non-European empires.

Any lingering doubts around the existing links between maritime raiding and slave trading were diffused as the mid-nineteenth century decades unfolded. These clear connections turned into a very convenient argument for imperialist powers to justify both diplomatic and violent moves all over the world. To do so, they consistently appealed to the Law of Nations, which they imposed onto others without hesitation. Through the application of the Law of Nations, European "parochial universalism" became a customary practice to subdue, to conquer, and to prevail over other nations, states, and peoples.[37]

The Law of Nations was a European product theorized, written, and, more importantly for those who opposed their expansionism in the nineteenth century, applied by the Europeans.[38] Jennifer Pitts drives home this point better than most: "Europeans alone managed to develop a body of legal doctrine that ought to be authoritative for the entire globe, and that they were therefore justified in imposing on others."[39] The Law of Nations was intrinsically associated with Europeans' beliefs in the superiority of their cultures and laws. Its enforcement by European imperial agents in faraway lands usually ignored the existence of numerous local laws wherever they arrived.[40] Crucially, as Lauren Benton has emphasized, thanks to such laws Western empires were able to claim a right "to intervene militarily anywhere in the world."[41] They did so by frequently generating "patterns of lawful extreme violence" that allowed them to blame "the victims because they had refused to submit."[42]

Such impositions were, of course, based on a belief that Europeans had reached a higher civilizational state, and that they were "in possession of universal moral and political truths" that others still lacked.[43] As these laws were imposed across the globe through the signing of treaties and the use of gunboats, they resulted in "the creation of multiple, regional 'legal spaces.' "[44] Calls "for universal jurisdiction for the punishment of pirates" were an inherent component of associated practices throughout most of the nineteenth century.[45] In this way, European—and eventually American—empires were able to justify the use of force whenever they desired to, in order to protect "European life, liberty, and property."[46] As Gerrit W. Gong has stressed, such practices were often vindicated by the resistance offered to Western civilizational endeavors by hostile non-European states and peoples, whose "standard of civilization" were considered not to be up to those of their white and Christian counterparts.[47]

The Law of Nations thus allowed for pigeonholing non-Western peoples into simplistic dualisms—for example, white and non-white, civilized and uncivilized, Christian and heathen—and it also allowed for defining what was to be considered as an act of piracy and what was the adequate punishment for those who had committed it. More relevant for this book, it enabled westerners to decide who was to be labeled as a pirate, thus legitimizing the use of violence to quell resistance and to occupy new territories, under the guise of protecting "legal" commerce, Western property, and life, and so on.[48]

Although there is no doubt that maritime predatory activities were extensive across each of the regions studied here, the concepts of piracy and pirate were not. This point was driven across by British administrator John Crawfurd in 1856 when he observed that among the Malay and the Javanese, "or indeed in any other native language" of Southeast Asia, there were no names "for piracy or robbery on the high seas."[49] Relying on their perceived civilizational superiority and on the Law of Nations, Western powers then bestowed upon themselves the right of filling out this conceptual gap, determining who was to be considered a pirate and who was not.

In the first decades of the nineteenth century, the romantic image of the Golden Age pirate continued to inform the ways in which people engaged in predatory activities at sea were to be judged by Western states. Although, as Amedeo Policante has noted, "the concept of the pirate that first emerged in the Atlantic of the eighteenth century travelled eastward, transforming itself in the process," Atlantic pirates were, in general terms, mostly westerners and Christians, even if their ferocious actions often challenged contemporary stereotypes associated with such origins.[50] In fact, and as Layton has pointed out, Atlantic pirates were defined "as economically-driven individuals, operating beyond the boundaries of sovereign authority," whereas "pirates" in other parts of the world did not necessarily fit such a rigid mold.[51] In these other regions, many had incorporated maritime predatory activities as part of their existence, and most were neither white nor Christians, and thus easier to stereotype, judge, and condemn using European laws as a base standard.

When it came to establishing who was a pirate, Western empires and their agents forced their ideas and protocols upon non-Western states, who often agreed to them through the signing of treaties or under the threats of superior gunpower.[52] White Atlantic slave traders, who were heavily involved in the plundering of other ships during these decades and who were in breach of international treaties that declared their slave-trading activities as acts of piracy, were often permitted to go without as much as a warning. The leniency shown to these men greatly contrasts with the severity with which non-white peoples in the Mediterranean, the Indian Ocean, China, and other parts of the world were often treated. The fact that many of the latter were also Muslims added a religious dimension to these deeply racist approaches.[53] Amirell's observation that piratical allegations against Southeast Asian seafaring peoples were "often linked to presumably 'innate' ethnic or racial traits of character" can be easily applied to the ways in which

Europeans referred to Muslim peoples from northern Africa, the Ottoman Empire, the Persian Gulf, and China.[54]

On occasion, there were better informed takes, although they were few and far in between. A case in question is the report about piracy in the Dutch East Indies produced by Christiaan Van Angelbeek in 1825, in which he presented "a more nuanced picture" of the phenomenon, revealing that maritime raiding among the people from Riau and Lingga was "part of a specific, traditional way of life, embedded in a pattern of dependence and servitude."[55] The case against Tunku Mohamed Saad a few years later also served to highlight how not everyone saw maritime raiding actions under the same light. Saad was charged with piracy, but a considerable number of people in Penang and Singapore did not agree with such an approach. Years later, Straits Settlements governor William John Butterworth recalled that during Saad's trial many had seen him as a "turbulent chieftain" and others considered him to be a "brave patriot," who was exercising his right of fighting the Siamese occupation of his land and those, like the British, who had supported Siam.[56]

For expanding Western—and occasionally non-Western—powers, labeling peoples as "pirates" or their actions as "piracy" became then a convenient modus operandi to make and consolidate all sorts of claims. Kim Wagner, for example, has highlighted one such case in his discussion of how, during the 1820s in India, the British began comparing thuggees with pirates, thus establishing "a new line of judicial argument" that permitted them to punish anyone whom they considered a thug, thus bending or ignoring their own laws.[57]

Such licenses opened the door for more abuses and misunderstandings of non-Western peoples. For example, James Brooke presented the Bornean Dayak to the British public as brutal pirates when he was laying claims to the region of Sarawak, of which he eventually became a ruler by force.[58] In China, Shap-ng-tsai was widely thought of and discussed as an individual, a pirate, rather than a seafaring predatory association, which emerged in the aftermath of the First Opium War, when scores of war recruits found themselves unemployed and struggling to make ends meet.[59] In fact, the case of Saad is also illustrative of how defining piracy could turn into a point-scoring game that would allow authorities to place the label upon anyone they saw as a troublemaker, even if, as in Saad's case, this person had been arguably undertaking actions of war against the enemies of Kedah, rather than attacking vessels of all nations, as a pirate would be expected to do.

Scholars have grappled with these same issues over the years. Until recently, for example, most historians felt comfortable using the terms "piracy" and "pirates" to refer to a wide array of maritime raiding undertakings without resorting to any sort of critical method to filter them.[60] As has been pointed out by both Bose and Layton, as recently as 1966 Charles Belgrave used the term "Pirate Coast" to refer to what would later become the Trucial States, reproducing nineteenth-century imperialist tropes without any real reflection and certainly without any hesitation.[61] Historical studies of Shap-ng-tsai constitute another example of such struggles, as until very recently some historians have continued to describe it as an individual rather than maritime association.[62]

Perhaps in no other region of the world has the phenomenon of maritime raiding in the mid-nineteenth century been better and more frequently researched that in Southeast Asia and the South China Sea. As a result, and not surprisingly, the best methodological tool to classify forms of maritime raiding was produced by one of the many scholars who have focused on these regions. In 1995, in an article published in the *Journal of World History*, J. L. Anderson broadly sorted maritime raiding into three types, according to its forms of expression.[63] The first type, *parasitic* piracy, represents the actions of groups that take advantage of busy seas to carry out their attacks, which are linked to the "volume of commercial shipping transiting the sea-lanes of the region."[64] The second, *intrinsic* piracy, refers to predatory activities which are an integral "part of the fiscal and even commercial fabric of the society concerned."[65] The final type, *episodic* piracy, is "occasioned by a disruption or distortion of normal trading patterns" and tended to be, to a significant extent, the result of Western expansionist activities.[66]

Although useful, with a few notable exceptions, these typologies of maritime raiding have not been widely applied outside the period and place studied by Anderson.[67] Such broad classifications could and should allow for a more fruitful dialogue among historians of maritime raiding, who often work on widely differing epochs and regions. In spite of its limited acceptance, thanks to Anderson's work we now have a conceptual apparatus that can help us in studying and understanding such predatory activities. The same, however, cannot be said about the suppression of piracy. Until the publication of works by Warren, Benton, Risso, Amirell, and Wilson, suppression activities were traditionally studied in a very parochial manner, both chronologically and geographically.[68]

Whereas there have been limits to the use of Anderson's typologies of piracy, they have arguably been well known for some time, which is more than can be said for the discussions and proposition of typologies of suppression of maritime raiding. In truth, although it would be possible to break the methods of suppression into more detailed typologies, perhaps this absence is due to the fact that there are two standing types of suppression that can be easily defined and described, namely, *diplomatic suppression* and *armed suppression*. Diplomatic suppression was often carried out with concealed but clear imperialist intentions; was almost universally implemented through the use of deception, coercion, and intimidation; and was executed through the signing of unfair and unbalanced treaties of commerce and peace.

Throughout the nineteenth century, numerous anti-piracy treaties were instigated by Western empires and forced upon other peoples. These treaties often included clauses that addressed slave-trading activities while guaranteeing various commercial and territorial privileges for those Western empires. As Jennifer Pitts has argued, these uneven treaties were forced on non-Western rulers and peoples precisely to facilitate their "dispossession and subjugation."[69] Here, too, it is possible to discern a significant discrepancy between treaties signed with other Christian countries, whose leaders were mostly white and "civilized," according to their own measurements, and those that were signed with the rest of the world. Consequently, treaties signed with non-Western peoples had a much more clearly stern and intimidating language than those signed with, for example, some of the new Latin American countries emerging from the wars of independence in the early part of the century. Again, Pitts has highlighted these differences while contrasting them vis-à-vis treaties signed with Asian and African states, although, as Julia Gaffield and others have emphasized, even in the Americas this distinction was crystal clear if one compares the ways in which Haiti was treated after the country declared independence in 1804.[70]

Between 1820 and 1870, European nations, led by Britain, relied more and more on the signing of anti-piracy treaties to establish and cement their superiority claims all over the world. The Spanish, for example, carved out new colonial territories in the Philippines by signing treaties with the sultans of Joló (1836), Mindanao (1845), and Baras (1850), among others.[71] For their part, the Dutch consolidated their authority over multiple territories in Southeast Asia during the same period by imposing treaties on Lingga-Riau (1818 and 1830), Pontianak (1819), Menado and Makassar (1824), Ternate and Tidore (1824), and Flores (1839). This strategy was complemented by the Anglo-Dutch Treaty of 1824, which included anti-piracy clauses, and accompanied by the use of extreme violence in the late 1820s during the Java war (1825–30) and other armed suppression actions, especially in Sumatra.[72] As Jean Pierre Cornets de Groot, a contemporary secretary to the minister for the colonies, explained, in "all the treaties signed with native princes, the Dutch Government always intended to include the repression of piracy" so that these princes would be left in no doubt as to what the consequences for engaging in, or supporting, piracy could be.[73]

Just as the Spanish and the Dutch did in their East Indies territories, so did the French, the Portuguese, and the British wherever their imperialist and commercial interests took them. These powers all concluded multiple treaties of "peace," which included anti-piracy clauses and dispositions, that were often signed under the menacing artillery of their cruisers and steamboats. After the British and the Americans had equated slave trade to piracy in 1815 and 1820, respectively, Britain began including clauses applying this principle in many of its treaties.[74] The Treaty of Amity and Commerce signed between Britain and Brazil in 1827 as much as suggested this link in its article 17.[75] More specifically, article 8 of the Anglo-French Treaty of May 1845, for example, established that actions connected to the slave trade in the Atlantic were "often accompanied by acts of piracy," which should be punished according to "instructions founded on the law of nations."[76] Similar clauses appeared in the treaties signed by the British with the Oriental Republic of Uruguay in 1839, the Republic of Texas in 1840, Portugal in 1842, and with the sultan of Borneo in 1847, among others.[77] As Patricia Risso has pointed out, "Piracy and the slave trade were linked because they were both illegal maritime activities."[78]

There is little doubt that many of these treaties were somewhat effective at curbing slave trade activities, but their real success rested on how they were used to open up countries to Western commercial interests, leading to new spheres of influence or colonial possessions. In fact, many treaties were signed after the use of armed suppression. The General Maritime Treaty, signed with Arab rulers at Ras Al-Khaimah in January 1820, was "an important milestone on the Persian Gulf's absorption into Britain's 'informal' empire."[79] Such a treaty was accepted only after the British bombardments of 1809 and 1819, in which, as Fashad Bishara has put it, "their ships were burned, their towns leveled, and their political and commercial ambitions decimated."[80] The treaty of 1820 is, of course, not an isolated example.

Diplomatic efforts leading to the signing of such treaties and to other lesser agreements were frequently concocted through a mix of misrepresentation, threats, and outright lies, and there was little interest in preserving the cultures and languages of peoples considered backward or inferior. When diplomatic suppression means failed, however, Western, and occasionally non-Western, pirate empires did not hesitate in resorting to military and naval force, showing little regard for the ways their actions could result in the recurrent displacement and annihilation of non-Western peoples.

Technological innovations in weaponry and warfare in the first few decades of the nineteenth century also contributed to the exacerbation of Western imperial endeavors across the world. For example, already by the 1820s, the British had used Congreve rockets in the Napoleonic Wars and in the bombardment of Algiers in 1816; they would use them again during the First Anglo-Asante War (1823–31) and First Anglo-Burmese War (1824–26).[81] New weapons—revolvers and other breech-loaded guns—were also widely in use since the late 1830s, while the carronade became the cannon of choice for most Western navies in their imperialist incursions.[82] The introduction in 1823 of Paixhan cannons, capable of launching explosive shells, and their popularization soon after led navies to give up on wooden vessels as the century advanced.[83]

By the 1850s, all navies operating outside Europe and the United States had introduced two main technological innovations that allowed for more daring attacks on any who resisted their advances in all corners of the planet, through the use of what historian Priya Satia has referred to as "mechanized killing" and "mechanized warfare."[84] The first important innovation was a direct result of the devastation caused by the Paixhan cannons on wooden ships: the introduction of ironclad war vessels, which became crucial for the success of maritime operations.[85] In fact, the first ship to be protected by an iron armor was one of the East India Company ships, the steamer *Nemesis*, used to fight maritime raiding in East Asia from the early 1840s, shortly after playing a prominent role in the First Opium War.[86] Closely linked to the development of ironclad vessels was the introduction of steam power, which allowed gunned warships to be significantly more lethal when attacking presumed pirates, both at sea and on land.[87] Many of the worldwide armed operations against amphibious populations that took place after 1840, which are discussed in the pages of this book, were carried out precisely by steam-powered vessels.

Armed suppression involved a significant degree of violence, occasionally on both sides. Violence carried out by pirate imperialist agents and their men was arguably more extensive and devastating than violence associated with maritime raiding or with actions of resistance against pirate imperialism. Even so, amphibious populations throughout the world resorted to violent means, on occasion extreme ones, whenever necessary. The sources produced by imperial perpetrators and witnesses leave little space for doubt about the fact that the use and abuse of armed violence was commonplace in the suppression of maritime raiding and in the resistance to it.

But, although pirate empires and their agents hardly had a monopoly on violence, they made use of it more systematically and in extreme ways. As Amedeo Policante has emphasized, once entire communities had been labeled piratical "they could be exposed to violence, persecuted and destroyed in a grey area between peace and war."[88] Western and, to a lesser extent, non-Western pirate empires then bestowed upon themselves the right to determine who was to be "endowed with sovereign rights" and who was to be "slaughtered without further ado."[89] Those in the latter category had their vessels destroyed, their villages and crops burned to the ground, and their communities displaced to distant locations under the guise of stopping them from going to sea and committing predatory actions.[90]

Armed suppression also had a financial dimension, accompanied by prospective military and naval distinctions in combat, that has not been broadly discussed until today. Suppressing maritime raiding, just like suppressing slave trade activities, could often turn into ferocious hunting expeditions of non-Western peoples, which resulted in multiple casualties and also in medals and bounty. As Anita van Dissel has noticed, the "prospect of a bounty after a successful venture and the increased chance of an honorable military decoration" played a role in the ways in which the Batavian ship captains and crews acted in the Dutch East Indies in the mid-decades of the nineteenth century.[91]

Ultimately, there is little doubt that "violence was a persistent feature of Imperial peace," and that Western and occasionally non-Western empires furthered their goals through dispossession, stealing, and burning—all practices historically associated with pirates.[92] Both the diplomatic and the armed types of suppression of maritime raiding were claimed to be absolutely essential for the spreading of civilization; for the implementation of the abolition of slavery and slave trade (although not for other forms of indentured labor); for the opening of foreign ports to the Western products, whenever possible at preferential prices; and, finally, for the consolidation of their colonial territorial gains. I discuss each of these piratical imperial reasons at length in chapters 1 to 4, demonstrating how the Western powers made use of means and deeds traditionally associated with piracy to expand and consolidate their empires. In chapter 5 I focus on the many ways these pirate empires cooperated as well as the times they fought over prospective markets and products, colonial territories, and cheap or free labor.

Unlike most books written about maritime raiding to date, *Pirate Imperialism* focuses not on piracy as a phenomenon but on trans-imperial responses to it. More specifically, it explores the various ways these empires found to suppress piracy across the globe, often employing very similar means regardless of the political or cultural background of the places they targeted. It is precisely the global scope of this book that sets it apart from other regional comparative studies, for example, those by Tarling, Al-Qasimi, Antony, Warren, and, more recently, Amirell and Layton.[93] By bridging the gap between the Atlantic, Indian, and Pacific Oceans and their subregions, in this book I establish the connections and divergences of suppression of maritime raiding in each of these corners of the world, attempting to provide a comprehensive interpretation of a phenomenon that interweaves with crucibles of colonialism, civilization, religion, race, and ethnicity.

There is little doubt that as they expanded across the world, Western empires, occasionally in tandem with their non-Western counterparts, treated diverse peoples differently. These selective means almost universally depended on subjective Western perceptions that related to the supposed levels of civilization and willingness to cooperate that each of these peoples offered. Their disposition to allow for the dissemination of free trading practices or to surrender their homelands to those same foreign empires could determine how they were perceived and dealt with. Lastly, their appearance, skin color, and readiness to embrace or, at the very least, mimic European cultural values, including Christianity, constituted crucial factors when deciding who was to be considered more civilized and thus less likely to be subjected to disproportionate levels of violent repression.

Atlantic maritime raiding in the middle decades of the nineteenth century, however, was nothing short of a sui generis paradigm. In the Atlantic, slave trade and piracy had been laid out approximately along the same routes, undoubtedly a result of links between slave trading and privateering in the early part of the century. Predatory and slave-trading practices and routes overlapped each other for most of the period. This allowed Western powers to link the slave trade to piracy as a means of justifying its persecution and suppression. And yet, even though they succeeded in making this connection in multiple transnational agreements, in practice Atlantic white slave traders were hardly ever brought to justice. Not even in those abundant opportunities when they were captured red-handed with their ships' holds full of enslaved Africans did they face charges of piracy. On the very few occasions when they were taken before European or American courts of law, it was because they had engaged in predatory actions against white European or American crews and passengers, or because they offered armed resistance to anti-slave trade patrol vessels.

Today it is easier to find documents relating to slave traders who resisted anti-slave trade patrol ships than about those who engaged in actual piratical actions while on their way to Africa, often attacking other slave-trading vessels. A combination of lack or jurisdiction over citizens of other countries, and a special regard for white Christian sailors, often allowed these human traffickers to walk away with only minor reprimands and, tragically, to join new slave-trading or piratical expeditions.[94] The situation was different elsewhere in the world, where non-white and non-Christian sailors considered to be pirates were repressed and massacred without as much as a second thought. In some well-documented instances, discussed in the pages of this book, the reasons could be as trifling as to having "offended" or "disrespected" the flag or the honor of one of the Western powers active in or around their homelands.

Most of the armed suppression actions—as well as some of the diplomatic ones—I consider in this book took place either at sea or close to bodies of water, by seashores and riverbanks. Furthermore, they often took place far from the seats of power or from any authority that could pass judgment on intrinsically vicious actions. When in 1849, in the aftermath of the battle of Batang Marau, James Brooke and Commander Arthur Farquhar went up the river Saribas "destroying everything" in their path, in an expedition that resulted in accusations of massacring the local amphibious populations, they did so far from any seat of British power.[95] Similarly, when in September 1851 men answering to the Ottoman governor of the island of Samos chased the notorious "pirate" Giorgos Negros and his crew to the desert island of Fournoi, they did so in the understanding that they would be allowed to use any means necessary, as they eventually did—killing him and all his men—without facing consequences from distant Constantinople.[96]

The story I recount here unfolds primarily on the water and joins an expanding body of work produced in recent years, which challenges what Marcus Rediker has critically referred to as the traditional "terracentric" approach to history. This new method of enquiry looks at the sea not as a realm of "unreal spaces" and "voids between real places" but as a historical place where processes and conflicts also occurred.[97] Oceans, seas, and rivers provided imperial powers with physical aquatic spaces where they could carry out excessive levels of oppression while avoiding the essential moral obligations and ethical behaviors expected from Western, "civilized" people.

Seen from this angle, the story is about the role of distance in enabling violence and lack of accountability. It was in these distant aquatic spaces that empires expanded their control of maritime expanses while consolidating modern global capitalist systems. The exercising of this control is what Marcus Rediker has referred to as "hydrarchy from above," a concept that originated from the discourse of the leaders of these very hegemonic powers, who saw resistance to their advances in the form of a many-headed hydra, nearly impossible to tame and kill. In their minds, as will be revealed time and again in the pages of this book, every time they "chopped off a rebellious head in one location, two more sprung elsewhere."[98]

By examining diplomatic and armed suppression at a global scale, I necessarily employ hydrarchy from above as a methodological tool to decipher and understand these phenomena. The examination of distant aquatic spaces, which is central to this book, and which has been critical in binding together the various regions of the planet that form the field of global history, lies at the center of every one of its chapters.

Unsurprisingly, the acts of diplomatic and armed suppression were much better documented by the scions of empire than were the acts of resistance performed by those amphibious communities they preyed upon. Even when documented, records associated with acts of resistance were deeply biased and imprecise. Although they feature in this book, to a significant extent the lack of balance encountered in the primary sources led me to focus on exposing Western and non-Western empires and their questionable piratical actions, rather than on the resistance that they frequently encountered. The fact that some of these empires were quick to criticize, complain, and attack other empires gives us a unique dimension of veracity, verging on exaggeration at times, that would have been difficult to find if the focus had been on those who resisted.

The preponderance of British documents that I encountered as I began my research soon gave way to a plethora of primary and secondary sources produced by other empires and written in other languages. The vast majority of these documents were produced by representatives of these same empires. In them we can see how frequently imperialist politics trumped ethical and moral considerations, and how lies, deception, coercion, and intimidation preceded almost every interaction between pirate empires and those they encountered across the world. They also reveal how the habit of stereotyping peoples was consistently used and abused to support claims associated with the moral higher ground of Western civilization to justify all sorts of actions, from the enforcing of ironically called "treaties of amity" to the displacement and slaughtering of entire amphibious populations under the banners of promoting peace, progress, and civilization.

Luckily, challenging opinions and even instances of internal dissent were not unusual after abusive diplomatic or armed suppression actions. Contemporaries of politicians and officers of empire who took questionable decisions, believing they would lead to an improvement of those they imposed themselves upon, were at times probed by direct witnesses of their abuses or by others at a latter day. George Bonham overruled the judicial authorities of Penang, ultimately with the support of the governor of India, Lord Auckland, on the grounds that Tunku Mohamed Saad was supposed to be a pirate, but many within the British colony questioned his authoritarian decision. And even within the British navy, some, like Sherard Osborn, an officer on HMS *Hyacinth*, accused the British of having "an adverse view of the Malay claim to Quedah" and European nations of "pushing them" into piracy.[99] Furthermore, Osborn also reflected that "no one seemed very well able to show" on "what grounds" they had been labeled as pirates.[100] This opinion had been publicly expressed before by Captain Edward Owen in 1831 or 1832 when he refused to treat the Malays from Kedah as pirates, stating that "no act of Piracy had been specifically alleged, or proof obtained" against them.[101]

By the middle decades of the nineteenth century, the image of the "pirate" continued to reflect allusions to both romantic heroes and hardy criminals. Alongside the fear that the skull and bones provoked, poems like "Canción del pirata" by José de Espronceda were published, and theater plays like *The Long, Low Black Schooner* were performed, conveniently keeping pirates and their exploits very much in the minds of the Western public.[102]

Maritime raiding in all regions of the world remained a formidable obstacle to Western and non-Western empires interested in expanding their formal and informal advances. In the name of civilization, abolition, commerce, and colonialism, Western, and occasionally non-Western, piratical empires used both diplomatic and armed means to put down those who attempted to stop their advances at distant, aquatic spaces. As Reverend George Percy Badger put it in 1861, while excusing the abusive behavior of the British resident at Bushehr, Captain James Felix Jones, "Stringent measures [were] necessary [on his part] to curb the turbulent and warlike spirit of the maritime Arab Tribes, as well for the security of our trade in the Persian Gulf, as for the general prosperity of the inhabitants themselves."[103] In other words, in the reverend's mind, as in the minds of his imperialist contemporaries, diplomatic and armed suppression of maritime raiding were essential for the prosperity of their empires and, oddly, for the good of the non-Western, less "civilized" peoples they preyed upon. This form of hydrarchy from above lies at the heart of the global narrative of this book.

CHAPTER ONE

Civilization and the Suppression of Maritime Raiding

On August 3, 1858, Fernando de Norzagaray, the Spanish governor of the Philippines, wrote a brief missive to the minister of state and overseas colonies in Madrid, informing him of the appearance of "célèbre pirate head" Palawan Dando before the governor of Zamboanga Province. Before concluding his short note, Norzagaray insinuated that it was likely that Dando's "piratical companions Paulima [Panglima] Taupan, Alip and other moors" would soon follow him, putting down their weapons and surrendering to the Spanish authorities.[1] As James Francis Warren has shown, Dando, Taupan, and Alip—and almost certainly fellow Balanguingui Samal leader Tumugsuc—had been engaged in a war of attrition with Manila. This conflict began shortly after the Spanish navy attacked on their base at Sipac fort in 1848, which resulted in the death of around 450 men, women, and children, many of whom chose to take their own lives rather than fall into Spanish hands.[2] For almost a decade, the men, now operating from Simisa, near Tawi Tawi, had attacked Spanish vessels and towns, taken captives, and become a true problem for the authorities in Manila and Madrid—and for their plans for expanding their territorial control over the Philippines.[3]

In the aftermath of the 1848 attack on Sipac the Spanish abducted around 350 people, mostly women and children, from Balanguingui, hoping to force Dando, Taupan, and other leaders to come before the authorities in order to be reunited with their loved ones.[4] Although the trick did not work then, nine years later when the Spanish attacked their new base in Simisa, again kidnapping all women and children and burning houses and crops to the ground, the "pirate heads" obliged.[5] One by one, Dando, Taupan, and Tumugsuc traveled to Zamboanga, where, taking advantage of the offer of amnesty they had received from Norzagaray, they surrendered themselves and also released dozens of captives as a goodwill gesture.[6]

The response of the Spanish authorities to this capitulation left much to be desired. Once Dando, Taupan, Tumugsuc, and other leaders walked into the government building in Zamboanga, they were arrested and unceremoniously thrown into the town's garrison jail, the promises of amnesty and reunion with their loved ones betrayed and ignored. Norzagaray attempted to justify why he had been forced to go back on his word, keeping these men in chains rather than allowing them to join their families as he had promised. In his mind, honoring his word could have immediately led to the liberation of the prisoners and their relatives, a circumstance that would have allowed them to go back to their former occupation.[7]

Norzagaray concluded his diatribe by questioning their "undoubted bad faith," while reflecting on the possible consequences of punishing men who had believed in his amnesty and who had presented themselves "wrapped in the Spanish flag, asking for forgiveness."[8] Ultimately, fears and prejudices prevailed over promises and Spanish honor, leading the captain general to believe that these men should be treated as enemies and held in custody. Over the next two years, the men and their families suffered several new setbacks.[9] Of them, only Tumugsuc eventually found his way back to his relatives; both Dando and Taupan died before their captors finally decided to relocate the rest of them to the Cagayan Valley in 1860.[10]

The cases of Dando, Taupan, Tumugsuc, and their families underline the hypocrisy of the civilizational discourses practiced by Western powers in their imperialist intrusions across the world during this period. In its details, the behavior exhibited by the Spanish authorities, officers, and navy in the story of the Balanguingui Samal surrendering parallels the usual litany of grumbles and accusations that Western powers used when discussing non-Western peoples involved in maritime predatory activities. There is no doubt that Norzagaray, and before him, in 1848, Captain General Narciso Clavería, did not shy away from using extreme force against men, women, and children during the attacks on Simisa and the Sipac fort. It is apparent too, that both men resorted to kidnapping women and children to use as bait, in order to convince Samal leaders to come forward and put down their weapons. Their offers of amnesty and reunification with their loved ones, which were ultimately taken by Dando, Taupan, and Tumugsuc, were nothing but a maneuver of deception, devised to lure the natives into a trap and cost them their freedom. Poignantly, these events occurred at a time when the same Spanish authorities and officers continuously lamented the perceived bad faith of the Balanguingui Samal, referring to them as savages who were deemed to be untrustworthy.

Be it through deception and plain lies or by the abuse of Spanish gunboats, the demise, imprisonment, and displacement of the Balanguingui Samal illustrates the manners in which Western imperialist agents saw themselves as civilizing heralds. The cases discussed in the following pages reveal a group of ambitious men who employed truly brutal and often deadly methods to expand their empires' spheres of influence, while cosplaying to be harbingers of civilization and Christianization. Believing themselves to be do-gooders, these men simultaneously "saw piracy as a manifestation of cultural anomie that needed to be stamped out if 'civilization' were to come to the region."[11] Acting on this supercilious belief, time and again and throughout the world, they took other peoples' lands while making substantial profits for themselves.

Balancing the notion of a supposedly superior Western civilization with the need to employ diplomatic and armed measures to suppress maritime activities among non-white, non-Western peoples presented a formidable challenge for the Western pirate empires.

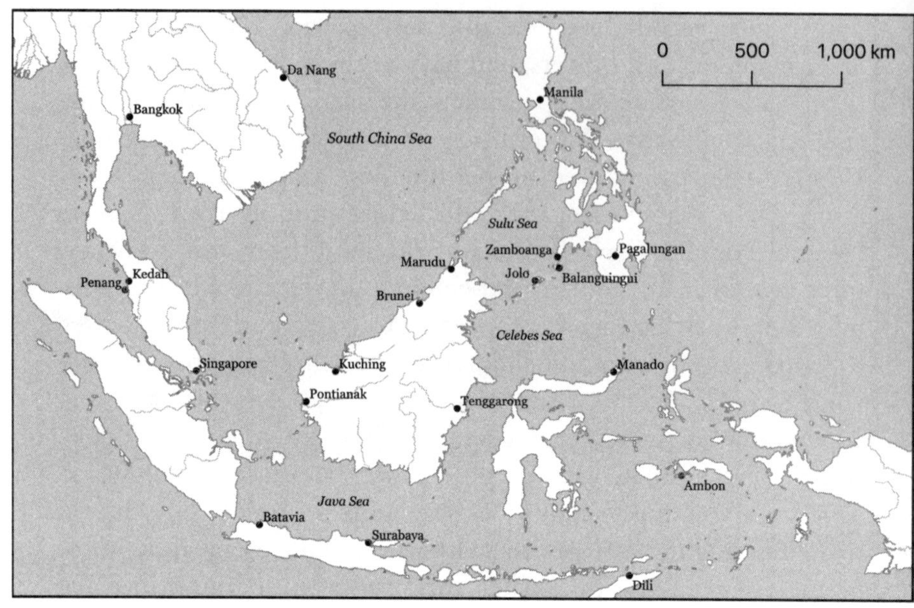

Southeast Asia

Maritime raiding carried out by non-Western peoples—read dark-skinned, non-Christians—presented them with what they saw as an opportunity to vindicate their hostile and often destructive actions. Colonial representatives of Western nations believed they had ascended to a higher moral ground, where they could confront conveniently labeled adversaries who, in their perceived backwardness, obstructed the path of progress and civilization. As we will soon discover, even when readily identifiable foes were absent, the Western powers became adept at fashioning new ones, casting trepang fishing and pearl-collecting communities, among others, as enemies to the entire human race.

The theoretical justifications for these actions were grounded in the Law of Nations, originally put forward by Emerich de Vattel in the middle of the eighteenth century. Furthermore, from the mid-1820s onward, these ideas were expanded upon and refined with the widespread adoption of James Kent's definitions of piracy and pirates. In his lecture 9, fittingly entitled "Offenses against the Law of Nations" of 1826, Kent attempted to simplify these definitions, providing some catchy phrases and literary figures that soon were widely known in the United States and across Europe. Among his many influential characterizations, Kent emphasized that piracy was done "in the spirit and intention of universal hostility," and he suggested that pirates had been and should be "regarded by all civilized nations as the enemies of the human race."[12] He also stressed that such crimes against "the universal law of society" should be "everywhere pursued and punished with death."[13] In just a few lines, Kent normalized Western suppression, including its violent kind, by defining non-Western amphibious populations as uncivilized and as enemies of the entire human race.

Characterizations like Kent's allowed for the perpetuation and reproduction of facile labeling of peoples who could and should be the object of violence, not so much as a last recourse but as a necessity that would eventually lead to their own improvement, providing they were not exterminated first. Establishing convenient stereotypes, through exaggeration and outright lies, was a cornerstone of pirate imperialist approaches. But the stitching together of stereotypes was just the tip of the iceberg. There were also various contemporary theories that predated the scientific racism of the late nineteenth century, which were conveniently used and abused to suppress amphibious communities throughout the world. Chiefly among these contemporary theories were ideas around polygenism and benevolent imperialism. The former suggested that the different human races had different origins; the latter attempted to present a benevolent image of Western imperial powers, based on ideas associated with their attainment of a superior civilizational stage. Both led to the acceptance of replacement theories and principles that were used to justify diplomatic and armed suppression activities.

In this drive to impose the superior principles of Western civilization nearly anything was permissible. Polygenism's popularity from the 1830s onward eventually mixed with social Darwinism in decades to come and added fuel to what was already a pretty violent and intense imperialist blaze. Polygenist ideas provided a theoretical scaffolding for the assembling of Western deterministic, at times fanatically expansionist, schemes and ultimately offered the basis for the brutal sort of scientific racism that became mainstream in the second part of the century. The needs to replace non-Western peoples, who were seen as nearly subhuman, with "superior" Caucasian ones was widely accepted by the middle decades of the nineteenth century. Such ideas were openly promoted by philosophers like Herbert Spencer, who went as far as stating, in unequivocal terms, "Wild races . . . cannot enter into a civilized state at all, but have to be supplanted by others which can."[14]

Benevolent imperialist ideas also turned mainstream in the middle decades of the nineteenth century, becoming even more popular than polygenist ones. Apologists of the British Empire in the mid-nineteenth century, among whom John Stuart Mill and John Bowring were perhaps the main exponents, were not fearful to remind anyone who would listen, or read any of their writings, about the advantages that Western civilization could bring upon non-Western populations.[15] Among these advantages were the establishment of Western laws and customs and the introduction of free trade, including an extensive trade on firearms.

An illustrative example of the double standards of these civilizational endeavors can be found in the writings of John Crawfurd. After visiting Siam and the Cochin China in the early 1820s, Crawfurd, a British imperial agent active in Southeast Asia at the time, was confronted with what could be only described as an arms-trade paradox. On one hand, traders from Britain, the United States, and other Western empires had realized that some parts of the world, including numerous Atlantic and Indian Ocean spots, were excellent places to sell firearms to the local populations. On the other hand, they quickly understood that such weapons could be used by their buyers against them, often at sea, in what they considered to be acts of piracy. Faced with this dilemma, Crawfurd tied himself to an impossible argument while trying to convince his readers that firearms had a "civilizing effect" on "the barbarous tribes."[16] To Crawfurd, the possession of firearms gave "the more intelligent and commercial tribes an advantage over their ruder neighbours," and he suggested that such an advantage unavoidably created power hierarchies that could not "fail to tend more or less to the diminution of anarchy, and the amelioration of law and government."[17] In reality, however, these weapons were sold and bought by anyone with means, and they often found their way into amphibious communities that then turned them against anyone they considered to be their foes.

Crawfurd's allusion to the need to civilize "barbarous tribes" was not an exception. For example, John Stuart Mill's view about the place of "barbarous peoples" became widely used; it served to standardize both the diplomatic and armed suppression of seafaring peoples all around the world whenever accusations of piracy were leveled against them. Not only was he clear in dehumanizing them when he stated that "barbarians" had "no rights as a nation," but he also endorsed and encouraged imperialist armed aggression projects when he claimed that in certain opportunities "civilized nations" were fully justified in attacking their "barbarous" neighbors.[18] Although these passages were published in the mid-1870s, Mill—just like his father, James—had been referring to non-Western peoples as "savages" and "barbarous" for decades.[19] Their ideas, or similar ones, spread further afield, toward other self-defined civilized Western nations, such as Spain, Portugal, the Netherlands, Prussia, and the United States.[20]

In France, for example, proponents of the *mission civilisatrice*, pleaded the case for an empire that would bring peace and advancement to non-Western peoples, even if violent means were necessary to achieve them.[21] In France, as in Britain, intellectuals associated with benevolent, liberal imperial approaches underwent a transition from opposing imperialism to supporting it. They convinced themselves of the benefits associated with bringing development and progress to "less civilized" peoples around the world, an approach that has been categorized as an "imperialist logic of liberal political thought."[22]

Imperial violence associated with ideas of polygenism and benevolent imperialism were also saturated by discourses that pointed to the race and religion of non-Western peoples as key impediments for their integration into Western civilization projects. Not surprisingly, then, race and religion were found at the center of replacement doctrines and schemes. As night follows day, racial and religious discourses associated with the universalization of Western civilizational principles shadowed imperial agents wherever they traveled. In the words of Lauren Benton, imperial agents dreamed of a "peaceful, white-dominated world," which could only be achieved "under the projection (or threat) of limited force."[23]

Naturally, imposing Christianity upon "heathen" or "pagan" populations proved simpler than attempting to reshape their racial identities, particularly for those whose skin color and physical features markedly differed from the fair skin and light-colored eyes traditionally associated with Western peoples. While missionaries and travelers could change minds—though at times they could lose their lives trying—and convince people to embrace Christianity, they could do little to alter the fact that racial features were a marker that often constituted an unsurmountable obstacle toward their fabled paradigm of civilization, even so for those who actively attempted to mimic their Western, white counterparts.[24] This is not to say that every population they reached could be easily converted or that the evangelizing task was straightforward. In fact, many amphibious communities refused to change their beliefs and often found renewed attempts to convert them to Christianity another reason to resist pirate imperialism.

Each of these approaches proved highly advantageous for Western imperial powers. A broad acceptance of philosophical arguments enabled them to label amphibious peoples as pirates and thereby justify the use of armed suppression whenever they deemed it necessary. As they extended their tentacles throughout the world, and interacted with non-Western amphibious communities, Western imperial agents increasingly displayed a wide array of bullish and forceful behaviors that resembled, quite dramatically, actions that they frequently associated with those they called pirates. While furthering imperial goals, they murdered, kidnapped, displaced, and dispossessed amphibious populations, burning and razing to the ground their villages and crop fields, all in the name of peace and order and through the use of their superior technological weaponry and means of transportation.[25] Imposing some of their symbols of civilization—for example, railways, roads, and agricultural knowledge—constituted part of their arsenal, alongside shiny steamboats, destructive carronades, deadly rockets, and other modern guns.

When examining pirate imperialism in action it is hard to disagree with Weng Ching's take on the slyness of the practices Western empires employed to take over the lands of other peoples. When he wrote "first the missionary, then the consul, and at last, the invading army," Weng Ching was exposing to the entire world what he considered to be the pirate imperialists' playbook.[26] Although this playbook was not always followed to the letter, and there were multiple variations on the ways in which pirate imperialist agents furthered their empires' interests, there is little doubt that the suppression of "piratical" activities carried out by supposedly savage peoples constituted one of its key foundations. Zeroing on these strategies opens a window that reveals the extent to which a deadly combination of deceit and violence allowed Western imperial powers to devastate amphibious peoples' lives and cultures, while doing so under the banner of civilization.

Extreme actions against maritime communities, such as the kidnapping of people undertaken by Spanish governors Clavería in 1848 and Norzagaray in 1857, were not uncommon during this period. In fact, not far from the Philippines, there was another remarkably similar case. In this instance, too, the perpetrators took care to document and then publicize their exploits, as if such actions were unquestionably indispensable to stop maritime raiding in the area. In a letter sent to Lord Palmerston in October 1849, James Brooke proudly stated that soon after carrying out a devastating attack on the "pirates" of the Skrang and Saribas Rivers, he had kidnapped their women and children and then asked for a ransom from their male relatives who had escaped alive.[27] Even though Brooke's inhumane actions were justly condemned, both in Singapore and London, he was still utterly gratified of his civilization-by-kidnapping tactics.[28] In a rare moment of honesty in the letter, however, he explained to Palmerston how his brutal tactics would allow him to "convey the impression of our humanity, and thus gain them over to the abandonment of their bad habits."[29]

Ideas advocating the need to bring amphibious peoples into the fold of civilization, while Western empires simultaneously consolidated their gains, were widely popular by this time. Stamford Raffles had made it clear in the early 1820s that "the diffusion of the humanizing arts [was] as essential to the character of our nation, as the acquisition of power and wealth."[30] At a more practical level, just a few years later and following a similar rationalization, Rear Admiral Edward Owen had made his feelings about the habits of the Malays transparently clear. From Owen's point of view, the

British government should consider implementing any viable measures to stop the Malays from resorting to piracy, as it was "an evil which [seemed] to have been a constant subject of complaint from the time of our earliest acquaintance with these seas."[31] The casual typecasting of amphibious peoples as pirates who resisted the advance of civilization and progress turned into a main discursive trope not just for the British but for each of these Western imperial powers.

British assumptions linked to ever-increasing imperialistic hydrarchic policies were far from unique; other Western powers competed against them in this race to "civilize" supposedly backward peoples around the world. In 1833, the Dutch criticized the "wretched form of government" and the "vices of robbery and murderousness" of amphibious populations throughout the Indian Ocean, and lamented the backward ways in which they abstained from adopting civilized customs, in spite of all the efforts made by European governments and agents.[32] A few years later, an article published in the Batavian newspaper *Javasche Courant* described the same communities as peoples who had been "pushed beyond the boundaries of civilized society, to seek, in lawless acts, a way of life more consistent with their moods," thus justifying any means of pacification that could be necessary against them.[33]

In some extreme cases, even having nautical knowledge or living out of the sea in a sustainable way could be misconstrued as uncivilized traits that needed to be stamped out. Cornets de Groot, for example, suggested that Southeast Asian amphibious communities were attached to piracy, "as if [it were] an industry that they had inherited from their ancestors."[34] He criticized them for choosing to "live preferably on water," and when discussing the Rayat people, whom he considered to be "very little civilized," he noticed the backwardness of their nautical knowledge, as, in his words, "They do not use a compass; to navigate they observe the stars at night; and by day, the sun."[35]

Similarly, a mid-nineteenth-century Spanish writer, Ignacio de Abenia Taure, referred to the Riff Coast in northern Morocco as "a country of outlaws, united in society just to be the scourge of mankind."[36] Another Spanish writer, José Manuel Diana, went further, accusing the inhabitants of living in a barbarous state in spite of being so close to Europe, a circumstance that made it likely that "sooner or later, they would be called to suffer under the weight of a dominating nation."[37] The people of the Riff were the frequent target of all sorts of accusations that went well beyond those of being pirates. Twelve years before these two Spanish judgments were published, Edme de Chasteau, French consul at Tangier, sent a letter to his foreign minister, François de Guizot, in which he referred to the Riff people as inveterate gossipers, who would "spread the news" of any event as soon as they would find out about it.[38]

This sort of simplistic pigeonholing was also applied by the French to another Mediterranean amphibious population, the Greeks. In 1854, the captain of frigate *Favin Lebèque*, who was part of a pirate-hunting expedition in the Aegean Sea, commented about the supposed laziness of Greek pirates, writing that they would "spend almost the entire winter season" at an island east of Naxos, resting, "eating and spending the fruit of their depredations."[39] "Laziness" was one of the main sobriquets employed by Spanish chronicler Emilio Bernaldez when he referred to the seafaring peoples fighting the expansion of Spanish imperialism in the Philippines as "lazy" and "ignorants."[40]

A closer examination of these labeling practices unveils how Western powers capitalized on the perceived imperative of civilization among their non-Western counterparts to advance their own objectives and to legitimize suppression activities. The examples are plenty. A particularly revealing case involves one of the sailors aboard the East India Company ship *Nitocris*, which had been tasked with the mission of suppressing piracy in the Persian Gulf during the 1840s. In December 1845, Henry Cole received permission to disembark during the ship's stop at Al Ma'qil. Contrary to orders to remain in the immediate vicinity of the vessel, he made his way to nearby Basra, where he indulged in several hours of drinking, becoming intoxicated. On his way back to the *Nitocris*, he stopped to purchase some eggs. Following an argument with the vendor, he became involved in a violent altercation with another man, which ultimately led to him shooting and killing the man.[41]

In the aftermath, while Cole was detained aboard the *Nitocris* with plans to eventually transport him to a British port for a court-martial, his superior officers found themselves compelled to enter negotiations with the locals, hoping to strike a deal that would prevent a violent escalation. To James Jones, the commander of the *Nitocris*, it was clear that for the Arabs, "for blood, blood is demanded," and he sought to find a way of compensating the relatives of the murdered man with what he referred to as "blood money" to serve as an "atonement for manslaughter."[42] In a second letter sent a few weeks after the event, and while Cole was still prisoner on board the ship, Jones went into a tirade of stereotypes of the "Arab Tribes," which in his opinion had an "uncertain temper," a "vindictive character," and an "eagerness for revenge," all character flaws that he saw as obstacles to reaching a satisfactory arrangement with the relatives of the murdered man. Ultimately, Jones flirted with the idea that it was really the Arabs who should be blamed for the entire episode, almost dismissing the fact that a British drunken sailor under his command had assassinated an unarmed Arab man.[43]

For Commander Jones and many others, it was not hard to disguise the piratical character of their activities overseas by blaming others for their own shortcomings and acts of rage. In fact, only a few years later, according to the British resident in the Persian Gulf, Arnold Burrowes Kemball, an anti-piracy patrol vessel officer had set his dog upon a slave, causing severe injuries and provoking a similar crisis because the injured man subsequently refused "their explanations, apologies and compensation."[44] Another British resident in the Persian Gulf, Lewis Pelly, went even further when discussing the shortcomings of the "Arab tribes," using, in 1868, the term "Pirate Coast" to refer to parts of the eastern shore of the Arabian Peninsula.[45] While repeating the usual epithets, including "vindictive" and "cruel," he blamed the Wahhabis in particular for compelling the other "tribes into plunder and piracy," thus justifying the need for the British to control and repress them.[46]

For Western pirate empires, learning to spin off their own crimes, and turning their instances of retaliation against non-Western amphibious peoples into acts of civilization and humanity, became a vital part of their overall imperial hydrarchic narratives. To them it was essential to create the impression that these so-called anti-piratical efforts were done reluctantly, at a high cost for them, and for the benefit of these amphibious populations. James

Brooke used such arguments extensively and repeatedly while suppressing maritime raiding—real or imaginary—along the northern coast of Borneo during the 1840s and 1850s. Brooke's definitions of piracy were unconventional even for his time, and they were questioned by his former business partner Henry Wise, as well as by British politicians like Joseph Hume, MP for Montrose Burghs. Hume, in particular, practically accused Brooke of turning the Sarawak Dayaks to piracy with each of his needless dreadful attacks. It is hard to argue that, to a certain extent, Wise and Hume were right, as Brooke himself acknowledged in a letter to Palmerston in April 1849. In this missive he casually mentioned how he had tried to starve the "pirates" by interrupting supplies of "salt, iron and other necessaries" during a blockade that ultimately led to the massacre of hundreds of Dayaks at the end of July, after they were left with no option but to defend themselves.[47]

Three years after Brooke's assault on the Dayaks at Batang Marau in 1849, his former partner, Henry Wise, wrote to British foreign secretary, Lord Malmelsbury, accusing Brooke of lying and confessing how he had instilled in him what he called a deluded "belief that the weak savage neighbours on whom he made war, were genuine and dangerous pirates," when in reality they were not.[48] Only a few weeks before, Joseph Hume presented the same charges, accusing him of destroying "more than a thousand innocent persons" just to further his own land-grabbing interests.[49]

Brooke's answers since the early 1840s to all these denunciations were, predictably, that all his actions had been legal, necessary, and for the own good of the local populations. When his murky dealings began to be questioned back in Britain, he assured everyone who would listen that he had obtained the Sarawak territory by nonviolent, legal means. In a letter to Malmelsbury, written in 1852, he vowed to have obtained these territories through "good will" only, and that he had had "no ulterior object, no prospect of any personal advantage" at the time.[50] Never mind that he also confessed in writing, in a very casual manner, that in order to secure his control over Sarawak he had "loaded the guns of the yacht" before securing an interview with Rajah Muda Hashim, who, not surprisingly, felt he had no other alternative but to cede the territory to the Englishman.[51] Adding insult to injury, Brooke presided over the looting of Dayak's treasures, "amongst which were some ancient jars, which the Dyaks hand down from father to son as heir-looms, and prize very highly, some of them being valued as high as 200*l*."[52]

By the late 1840s Brooke had come to believe his own civilizing and provider-of-peace hype. By 1848, he was blaming the increase of piracy in the region on his absence from Sarawak and on "the length of time" that had "elapsed since their last punishment," clearly referring to his previous preemptive expedition undertaken alongside Captain Henry Keppel in 1845.[53] As pressure against him mounted in the early 1850s and a public enquiry was set up, his answers to critical questions continued to be evasive and, in Hume's words, "mythical."[54] In spite of the overwhelming amount of evidence demonstrating his wrongdoings, Brooke was let off by the British government time and again, as his skillful services as an imperial agent had brought not only Sarawak into the British sphere but also the strategic island of Labuan in 1846.[55]

Although Brooke is perhaps the best-known truth-twisting speculator of his time, he was hardly the only one to justify atrocities against non-Western amphibious populations on the basis that they were absolutely essential for the benefit of those they displaced, kidnapped, injured, and killed. Years before, another British adventurer, a Mr. Dalton, engaged in serious discussions with the Dutch government in Batavia in the hope that they would "send a force to dethroning the present Rajah" of an undetermined region of Borneo, probably Pontianak, "establishing influence in that part of Borneo by means of the individual whom he recommended to replace the Rajah."[56]

Likewise, around the same time Brooke found himself defending his actions in London, the Ottoman governor of the island of Samos, Georgios Konemenos, ordered a deadly attack on a group of "pirates" who had been raiding the western coast of Turkey for years. The attack ended in a slaughter, with not one person surviving. Writing to the foreign minister of the Sublime Porte, Ali Pasha, soon afterward, Konemenos excused himself for authorizing the use of excessive force and confessed that he sought "consolation in the idea that the world [had] been delivered from a great scourge."[57] In a similar vein, Spanish missionary Ylario Alcazar attempted to justify the French bombing of Da Nang in 1856 by blaming the Annamites for being "ignorant magnates" who could not be persuaded that the French came with "friendly purposes"—in spite of the very obvious fact that they had just unleashed their canonry on the three forts that protected the city.[58]

This idealization of Western incursions overseas as benign operations was, at times, rationalized by some of these imperial agents. Two cases in question are those of William Dallas Bernard and Scott Beresford, both of whom honed their ideas during the armed suppression of amphibious populations in the South China Sea following the end of the First Opium War. In a two-volume narrative of his time on board the famous steamer *Nemesis*, Bernard wrote, not without irony, that he hoped that the conquerors' "example of humanity and forbearance" would serve "to modify the barbarous ideas of war" which the Chinese were attached to.[59] By doing so, he expected that after being severely chastised, they would learn "to respect and admire the principles of the advanced civilization" of the Europeans who had invaded them, occupied their towns, and in some instances, massacred their people.[60] Beresford's opinion was even more disconcerting than Bernard's. In a volume published in 1851, he expressed the hope that the ways in which the English had imposed themselves over the Chinese would present "a great moral lesson."[61] To Beresford, the British had done nothing but sacrifice themselves and risk their lives, "ridding the coast of the destroyers of their commerce."[62] Both Bernard and Beresford saw the war and its aftermath as a civilizing endeavor. At the same time, they saw the Chinese as an ungrateful partner who did not appreciate what European gunboats had done for their benefit, by suppressing maritime raiding activities that the Chinese had, to a considerable extent, provoked when they unleashed a war to protect their drug-trafficking operations.

To all Western pirate imperial powers engaged in projects they saw as civilizing amphibious communities, their efforts on occasion entailed the introduction of supposed benefits for those who had survived the initial violence. Such benefits could arise through the introduction of new technological developments or, simply, from setting up trading or transportation networks, of which, later in the century, railroads would become imperialism's pride and joy.

An illustrative example of this kind occurred in December 1860 when a large Dutch force chased down a group of maritime raiders who had been active for months, maybe years, in the Makassar Straits. After they were finally tracked down to a small island in the Celebes Sea, "a multitude of robbers [were] shot down" by the guns and crew of the steamer *Reinier Claeszen*.[63] Subsequently, in an attempt to "eradicate that robbers' nest completely," the Dutch commander, W. G. Willinck, ordered that "the whole island [be] intersected with roads," so that no future sanctuary could be found on it by any party that threatened Dutch control in the Celebes Sea and the Makassar Straits.[64]

Turning maritime raiding communities into agricultural ones was also a favorite system used by Western empires. In the 1820s, the Dutch relocated entire seafaring communities to agricultural regions in the Moluccas, forcing them to abandon their amphibious lives and cultures and learn new productive skills that fitted better with the capitalist needs of the Dutch East Indies.[65] Likewise, after the kidnapping of their relatives, Fernando de Norzagaray banished most of the "sea-robbers" of Tawi Tawi, and their entire families, to the Cagayan Valley in the northernmost part of the Philippines, where they were forcefully turned into agricultural laborers.[66] To westerners' minds, another civilizational tool was the foment of commerce, which they saw as a means to acquire wealth and as an antidote to maritime raiding activities.

In chapter 3 I discuss the relationship between commerce and maritime raiding at length, but it is worth noting here one representative instance that reveals the ways in which Western imperial actors attempted to "civilize" while simultaneously grabbing peoples' lands and waters by force. In a missive sent to London in June 1856, the British consul in Tangier, John Hay Drummond Hay, wrote about a conversation he had had with the Spanish governor of Melilla, Brigadier Manuel Buceta. In this informal exchange, the latter had offered a few candid opinions about the relationship between the town under his command and the local "piratical" populations of the Riff Coast.

According to Drummond Hay, the Spanish governor was wary of the ongoing conflict between Melilla and the Riffians and had decided to set up a customs office at the Melilla garrison to stop the smuggling across the border with French Algeria and, more important, to encourage "the industry and trade of the Reefians."[67] In Buceta's mind, the encroachment and occupation of their lands was not the main source of friction with the local population, and neither were his repeated expeditions against the maritime communities of the Riff, where he had reputedly sank at least forty-four of their vessels in a short period of time.[68] Instead, Buceta believed that reorganizing steps were needed as they "would help to civilize them and afford them means of enriching themselves and of obtaining the produce of European manufacturers, [rather] than by *piracy*."[69]

Self-righteous views about the civilizational and liberating character of European efforts in northern Africa, China, and other parts of the world were shared by imperial agents of most, if not all, Western pirate empires. For instance, a few months before the start of the Second Opium War, French politician Melchior-Honoré Yvan naïvely commented that whenever "the flag of a civilized power" appeared in the seas of China, pirates' captives saw it as "an ark of deliverance that floats in the horizon."[70] Likewise, while discussing maritime raiding events before and during the Spanish invasion of Morocco in 1859, Evaristo Ventosa contrasted the "acts of savage piracy" of the Moroccans with the "Spanish magnanimous generosity."[71] Almost immediately afterward, Ventosa saw fit to point out that such "piratical" acts had forced the Spanish to take "some measures of rigor," which, as is well known, amounted to nothing short of war crimes.[72]

Beliefs in Western imperialist benevolence also served as a footing for calls to implement replacement theories. In 1856, French author H. de T. D'Arlach bemoaned how civilized nations had "shown such a long patience in the presence of acts odious piracy that is perpetually committed on the coasts of the Riff."[73] In his opinion, the only way to "punish these pirates in a salutary manner" would be "by the complete extermination of these hordes of savages."[74] Like D'Arlach, John Bowring, a disciple of Jeremy Bentham and James and John Stuart Mill, did not mince words when he wrote that "the savage and least improvable races will continue to be supplanted or absorbed by those of a higher intelligence."[75] To Bowring, only by entering into contact with a greater civilization could the "semi-civilized" populations survive the encounter between cultures provoked by nineteenth-century expansive Western imperialism. In fact, Bowring's and D'Arlach's ideas were destined to make a similar point; in the words of the latter, in the "struggle between civilization and barbarism, victory [of the Western imperial powers] is not in doubt."[76]

Races and religions that were perceived as inferior and backward, then, provided aggressive imperial powers with an extra layer of typecasting imageries, which were often used and abused to rationalize all sorts of atrocities. Dark-skinned peoples in particular were associated with regressive traits and behaviors that made it easier for westerners to label them accordingly. Non-Western amphibious communities in many of the regions discussed here, likely to be dark-skinned, were readily considered to be "piratical" the moment they offered any sort of refusal or resistance to Western ideas or practices. When the royal commissioner Charles Robert Prinsep submitted his report on the accusations against James Brooke for massacring the people of Batang Marau, he felt compelled to first point out that the punishment that Brooke had inflicted on them had been adequate, "with a view to the repression of their atrocious outrages."[77] But Prinsep did not stop there. He further shored up his argument by brushing aside the human lives lost due to Brooke's attacks, principally due to what we can only refer to as racial considerations: "So far, as regards the loss of life inflicted on them, there does not appear any reasonable ground for sympathy with a race of indiscriminate murderers."[78]

Terms such as "race of pirates" or "bloodthirsty races" were frequently used by Western agents before, during, and after their encounters with non-Western amphibious peoples accused of being pirates. In 1838, William Norris, referred to the Iranun as a "notorious and formidable race of Pirates," who had "carried on their depredations on an extension scale and from the earliest times."[79] The Spanish general Rafael de Echagüe, who had fought amphibious peoples along the northern coast of Africa in the late 1850s and who was appointed governor general of the Philippines in July 1862, reported only a few months after taking up his new post that he had overseen the destruction of the "pirate towns" of Carondong and Patián. In this report he emphasized that the victory obtained by the Spanish forces was over "bloodthirsty and warring races living in the south of this archipelago [the Philippines]."[80]

In a letter to the ministers of war and marine, written soon after one of the many incidents of maritime raiding in northern Moroccan waters in the 1840s and 1850s, Spanish secretary of *ultramar*, Juan de Zavala, referred to the peoples of the Riff as "a numerous race, who sees in piracy a profession both profitable and glorious."[81] Similarly, Captain Henry Giffard used transparent racial terms when he described the same communities as a "numerous, daring, warlike and brave race of people."[82] Such racial stereotypes were applied by the representatives of pirate imperialist powers not only to the Riff and Southeast Asian communities but to amphibious populations from all over the world.

Those living in the surroundings of the mouth of the river Indus, particularly the Zingan, were described as a "race of pirates" by James G. Percival, in the "Appendix of the Varieties on Human Race," published in 1826.[83] Exactly the same moniker was used by W. S. Bridges thirty years later, in 1856, when he presented a group of suggestions for the suppression of piracy in the China Seas to the British secretary of states for the colonies. In this document, Bridges referred to the islands in the vicinity of Hong Kong as the "haunts & nurseries of the present race of pirates."[84] The French, too, classified seafaring groups engaged in "piracy" activities along the Albanian coast in terms associated with Islam, such as "Ottoman Turks."[85] In doing so, they made sure that their non-Christian origins were highlighted as a marker of difference from white, Western, Christian people, thus preemptively justifying any violent armed actions that could be taken against them.

As a matter of fact, alongside typecasting of a racial, racist nature, pirate imperialist agents and governments frequently made a point of singling out Islam and other non-Christian religious beliefs by portraying them as backward and as a main reason for the continuous uncivilized and ferocious character of the seafaring populations they encountered all over the world. Islam as a religion and Muslims as a group were repeatedly targeted with all sorts of clichés by every Western pirate empire that came into contact with them. Even in exceptional opportunities when the influence of Islam was praised, barely a few lines later some aspect of their creed was likely to be belittled or demeaned. This was the case of Stamford Raffles, who in 1823 commented that the "states more advanced in civilization have embraced the Mahomedan faith," somehow implying that they had benefited from doing so. Sadly, shortly afterward, he referred to "Mussulman teachers" as "little more than manumitted slaves" who assumed the titles of "Syeds or Sheiks."[86] Lewis Pelly, British resident in the Persian Gulf who, as we will soon see, held some positive opinions about the inhabitants of this region, criticized Islam, and more particularly its Wahhabi version, whose "religious idea" had "fused them into an aggressive mass."[87]

The Dutch had similar views about the influence of Islam among those they considered to be engaged in maritime raiding in the Eastern Archipelago. In a letter to the governor of the Dutch East Indies in 1833, Jacques Nicholaas Vosmaer disparaged their "fanatical religious principles" and their "stupidest superstition," which kept them engaged in robbery and in a state of "backward civilization."[88] Such ideas were echoed decades later on the pages of the Dutch East Indies newspaper *De Oostpost.* In an article published in 1857 and titled "De Zeerovers in den Indischen Archipel" (The Pirates in the Indian Archipelago), the writer blamed "Arabs from the Red Sea and the Persians" for introducing the practice of piracy in Southeast Asian waters.[89] More specifically, the article claimed that "conjugated by the evils of religion, these Mohammedan adventurers supported one another against the natives," making conquests and becoming rich in the process.[90] Some colonial officers agreed with these views. In his *Notices Historiques* Cornets de Groot made a point of accentuating the "kind of religious fanaticism maintained by the most stupid gullibility" as one of the main reasons that led Dutch East Indian amphibious populations "to make trade of piracy."[91]

And so did the French, the Spanish, and the Americans. The former used all sorts of derisive language against the Muslims during the North African campaigns in the nineteenth century. French diplomat Alexandre de Miltitz discussed, in his *Manuel des Consuls*, how and why the Muslims of northern Africa had turned to piracy and the role that their faith had played in this process. In his words, "Under the banner of the Crescent, they had become excellent sailors, and their leaders, who had made Algiers the main place of arms, had given a color of sanctity to their piracy by means of religious fanaticism."[92] The Spanish, too, repeatedly mocked Islamic beliefs as "criminal" and blamed Muslims' fanaticism for their religious intolerance, a circumstance that served as a perfect excuse for Spain to attempt the conquest the whole of the Riff.[93]

Just like the French and the Spanish, American imperial agents held contemptuous views about non-Christian religious beliefs, not limited to Islam, that were practiced by non-Western, darker-skinned peoples. A case in question is that of American missionary Adoniram Judson, who dismissed Buddhism as backward and uncivilized when he referred to Burma as a "land of darkness" with "towering pagodas and a rude filthy population."[94] In another representative example, the American consul in Amoy (Xiamen), Charles William Bradley, attempted to exonerate Robert Brown, captain of a ship, after a large contingent of Chinese coolies, whom he was transporting to Peru, took arms against him and his crew, killing some of them and taking the vessel back to China. To Bradley the main reason for the uprising, which was eventually deemed to be an act of piracy, had been the attempt of the captain to clean up the coolies, having them "scrubbed by the crew" and cutting off the tails of more than two hundred men, which, he admitted, had been a mistake.[95] However, even though he acknowledged that the comportment of the captain and crew had included actions that they could not "easily forgive," Bradley did not hesitate to dismiss the sentiments of the coolies as some sort of "superstitious feeling," and nothing else.[96]

Racial and religious prejudices allowed, on occasion, for the development of civilizational hierarchies that could be used to determine to what extent particular populations could be targeted for land expropriation, displacement, colonial occupation, and so on. For example, dark-skinned communities, particularly Africans, were frequently described with pejorative appellations that could infantilize or dehumanize them. Islamic peoples, too, were sometimes readily associated with extreme violent behaviors that could justify their repression with similar or even greater levels of ferocity.

On occasion, some notable British imperial agents of this period attempted to rationalize these views by resorting to highly speculative, pseudo-intellectual, racist tropes. Notably, John Bowring, who was a proponent of replacement theories, conjectured in the late 1850s about how a "middle race" like the Chinese was, at that time, "advancing the work of civilization" by facilitating the emigration of millions of their men, women, and children to places as far away as Peru and Cuba.[97] Bowring's use of "middle race" to refer to the Chinese, while contrasting them to the populations that inhabited the nearby Philippines, constituted a case in point that reveals how some mid-nineteenth-century Western imperialists saw non-Western populations through their own distorted segregating lens.

John Crawfurd, who had earlier argued for the need of selling firearms to Southeast Asian peoples in order to improve their chances of development, was even more explicit in his hierarchization of the peoples of the world. In his own words, it was all "a mere affair of civilization."[98] To Crawfurd, the Hindus were inferior to the Europeans and the Chinese "in real skill and intelligence," and yet, he remarked, they were "no savages."[99] In the mind of this influential British imperial representative, the Hindus were "far more civilized than the Mexicans and Peruvians ever were," which, he concluded, suggested that there was "little ground to expect their extermination."[100]

Stereotypes such as the ones discussed above were further driven by more specific depictions of the "looks" of non-Western seafaring peoples. These descriptions usually presented "uncivilized" characteristics in all their glory and were found in writings and drawings published in European and American newspapers and magazines. For example, multiple engravings of Malay and Iranun "pirates" published in the *Illustrated London News* during the 1840s and 1850s presented these peoples as mostly uncivilized and warlike, thus supporting descriptions that had been made by Brooke, Keppel, and others to justify their repeated attacks on them.[101] Chinese and Riffian maritime raiding leaders, such as Chui-a-poo and El Hadji Taradji, were portrayed in British and French newspapers, alongside narratives of their alleged crimes and the sacrifices made by European nations to bring their depredations to an end.[102]

Chui-a-poo, the Chinese pirate. *The Illustrated London News* (June 14, 1851).

Diverse portrayals of non-Western seafaring peoples considered to be engaged in piratical activities appeared in assorted types of sources; they were common in both published literary works and official correspondence between imperial agents. In a book published in 1861 and after resorting to the usual pejorative terms used to refer to the Malay (e.g., little civilized, stupid, unintelligent), Alfred de Moges offered a physiognomic description of these "pirates." Referring specifically to the Malays from Sumatra, he commented that there was "something wild and stern in the look of these natives."[103] He then leapt to facile conclusions associating these looks with what he thought a "race" like theirs could do for a living: "They have quite the appearance we should expect to meet in a race of hardy and relentless pirates."[104]

Fellow French author Melchior-Honoré Yvan was more precise in his description of the "pirates" of the Sunda Islands and the Sulu Archipelago. In his words, these men always carried

El-Hadji Taradji, pirate of the Riff. *L'Illustration: journal universel* 25 (October 18, 1856).

"their kriss in their belts" and "their spears in their fists."[105] According to Yvan, their "naturally rough physiognomy" took on "a formidable character, when their long hair half veil[ed] their features"; behind the veil of hair one could see "their blood red lips, their black teeth," which had been purposedly filed by them with a black "empyreumatic preparation" that had destroyed their enamel.[106] Portrayals of this kind often made it into the pages of newspapers and magazines with a large circulation, informing public opinion arguably more than books like those by de Moges and Yvan. In 1857, for example, *De Oostpost* focused not only on the overall looks of these people but also on their assorted types of weapons, which included the kriss or male dagger, the klewang, two-sided swords, lances, bows and poisoned arrows, grappling hooks, and riffles.[107]

A similar description of the amphibious communities of the Sulu Sea was given by José García y Ruiz, a former Spanish governor of Zamboanga. García y Ruiz also referred to the weapons carried by the "moros" of Joló, mentioning the kriss and the campulan, well-built swords that often featured handles made of ebony, ivory, and silver.[108] Equally, he made a point of conveying to his readers an image of savage, desperate people, who would fight to death rather than surrendering to the better armed and organized Spanish troops. García y Ruiz was at pains to point out that they did not "shave the hair" as most other Muslims did; instead, they let it grow to the base of their necks, to the point of coming out of their turbans, as a "signal of the warriors" they were.[109]

Comparing these amphibious peoples to animals or going to extremes to portray their behaviors as beastly was a recurring argument made by those who came into contact with them. For example, soon after a successful attack against a supposed group of "pirates" in Tawi Tawi in 1862, Antonio de Mora reflected on the bravery of the men of the *Santa Filomena* and *Samar* war vessels, who, in his words, "dared to enter in the hidden and frightening den of the crueler than wild beasts pirates."[110] Likewise, Captain General Antonio de Urbiztondo reported on a raid against a group of "pirate boats near Paragua" in 1851, which, in his words, had resisted in a way that "could not be more ferocious and hostile."[111] In a missive sent only a few months before, Urbiztondo had used the term "Argelians of Asia" to refer to those "moors" who were plundering the area under his command, establishing a clear link between maritime predatory activities and their suppression in two very different parts of the world.[112] A similar description was provided to the authorities of Gibraltar by the skipper of the felucca *Mary*, who had come under attack by Riffians "uttering fierce cries" only days before.[113] De Abenia Taure also used animalistic terms to refer to the Riffians, going so far as to consider them as a "people of beasts" that "crawls through the ground as a panther, to close on the prey that wishes to devour without being seen."[114]

Likewise, Western imperialist agents frequently depicted seafaring peoples who stood in their way as treacherous or cowardly enemies, always ready to use their ferocious and ruthless ways to attack and destroy. In June 1856, the commander of HMS *Ariel*, in a letter sent to his superiors after returning from the Riff Coast, commented that he had been forced to use "the utmost caution" while approaching the coast, as the inhabitants were "treacherous and unscrupulous."[115] Likewise, while dealing with the aftermath of the first attempt by the Malays to retake Kedah from the Siamese in 1831, the British governor of the Straits Settlements, Robert Ibbetson, celebrated the captured of one of the Malay leaders, Tunku Kudin, whom he considered to be not just a pirate but also "a treacherous and troublesome neighbour."[116]

Another British officer, Appleton Oaksmith, had a similar experience four years earlier when, during a stop at Shark Point near the mouth of the Congo River, his ship, HMS *Dolphin*, was attacked by a group of "African pirates." Though the crew of the vessel was forced to fight back, Oaksmith commented that they did not think much of the attack, "attributing it to their natural cowardice."[117] Along the same lines, Spanish officer Eusebio Salcedo used the word "coward" to refer to the resistance he had encountered during an attack against maritime raiding populations in Tongkil in 1862.[118] In another case, in 1847, a Dutch East Indies newspaper saw fit to repeat a number of tropes associated with the maritime communities of this region. Not content with resorting to the usual stereotypes, which included presenting them as "rather cowardly in nature," the article pointed out that they lacked "the careless bravery and fearlessness that distinguished the European buccaneers" of the Golden Age of Piracy in the Atlantic.[119]

In parallel with such widespread ways of pigeonholing seafaring populations, Western imperial agents were expedient in adapting those views and even turning them around when members of these communities decided to embrace or mimic Western ways and religious beliefs. Jacques Nicolaas Vosmaer, writing in 1833, considered these groups more an exception than a common occurrence. To him, on "those fortunate lands where Europeans [had] established their influence," the same people who would normally be considered as uncivilized and savage had attained "a superior character and state."[120] Similarly, Spanish officer Antonio de Mora, who had been highly critical of the character of amphibious communities in the south of the Philippines, found it in himself to praise a group of "subordinate moors" who had fought shoulder to shoulder with the Spanish troops under his command, and who had spilled and mixed their blood with their Spanish counterparts during their anti-piratical campaigns.[121] To de Mora, these men had "stamped their love for the civilizing principles" by choosing to join Spain in an attack against those who had been, until recently, their brothers.

The British, too, argued that their imperial endeavors could have a positive effect among previously uncivilized populations and their leaders. In 1831, for example, the British resident in the Persian Gulf, David Wilson, referred to the imam of Muscat's "comparatively enlightened views" and to his role in "advancing civilization in that part of the world," which should aid "in putting down piracy" in the region.[122] Before concluding this letter, Wilson made sure of pointing out that these civilizing views were nothing but the result of his decision to form an alliance with Britain.[123]

In fairness, a small number among the many imperial agents cited in this book did have a mixed outlook when it came to the amphibious communities they came into contact with. Some, for example, Lewis Pelly, revealed in their correspondence various levels of admiration for non-Western peoples and cultures. Pelly was particularly impressed by how the Arabs he had met had a symbiotic relationship with their environment, which he admired and respected. In a letter written in 1868, he observed that the Arabs had "a mutual confidence" with all animals, including horses and greyhounds, and that these "beasts" seemed "so thoroughly to comprehend language addressed to them by men."[124] Pelly also reflected on the former grandeur of the Arab conquests, stating that meeting them (the Arabs) one could "readily comprehend how they once stormed across the world," and be "persuaded that they still possess[ed] qualities" which could "again render them renowned, should outward circumstances favor."[125]

In spite of some earlier criticism of their form of life and their maritime raiding activities, Sherard Osborn, too, strived to highlight the positive aspects of the Malay character, going as far as to compare it favorably with that of his European fellow crew members. Osborn commented on how in the Malays' "practical jokes or witticisms, there was none of that grossness or unbecoming language which European sailors, be their nation what it may, would assuredly have indulged in."[126] At some other juncture, Osborn even implied that the main reasons behind the seafaring Malays turning to piracy were the persecution and harassment they had been subjected to by the Dutch and the Siamese empires "in days long" ago and by the British in more recent times.[127]

Stereotyping also happened in reverse, as non-Western peoples saw their Western agents of pirate imperialism through racialized and pejorative prisms. They recorded their opinions on occasions numerically limited when compared to those left by their Western counterparts. In these instances, and not without reason, they pointed out the ways that westerners behaved and, unsurprisingly, accused them of a variety of crimes, including piracy. As Amirell has recently noticed, in 1860 the Vietnamese emperor Tu Duc accused the French of being "pirates, equally incompetent and cowardly," while also labeling them as "dogs."[128] By the time Tu Duc made these accusations, the Vietnamese had endured several American and French attacks, dating from the mid-1840s onward and including a recent bombardment of the port and city of Da Nang. In 1845 and 1847 naval squads commanded by John Percival and Charles Rigault de Genouilly, respectively, shelled their cities, kidnapped some of their mandarins, and caused numerous deaths among their armed and civilian population.[129] Tu Duc had also been forced to deal with numerous instances of maritime raiding originating in China and other parts of the South China Sea and Southeast Asia, as recently demonstrated and extensively discussed by Nguyen Thi My Hanh.[130]

It was in China, in the aftermath of the First Opium War, where more opinions about westerners were recorded, both within Chinese documents and also by European witnesses, who at times struggled to understand the terms chosen by the Chinese when referring to Europeans. Of these, perhaps the most relevant to this discussion is "barbarians," which the Chinese used extensively when referring to the Western invaders in the decades that followed the British imperialist invasion of 1839.

In a volume in which he reproduced various original accounts written by Chinese witnesses to the British invasion, Arthur Waley included a number of these references to Western barbarians, and others that presented westerners in equally unflattering ways. One document was produced by Commissioner Lin Zexu, the Chinese mandarin who was the main antagonist of Canton-based British drug lords William Jardine and James Matheson and who played a central role in the events leading to the outbreak of the First Opium War. Not surprisingly, Lin's opposition to the illegal importation of opium into China meant that he was maligned and denigrated by British drug lords and government agents alike; they consistently blamed him for the outbreak of hostilities in 1839. Lin was very critical of the manner in which the British had been exporting opium into China, and in one of the many passages condemning their actions he compared their opium to poison and lamented the "barbarian smoke" that now filled his country's markets.[131] Lin was also quite critical of the habit that Europeans had of "marrying people with the same surname," which in his eyes was "indeed a barbarous custom."[132] In another passage, he described the Europeans he had met in Macau as having the look of "devils," also making reference to their dark-skinned enslaved peoples, whom he called "black devils."[133]

Another author cited by Waley, a poet named Chu Shih-yun, used the term "black devils" repeatedly while discussing the violence caused in Chinkiang by some Indian troops that had accompanied the British in their invasion.[134] Both Chu Shih-yun and another author, who went by the name of Ts'ao Sheng and who experienced the devastation caused by the British in Shanghai, described how the "barbarians" had looted and raped as they had pleased during the occupation that followed the First Opium War.[135]

Commissioner Lin, being a prolific writer, left the most extensive critical commentary on the British and their actions before, during, and after the First Opium War. Lin considered opium to be a poison and the British drug dealers in China to be men of a very questionable character. He accused the likes of Jardine and Matheson of "tempting fools to destroy themselves, merely in order to reap profit," and on a couple of occasions he went as far as pondering whether they were engaged in much more sinister operations.[136] For instance, after hearing about the British "buying little pigs" in Canton, he wondered whether this expression was but a euphemism to cover up child-trafficking operations, which, he lamented, was very difficult to confirm.[137] On another occasion, Lin discussed how

British opium was processed, questioning a rumor that suggested that the poppy juice being sold in China was mixed with human blood and concluding that in reality the juice was being mixed with a less ominous ingredient, namely the "corpses of crows."[138]

Edward H. Cree, a surgeon in the Royal Navy, who participated in the First Opium War and who left a significant number of watercolors revealing the destruction and death created by the British invasion in 1839, also commented in his journal about the ways the Chinese employed the term "barbarian" when talking about the British. On January 14, 1841, for example, he denigrated the Chinese authorities of Ningbo for sending an insolent message to his commodore, in which they addressed the British as "the English barbarians, the most inferior natives."[139] Even when commending the Chinese for their friendliness, Cree was forced to record how some of them had decided to stay behind, rather than fleeing from the war, because, in his words, "they had confidence in the barbarians."[140]

Ultimately, and in spite of having only fragmentary evidence, it is possible to affirm that westerners' beliefs about the superiority of their civilization and religion, which provided the rational justification for diplomatic and armed suppression activities around the world, were questioned and challenged virtually everywhere they attempted to make them stick. In a letter to Lord Palmerston, sent in 1840, the British representative before the Sublime Porte, Viscount Ponsonby, bid the foreign secretary understand that even though the Turks may have believed them "to be their superiors in the Sciences, Arts and in Arms" they were "very far from thinking our wisdom and our morality [to be] greater than their own."[141] Just as the British foreign secretary was compelling nations across the world to embrace abolitionist policies, while simultaneously ordering the bombing of Chinese cities so that drugs could keep flowing into their country, one of his own ministers was pointing out to him that the ways the British saw themselves did not necessarily match how they were perceived the by others.

Among the papers of James Brooke, held at the Bodleian Library at Oxford University, is an undated piece of prose entitled "Damning a Brooke." Probably written by one of Brooke's contemporaries, the document makes virtually every major argument developed in this chapter within a few lines. It begins, "There are so many James Brookes in the world,—so many men looking out for pirate tribes to put down . . . and savage races to civilise," stressing the correlation between Brooke's imperial ambitions and his use of the suppression of piracy—real or imaginary—to further his own aims.[142] But it does not stop there. Soon after, the author refers to "straggling villages of a few hundred inhabitants to convert into well-ordered towns with their twenty-five thousands of populations" and to "export traders to create out of nothing," highlighting the role that colonialism and commerce played in this tragedy.[143] Finally, the author moves on to "violence to extirpate by law, and heathendom to drive out by Christianity," clearly turning the focus on the role played by European laws and Christianity as an effective supporting cast in this pseudo-civilizing saga.[144]

Pirate empires and their agents saw their "civilizing" efforts as forerunners of peace, happiness, and progress. Or as Lauren Benton has recently put it, "A future conditional peace was firmly and increasingly associated with utopian visions of civilization."[145] In reality, even when their "civilizing" actions were done in good faith, imperial agents were more likely to usher in suffering, displacement, penury, and death for the amphibious communities with whom they made contact. From the dehumanization of non-western peoples so that they could be "civilized" to the countless deaths caused by pirate imperialist armies and navies claiming new lands and seas, such ideas and associated practices pervaded the encounters between western and non-western peoples during the entirety of the period studied here.

The kidnapping of women and children to use as ransom, the bombardment of seafaring populations, the razing of crops and villages, and even the belief that assimilation or extermination were the only available paths forward for peoples they considered to be "savages" were all distinctive indicators of diplomatic and armed suppression of maritime raiding during this period. These policies often amounted to nothing short of true piratical actions. The fact that empires repeatedly chose to suppress piracy by using piratical means raises the question of whether Western empires were indeed the more civilized party. John Guard, a former convict who ended up as commander of the ship *Harriet,* wrecked off the coast of New Zealand in 1834, revealed such pirate imperialist views perhaps better than anyone else when he suggested, "A musket ball for every New Zealander [was] the only way of civilizing their country."[146]

CHAPTER TWO

Abolition and the Suppression of Maritime Raiding

On the morning of November 25, 1835, following the two-week-long trial of the crew of the Spanish schooner *Panda*, the United States Circuit Court in Boston, Massachusetts, reconvened one final time. The *Panda*'s captain and sailors had been accused of attacking the American brig *Mexican* in the vicinity of the Azores Islands in late September 1832, robbing the crew of everything they had and attempting to sink the ship, putting into practice the old adage "dead men tell no tales" often associated with the Golden Age of Piracy. The trial of Captain Pedro Gibert and his crew captured the attention and imagination of the American public. Soon after the trial took place, and even before the resulting death sentences had been carried out, multiple illustrated articles and books were published discussing the particulars of the case.[1]

The story of the schooner *Panda* was not unique or even uncommon, as we will soon see. The *Panda* was a vessel that had participated in various slave-trading expeditions under various names, and so had its captain, Gibert.[2] After the pillaging of the *Mexican*, the *Panda* had sailed for its original destination in the river Nazareth, near Cape Lopez, where the crew was expected to take on illegal

Scene from the trial of the schooner Panda in Boston showing one of the pirates being attacked in court by one of the sailors of the *Mexican.* *The Pirates' Own Book or Authentic Narratives of the Lives, Exploits, and Executions of the Most Celebrated Sea Robbers* (Portland: Sanborn & Carter, 1844).

human cargo and return to Cuba, hoping to make a hefty profit. Unforeseen and severe health problems, however, forced Gibert to take the schooner to Principe Island, where it was spotted by British cruiser HMS *Curlew*, which ultimately followed it to the river Nazareth, attacking it and capturing Gibert, his second mate Bernardo de Soto, and a number of its sailors.[3]

After a transatlantic journey that took over two years and led them to Fernando Po, Ascension Island, and England, the crew of the *Panda* was finally extradited to the United States in 1834 to face trial for their act of piracy on the high seas. In spite of all the evidence gathered against them, including the testimonies of firsthand witnesses, the crew of the *Panda* received public support from Spain, Havana, and even from some quarters along the East Coast of the United States. They were defended by none other than David Lee Child, an abolitionist who, for reasons that are hard to determine, chose to represent them. Numerous public figures stepped up either to defend them or to question the accusations against them. This group included several hundred citizens from Boston and Watertown, who sent a letter to Andrew Jackson, inquiring about the evidence presented against the Spaniards.[4] In fact, President Jackson felt compelled to intervene after the sentences had been handed down. He pardoned the second mate, Bernardo de Soto, after meeting his wife and receiving multiple letters from the illegal slave-trading community of Havana attesting to his good character.[5]

When contrasted with the ways in which non-Western, nonwhite seafaring peoples were summarily attacked, displaced, and massacred, often without the right to a fair trial, the proceedings against Gibert and his mates reveal a categorically different way of dealing with those accused of piracy throughout the Atlantic world. Although much less studied than the same phenomenon in previous centuries, Atlantic piracy continued to be a problem for all nations sending ships out to sea during the first few decades of the nineteenth century.

After a transition period that took the best part of the decade of the 1820s, privateering activities linked to the wars of independence in the Americas gave way to forms of maritime predatory violence carried out by disavowed former privateers, who turned to the slave trade as an alternative economic activity. Many of them did, at least for a while, roam the ocean "in the double capacity of pirate and slave dealer," as Alexander Bryson pointed out in 1847. This was not particularly surprising as both activities were overlapping, illegal, and in some cases, thanks to bilateral treaties and national laws, considered to be the same crime.[6]

In the Atlantic, and arguably beyond, maritime raiding and slave trading were oftentimes overlapping, complementary activities. Atlantic slave traders often resorted to piracy, including raids on fellow slave traders, and former privateers turned to the slave trade from the 1820s onward, while continuing and even expanding their predatory undertakings. Along the Atlantic and Indian Ocean coasts of Africa, local rulers in tandem with Western slave dealers continued to supply enslaved men, women, and children to be carried to places as far away as the United States, Cuba, and Brazil, while also humoring the piratical desires of many of the ship captains and crews that they did business with. On the American side of the Atlantic, authorities in places like New York, Havana, and Rio de Janeiro indulged maritime raiding as an acceptable economic activity. As the century unfolded and slave trading became more and more a synonym for piracy, they continued to support the pursuits of slave dealers, showing little regard for the possible consequences of their actions.

Subsequently, Western governments involved in the abolition of the slave trade were confronted with a new reality: slave trading and maritime raiding were often hard to disconnect, thus making the persecution and condemnation of slave trade vessels much harder. Led and, at times, forced by Britain, many Western and non-Western states began to adopt measures that coupled both illegal activities, ultimately turning them into a single one.

The case of the *Panda* highlights this consolidating process, both from the viewpoint of the slave dealers/pirates and from that of those engaged in abolishing human trafficking and maritime raiding in the Atlantic and beyond. In order to develop and expand these anti-piratical and anti-slave-trading policies, the British began a relentless push to persuade other states to commit to this double mode of abolition. All over the world, but particularly in the Atlantic, Britain either induced others by diplomatic means to equate the slave trade to piracy or, alternatively, imposed such views through bilateral treaties that were often signed within sight of their gunships. Within a few years, many of those who had been originally forced to implement abolition practices did embrace these views, and at times they even challenged British supremacy on the high seas, fighting both slave traders and pirates. The French, for example, managed to outnumber the British Anti-Slave Trade Squadron after 1845, becoming the main anti-slave-trading naval force in West African waters for a while.[7]

By the time Britain imposed its first treaties against piracy and the slave trade upon other states, it (1815) as well as the United States (1820) had passed internal laws condemning the slave trade and equating it to piracy. The aim of these laws was obvious. By turning human traffickers into pirates, it was hoped they could be judged by the rules established by the Law of Nations, which in practice meant that they could be sentenced to capital punishment without much ado. In the James Kent–inspired words of Justice Joseph Story of the American Supreme Court, pirates were nothing but "hordes of needy adventurers" and "the enemies of the human race." To Story, a judge who coincidentally presided over the trial of the *Panda* and who years later delivered the Supreme Court verdict on the famous case of the *Amistad*, there was only one suitable punishment for this type of crime, that of being "punished with death."[8] Even though, as we will soon see, the efficacy of measures likening one of these illegal maritime activities to the other was soon brought into question, new laws and treaties continued to be passed and signed until the transatlantic slave trade finally came to an end in the late 1860s.

Other Atlantic states followed Britain and the United States in passing laws that banned the slave trade and included provisions likening it to piracy. In 1824, a new law declaring "the traffic of negroes on the Coast of Africa" as piracy was passed by the Junta of Representatives of the province of Buenos Aires, and in October 1842 the Congress of the Republic of Chile determined that any citizen involved in one way or another with the slave trade would be liable to the "penalty for piracy," as enshrined in law 18, chapter 14, paragraph 72, of the laws of the republic.[9] A crucial decree declaring the slave trade as a piratical activity was passed by the Portuguese in July 1842, shortly after the British Parliament had revoked the Palmerston Act of 1839 and signed a bilateral agreement with the Portuguese crown for the effective abolition of the transatlantic slave trade.[10] Perhaps the most noteworthy of all these laws was passed by the Brazilians in 1850. In the so-called Eusébio de Queirós law any participation in slave-trading activities by Brazilian subjects was deemed to be an act of piracy and was expected to be punished accordingly.[11] As a result, and within a short period of time, Brazilian slave traders began to abandon their involvement in the traffic of human beings from Africa.[12]

Just as local or national laws had been enacted from the early 1820s, international, often bilateral, treaties played a central role in the process of turning slave traders into pirates, not just in the Atlantic but also beyond. In fact, one of the first treaties where the link between these two illegal activities was established was signed in 1820 between Britain and a number of rulers of the Persian Gulf, soon after the second bombardment of Ras Al-Khaimah. In this case, however, the main objective of the British was to stop predatory activities in the gulf, as it had been having an adverse effect on their trade with India for years. In its article 9, the treaty clearly stipulated that the "carrying of slaves, men, women or children, from the coasts of Africa or elsewhere" would thereafter be considered to be "plunder and piracy."[13] Consequently, "friendly Arabs" were dissuaded from participating in any sort of transportation of people.[14] This treaty, like many others that followed, specified that the suppression of maritime raiding and slave trading was, in fact, the responsibility of non-Western rulers. In practice, such agreements provided the British and other Western imperial powers with a license to use diplomatic or armed means to suppress these activities within their cosignatories' territories as they saw fit.[15]

The General Maritime Treaty with the Arab tribes of the Persian Gulf was followed by numerous others, all of which attempted to liken slave trading with piracy, in the hope that threats of capital punishment for those found guilty would discourage slave traders. Several states agreed to clauses in bilateral treaties signed with Britain during this period, including Brazil in 1826, Uruguay in 1839, Texas in 1840, and Mexico in 1841. Other treaties that did not incorporate such equating terms were worded to suggest that captured slave traders could be subjected to new worrisome measures. For instance, the Webster-Ashburton Treaty, signed between the United States and Britain in 1842, promised that both nations would work together to deliver to justice any persons engaged in criminal activities, including slave trafficking and piracy.[16] The treaty signed between Britain and France in 1845 also made a direct reference to how the transatlantic slave trade was "habitually carried on . . . accompanied by acts of piracy," subsequently committing the navies of both nations to stop these depredations in accordance with the Law of Nations.[17] Two other treaties signed that same year by the imam of Muscat with the French and the British were drafted keeping similar insinuations in mind.[18]

It could be argued that attempts at diplomatic suppression through the signing of treaties declaring the slave trade as piracy were ultimately successful. However, it took decades for them to have any serious effect on the transatlantic slave trade and the parasitic sort of predatory activities that came alongside it. Firstly, there were various nations that refused to agree to mutual searching rights with the British, particularly the Americans but also the French for a considerable part of this period. In other cases, notably with the Spanish, adding a clause declaring the slave trade as piracy to the anti-slave trade treaties signed in 1817 and 1835 became impossible. In fact, in spite of British pressures since the late 1810s to equate both activities in the laws of both countries, the Spanish held out until the 1860s. It was only in July 1861 that the governor of Cuba, Captain General Francisco Serrano, requested that the Spanish government declare the slave trade a form of piracy and punish engagement in it accordingly. Even then, and in spite of Serrano's appeal, it took another five years for the Spanish Cortes to pass the Law for the Repression and Punishment of the Slave Trade in 1866, after foreign minister, Antonio Cánovas del Castillo, brought it forward for debate.[19] Although the law, as Jesús Sanjurjo has clarified, did not include the word "piracy" in its text, its wording, in essence, likened both activities and established the same punishment for those who practiced either slave trading or piracy.[20]

Thomas Fowell Buxton, perhaps the foremost abolitionist in the 1830s in Britain, was well aware of the shortcomings associated with any laws or treaties declaring the slave trade as piracy. In *The African Slave Trade and Its Remedy*, published in 1840, his pessimism was quite transparent when he noted: "I am afraid that there is not the remotest probability of inducing all nations to concur in so strong a measure as that of stigmatising the Slave Trade as piracy."[21] In this reflection, Fowell Buxton was to an extent digressing about what James Kent had pointed out in *Commentaries on American Law* in 1826. For Kent, who at the time was one of the most respected authorities on the legal corpus regulating international relations in the United States, in order for the slave trade to be considered as piracy, it would have to be treated as such "in practice by all civilized states, or made so by virtue of a general convention."[22]

For a while Fowell Buxton had been skeptical that things would change at all, even if they could meet such challenging demands and manage to get all nations to declare the slave trade as piracy. To him, it had been evident that equating the slave trade to piracy had failed to stop countries like Brazil and the United States from slave trading, or to limit their involvement, noting that threats of treating slave dealers as pirates before their courts had been just that: threats. In Brazil, he noted, "not one has suffered under the law of piracy," and for the United States, he lamented, "I have yet to learn that even one capital conviction has taken place during the eighteen years that have elapsed since the law was passed."[23]

Fowell Buxton was scarcely alone in seeing the flaws in this sort of treaty. Commander Henry James Matson, who was one of the main protagonists in the capture of Gibert and his crew in 1833, and who after spending over two decades involved with Royal Navy abolition efforts in Africa and the Americas had acquired a firsthand knowledge of all the stratagems used by slave dealers throughout the Atlantic world, fully agreed. In a book published in 1848, Matson acknowledged that the inclusion of the word "piracy" in the treaty signed between Britain and Brazil in 1826 had left Brazilian slave traders "very much frightened."[24] Unfortunately, he observed, "they quickly found that it was only pen and ink," and in the following years their involvement not only continued but in fact increased.[25] In spite of these drawbacks, Matson still considered in 1848 that "Brazilian slave traders should be treated like pirates," as such measure would likely lead to the end of their involvement in the slave trade sooner or later.[26]

William Gore Ouseley, who served as British consul in Rio de Janeiro at the height of the Brazilian slave trade in the 1830s, also lamented that the treaty of 1826 had not had the desired effect. In a book published years later, in 1850, Ouseley recalled a conversation in which the Marquis of Barbacena, one of the most influential members of the Brazilian emperor's court, had shared with him what he considered to be "a ready method of putting a stop to the traffic."[27] Presented with this proposition, Ouseley sought out further details. Barbacena obliged, promising that "the master, mates, supercargo, and crew, at the yard-arms" would be hanged on the deck of the first vessel that they took that would afford them "a good reason, whether by resistance, killing your men, throwing their Africans overboard, or some such acts."[28] The marquis assured Ouseley that thereafter the traffic of enslaved peoples across the Atlantic would stop right away.

Equating slave trade activities with piracy through the passing of national laws and the signing of international treaties was a process fraught with difficulties. Although the strategy eventually contributed to the end of human trafficking in the Atlantic world, it was effective only when these laws and treaties were followed by actions. For example, in the case of Brazil, the implementation of the Eusébio de Queirós law forced Brazilian slave traders either to divert their business interests elsewhere or to relocate to other Atlantic spots—Havana, New York, or along the coast of Africa—where they were able to carry out their slave-trading endeavors for a few more years.[29]

Ultimately, the coup de grâce of the Atlantic slave trade also took place in a North American court of law, when another cause célèbre, that of Nathaniel Gordon, brought upon slave traders the realization that the Act of 1820 was a dead letter no more.[30] For years the United States had been presumed to have zero tolerance toward the transatlantic slave trade, while it failed to stop national and foreign traders from using its ports as a base for their expeditions.[31] In fact, American shipyards also constructed purpose-built vessels, featuring state-of-the-art technological developments, often upon commission, for notorious human traffickers until the final years of the transatlantic slave trade.[32] Nathaniel Gordon was one man among a crowd of speculators who continued to engage in this inhumane commerce, even as more and more nations committed to abolishing it. He had been engaged in slave voyages before being captured and imprisoned in 1860, and could have been forgiven for thinking that at worst he would receive a short jail sentence for his participation in this traffic. Instead, and for the first time ever, the United States decided to prosecute and sentence one of its own under the stipulations of the 1820 act that declared slave trade as a piratical action.[33]

It could be argued that Gordon was not the first slave trader sentenced by an American court. After all, the captain and crew of the *Panda* were originally bound for the coast of Africa on a slave-trading expedition. But in cases like the *Panda*'s, slave traders were prosecuted not for trading in human beings but for committing actual predatory actions against American merchant vessels. The Spanish slave dealers of the schooner *Panda*, and those of the *Amistad* a few years later, did not face charges for their participation in the slave trade, even though in both opportunities they were heavily criticized for it by Justice Story of the Supreme Court.[34]

This tale repeated itself all over the Atlantic world during these decades. Even after offering stern resistance to anti-slave trade patrols, slave traders would be let go with minor reprimands; only in exceptional cases, where violence was excessive, would they face charges of piracy. Even then, in every known case bar Gordon's, they were freed, often finding a way back on to other slave vessels. Committing piratical actions, however, was a different subject altogether, as the prosecutions against the sailors of the *Panda* in the United States, the *Defensor de Pedro* in Cádiz and Gibraltar in the late 1820s, and the *Felicidade* and *Eco* in Exeter in 1845 revealed.

The stories of the *Defensor de Pedro* and the *Panda* had a lot in common. The *Defensor de Pedro*, like the *Panda*, was a slave ship bound for the coast of Africa, more specifically for the port of Woe, near Accra, on the Gold Coast. Its crew was formed by a truly international cast that included Spaniards and Frenchmen who had been involved in privateering activities in the Caribbean until the summer of 1825, when the arrival of the American West Indies Squadron brough most maritime raiding in the Caribbean Sea to a halt.[35] During the stop at Woe, and while the captain and first mate were on land procuring a human cargo, the sailors took up arms against the rest of the Portuguese-speaking crew, while screaming "down with the Portuguese."[36]

Once in charge of the vessel, and under the command of Galician sailor Benito de Soto, the renegades on the *Defensor de Pedro* attacked and sank multiple merchant vessels in the vicinity of Ascension and the Azores, while also murdering and raping numerous people. The surviving crew of one of the ships they pillaged, the British frigate *Morning Star*, which had been on its way from Ceylon to England with a cargo of coffee and cinnamon, managed to retake control of their vessel and steer it to safety. The survivors of the *Morning Star* spread the news about their encounter with the *Defensor de Pedro*, placing authorities across the Atlantic on guard. Within a few months, and after a short stop at the Galician port of El Ferrol, the men on the *Defensor de Pedro* beached the ship near Cádiz and made for the Spanish city in the hope that the news of their actions had not reached there yet.[37]

Most of the sailors were soon seized, interrogated, and put to trial in Cádiz. Their captain, Benito de Soto, ran away to the British enclave of Gibraltar, where he was arrested, after a number of items belonging to the *Morning Star* were found among his belongings.[38] After a criminal trial, which involved a significant amount of cooperation between the Spanish and British authorities in Cádiz, Madrid, Gibraltar, and London, ten of the *Defensor de Pedro* sailors were hanged in Cádiz in December 1829.[39] Seven of the corpses were dismembered, and their heads severed and mounted on pikes in public spaces as a warning to anyone who might think of following in their footsteps.[40] Benito de Soto's trial in Gibraltar came to an end just a few days later. He was hanged, on January 25, 1830, barely a month after his shipmates.[41] Like Pedro Gibert, Benito de Soto achieved fame, making it into virtually every book on pirates published after his death. Allegedly, he served as the inspiration for José de Espronceda's famous poem "Canción del pirata," and even today his crimes continue to be of interest for historians of piracy.[42]

Another case from this period, when slave dealers were rigorously put to trial for resorting to piratical actions, was that of the Brazilian ships *Felicidade* and *Eco* in late February 1845. The former, without enslaved peoples but fully fit for the transatlantic slave trade, was seized by HMS *Wasp* in the Bight of Biafra while preparing for a slave trade voyage. Almost as soon as the prize officer, Lieutenant Robert Stupart, had taken control of the ship, he was ordered to give chase to another suspicious vessel, the *Eco*. It was soon captured and discovered to have more than four hundred enslaved men, women, and children on board. Being obliged to split up his own crew and the crews of both slave ships, Stupart decided to stay on board the *Eco*. He sent Midshipman Thomas Palmer to take the *Felicidade* to Sierra Leone, in the hope that both ships would be charged with involvement in the transatlantic slave trade.[43]

Stupart and the *Eco* made their way to Freetown without much trouble, but the slave trade crew under Palmer's supervision on the *Felicidade* rebelled, murdering him and the other British sailors on board. As they tried to escape they were spotted by another British cruiser, the brig *Star*, seized, and then carried to England, where seven of them were found guilty of piracy and sentenced to death by a court convened in the town of Exeter in late 1845.[44] Before long, however, their sentences were reviewed and, to the public's surprise, overturned, following claims that the Spaniards had been wrongly convicted "on the ground of want of jurisdiction in an English Court."[45] The ruling was not unanimous, with judges Joseph Denman and Thomas Platt disagreeing with the new outcome. To Denman and Platt, the British vessel that had seized the pirates had acted according to international treaties and, as such, the original capital sentence should have stood.[46]

That the slave traders of the *Felicidade* and *Eco* found a way to escape punishment, in spite of definitive proofs of their piratical actions, was not unusual. As patrols were sent out to the Atlantic to search for slave traders by a number of nations—including Britain, France, Portugal, the United States, Brazil, and Spain—slave traders resorted more and more to violent means to resist capture, and yet, in every known case where they were arrested, sooner or later they were freed. This fortunate treatment of mostly white, Western pirates in the Atlantic offers a stark contrast with the treatment of non-white, non-Western peoples accused of piracy elsewhere during the same period, a time when Western empires were expanding their territory and spheres of influences beyond the Atlantic realm. This contrast becomes even clearer when slave trading and slavery are factored into their stories, irrespective of where in the world they were recorded. Between the signing of the first international treaties allowing for the right to search between Britain and other nations like the Netherlands, Portugal, and Spain, and the ending of the transatlantic slave trade in the mid-1860s, numerous cases of this sort were recorded.

In fact, even before Britain obtained the permission of other countries to stop and search their ships, they carried out a number of arrests that saw violent actions of resistance on the part of crews that went unpunished. Slave traders, especially the Spanish and the

Portuguese, complained profusely about these abuses of the Law of Nations, going as far as to suggest that these violations amounted to acts of piracy. In a letter written in 1816, Juan José Zangroniz, who would soon become one of the main Atlantic slave traders out of Havana, complained about British actions against his slave ships, suggesting that the British would resort to any "indirect means" and "oblique paths" in order to stop the Spanish from engaging in the "commerce of blacks" in Africa.[47] Zangroniz complained in writing, but quite a few of his fellow slave traders resisted with their guns.

Among them was the schooner *Apodaca*, which offered resistance for over four hours to a British man-of-war north of the river Sestos, in 1815.[48] Likewise, also in 1815, in January, the schooner *La Rosa* engaged in a fifteen-minute gunfight with a British ship. Although the crew of *La Rosa* managed to guide the vessel into the river Gallinas, a few days later, now having 270 enslaved Africans on board, the ships found each other again, and this time the captain was forced to surrender after a gun fight that lasted for more than thirty minutes.[49] In all cases, captains and crews made it back to Spanish territories, where they then proceeded to open lawsuits against the British. It is only thanks to the paperwork produced by these legal cases that we know about each of them today.

Once Britain succeeded in forcing a number of nations involved in the transatlantic slave trade to allow for mutual rights of stop and search, cases like these became more common, and accusations of piracy against slave traders who fought back, more credible. Actions of resistance by slave trade captains and crews, often resulting in casualties on all sides, were frequent, but even in the most lethal cases, slave traders were rarely prosecuted or convicted. The principal reason behind such a restrained approach was, in the main, the fact that while these treaties allowed for stop and search rights, and for vessels to be taken to Courts of Mixed Commission established across the Atlantic, they did not sanction the prosecution of foreign nationals.[50] Whereas in places like the Mediterranean, the Persian Gulf, Southeast Asia, or the South China Sea, those suspected of engaging in maritime raiding activities were either unceremoniously prosecuted and convicted, or simply exterminated, in the Atlantic, their citizenship rights were almost universally observed, and thus, they were rarely subjected to similar treatments. An in-depth comparison of the treatment of people accused of maritime raiding in the Atlantic and other parts of the world reveals how Western imperial powers adopted different approaches to dealing with such cases, methods that were arguably based on theories associated with standards of civilization and fueled by racial and religious prejudices.

When in 1846 HMS *Wasp*, the same vessel that had come across the *Felicidade* and *Eco* in 1845, attempted to stop and search two Brazilian slave ships within a short period of time, there was firm resistance from their crews.[51] These two vessels, the brig *Galgo* and the schooner *Gaio*, were both arrested while en route to the coast of Africa from Salvador de Bahia and Rio de Janeiro, respectively.[52] In spite of wounding ten British sailors between them during their actions of resistance, the crews of both ships were ultimately released after several letters and opinions were exchanged between the *Wasp*'s captain, the authorities in St. Helena, where the vessels were taken for adjudication, and the British government in London.

Upon their arrival in St. Helena in April 1846, the crews of both vessels were remanded in custody, then put to trial in June.[53] John N. Firmin, the queen's advocate in the island's capital, Jamestown, followed procedure to the letter, in order to secure the conviction for "piracy and felony" of those who had fired and wounded several Royal Navy sailors during the two high seas battles.[54] Although the sailors were convicted, a few days later, Diogo Ignacio Tavares, captain of the Brazilian corvette *Bertioga*, challenged the verdicts on behalf of the owner of the *Galgo*.[55] As a result, the papers of the case were sent to London, where the queen's advocate, John Dodson, determined that the sailors had been wrongly convicted. Dodson did not consider that "firing at, and killing British subjects under the circumstances stated in this case, would be held to amount to piracy by the General Law of Nations."[56]

To support his decision, Dodson referred to the case of the sailors of the *Felicidade*, who, after being convicted the previous year at a British court at Exeter, had been released due to similar jurisdictional issues. Just as in the case of the *Felicidade*, Dodson concluded that although the crews of the *Galgo* and *Gaio* had been tried and convicted for "piratical acts," their acquittal was appropriate "on the grounds of being foreigners and not amenable to British Law."[57] The evidence of violent piratical actions was overwhelming, both in the case of the *Felicidade* and in the cases of the *Galgo* and *Gaio*, but convictions were overturned, as the rights of Spanish and Brazilian subjects were protected and respected under the Law of Nations, a privilege that most "pirates" beyond the Atlantic seldom received.

In many other cases, such as that of the *Principe de Guiné* in 1826, taken by HMS *Maidstone* after offering a stern resistance that caused the death of at least fifteen enslaved Africans, a similar outcome followed.[58] Another Spanish ship, the *Formidable*, offered "a spirited resistance" that resulted in the deaths of three British sailors in 1834.[59] Although the *Formidable*'s crew faced trial in Freetown, all were released a few months later.[60] Then, there were the cases of the *Midas*, seized by HMS *Monkey* in the Straits of Florida, north of Havana, in 1829, and the *Patacho Veiga*, apprehended by HMS *Cyclops* off the coast of Angola in 1850.[61] In each of these occasions, deadly resistance did not lead court trials or convictions, and captains and crews were released after short periods of incarceration. Even in the case of the *Arrogante*, a vessel captured by HMS *Snake* west of the island of Cuba in 1837, after resisting and attempting to flee, and in which there were multiple accusations of brutality made by the Africans against the sailors, including one of cannibalism, the crew did not face any consequences.[62] The *Arrogante*'s captain, crew, and passengers—including notorious slave dealer Pedro Blanco—were released at the first opportunity, when the *Snake* and the *Arrogante* briefly stopped at Jagua Bay in southern Cuba, while on their way to Kingston and Freetown, respectively.[63]

It was not only the British who let slave traders engaging in piratical actions walk free. The French, for example, exhibited similar limitations. The case of Denis de Trobriand, a former French naval officer, turned slave dealer and pirate, illustrates the frustrations of French officers on both sides of the Atlantic who attempted to indict and convict Trobriand in the second half of the 1820s. Trobriand, who hailed from an illustrious family of naval officers, abandoned the French navy sometime before 1825, when he was enlisted by slave trade speculators on the Caribbean island of

St. Thomas to serve as captain of the slave vessel *Z*. The instructions he received in May that year suggest that he may have been involved in previous slave voyages, since the consignee of the ship left most details of the voyage to him.[64] As it happened, their human-trafficking venture resulted in capture and adjudication by the Anglo-Dutch Mixed Commission Court of Sierra Leone, where the vessel was taken after being found flying a Dutch flag. Trobriand, however, did not wait for the outcome; he left for the United States on the first vessel he was able to find.[65]

Two years later, in 1827, Trobriand found himself awaiting trial at Gorée Island, after being captured by the French frigate *La Flore* while on another slave voyage to the coast of Africa. On this occasion, too, his ship was condemned by the local court, and he was said to have been punished for being considered "a Négrier."[66] In spite of his conviction, Trobriand found a way to freedom, and in 1829, he arrived in the city of Matanzas, in charge of a French slave vessel but once again flying a Dutch flag. His arrival on the ship *Le Martin* was duly noted by Louis de Magnan, the French provisional consular agent in Matanzas. In a letter to the French consul in Havana, the Marquis de Vins de Peysac, de Magnan reported not only his participation in yet another slave voyage, but also his involvement in an act of piracy off the African coast. According to de Magnan, Trobriand had sought the help of some British officers when some of his crew rose against him, but once he realized that the British had noticed that his ship was destined to take enslaved Africans across the Atlantic, he had taken back the command of the brig, put the British officers on a boat, and headed for Santiago de Cuba, where he had landed his human cargo.[67]

Upon being pressed by de Magnan, Vins de Peysac attempted to have Trobriand arrested on the charges of using a foreign flag while engaged in an illegal slave trade voyage, but his requests to the Cuban governor, Captain General Francisco Dionisio Vives, fell on deaf ears, and Trobriand, once again, managed to escape.[68] Years later, in 1836, Trobriand published a short memoir about his life as a slave trader. In it he described fighting back against another ship—possibly a British man-of-war—whose occupants had tried to board Trobriand's ship to stop it from completing a slave voyage across the Atlantic.[69]

Perhaps the most representative example of how slave traders were able to resort to piracy without facing major consequences is the interconnected stories of the Spanish slave ships *Veloz Pasagera* and *Destemida*. Between 1828 and 1830, both vessels were involved in significant maritime raiding incidents along the African coast, the former resisting capture, and the latter attacking a British schooner. In both cases captains and crews escaped conviction in spite of British attempts to pursue and punish them.

The *Veloz Pasagera* was captured after a fierce resistance against HMS *Primrose* in early September 1830. The confrontation at sea yielded three sailors killed and thirteen wounded on the part of the British, and forty-three killed, twenty wounded, and six lost, probably fallen overboard, on the *Veloz Pasagera;* the captain, José Antonio de la Vega, lost one of his arms in the battle.[70] This clash was widely considered to be one of the most remarkable encounters between slave traders and a British ship at the time, particularly due to the numerous casualties, including deaths, among the British crew. Nonetheless, in its aftermath, most of the sailors involved in the battle were "supplied with a boat and provisions, shortly after capture, and sent away to the nearest land they could make."[71] The rest of the crew, including the captain, were sent first to Sierra Leone and then to England to face trial for piracy.[72] As with the cases discussed above, the British soon found out that they were powerless, according to existing laws, to prosecute them.[73] The men were sent to Spain, in the hope that they would be put on trial for their actions. In reality, however, they all seemed to have walked free within a very short period of time. The captain, José Antonio de la Vega, was reported to be in command of another Spanish slave ship, the *Catalana*, on a voyage to Africa in 1832, and four years later, in 1836, he was again leading another slave trade expedition, this time as the skipper of the *Llobregat*.[74]

The *Destemida*, a vessel that was also known as the *Despejado*, was another heavily armed vessel deeply linked to the *Veloz Pasagera*.[75] Between 1828 and 1830, some sailors swapped vessels while waiting to embark enslaved Africans at Whydah. This ship had left from Barcelona in the summer of 1828 under the command of Antonio Constantí, stopping at Gibraltar for supplies before being forced to run away when the British authorities realized the ship was fitting for a slave-trading voyage under their own incredulous eyes.[76] In the next few months, the *Destemida*, or *Despejado*, touched at some notorious slave factories along the coast of West Africa, like those at Gallinas and Little Bassa, before finally arriving at its predetermined destination, Whydah, on December 6.[77]

Over a year later, in March 1830, while Constantí was dining on board another slave vessel, and as his first mate, José de Vilardaga, was recovering from a bout of fever on the *Veloz Pasagera*, the *Destemida* was said to have disappeared from the Whydah roads, along with one of Constantí's close partners, Raimundo de Arribas.[78] Although Constantí went to lengths to denounce the theft of the ship, all evidence points to a cunning inside job, where both he and Arribas, and very likely Vilardaga, worked together to steal the vessel from its Catalonian owners. Not only did Constantí suspiciously give all his nautical charts and documents to Arribas right before both he and the ship vanished, but about a month later notorious slave dealer Francisco Félix de Souza messaged Arribas discussing a cargo of fifty elephant teeth, clearly a euphemism for enslaved Africans, for him to take to Salvador de Bahia.[79]

Barely a few days after its disappearance, the *Despejado*, or *Destemida*, materialized, this time attacking the British schooner *St. Helena*, which was sailing off the coast of West Africa on its way from St. Helena to Sierra Leone. Of the twenty members of the *St. Helena*, only seven survived what they described as a vicious attack. The captain and the doctor were tied together and thrown overboard, and the others who died were either killed as they fought back or thrown into the sea as well.[80] Following the paper trail left by Arribas, it is possible to assert that a few months later, the vessel steered for Salvador de Bahia with the cargo of fifty enslaved Africans (the ones previously referred to as "elephant teeth") provided by Francisco Félix de Souza. They were spotted in transit, given chase, seized by the British cruiser HMS *Druid*, and subsequently taken for adjudication before the Mixed Commission Court of Rio de Janeiro. There, after a process that did not conclude until January 1831, the ship was condemned for being engaged in illegal human trafficking and the fifty Africans were liberated.[81]

In spite of the significant amount of evidence against Arribas, Vilardaga, and Constantí, all of whom had played important roles both as slave traders and as pirates, none of them were convicted for their actions. Soon after the condemnation of the vessel in 1831, Arribas found his way back to Havana, where he took the command of another slave vessel, the brig *Zafiro*.[82] José de Vilardaga also continued his involvement with the slave trade: in 1834 he was captured by HMS *Dispatch* while carrying 290 Africans on the schooner *Rosa* and taken to Havana, where the ship was condemned for being engaged in the slave trade.[83] Constantí, for his part, was still trading in enslaved Africans in 1834, when he was reported to have arrived in Salvador de Bahia from the Gold Coast on the Portuguese ship *Fortuna*, in ballast, another common euphemism that suggested that the vessel's human cargo had been landed elsewhere along the coast, before entering port.[84]

While the British, the French, and to a lesser extent the American and the Portuguese at least attempted to disrupt the extensive human trafficking carried out across the Atlantic at the time, the Brazilian and the Spanish actually allowed and protected these sorts of activities and behaviors. The American consul in Havana in the late 1830s, Nicholas P. Trist, who was himself more than once accused of covering up for slave traders, noticed how the Cuban slave trade was "carried out with the good wishes of the authorities themselves."[85] A few days later, in a letter discussing how the news of the Boston trial against Gibert and his crew had been received by the slave-trading community in Havana, he wrote that he had learned that the owner of the *Panda* was not really upset about the act of piracy but about the financial consequences of the capture and loss of the schooner. Trist also observed that "had he made a successful voyage of it, the piracy would have been a feather in his cap," and that this was "an additional reason for not affording to these scoundrels any ground for believing that they may with impunity, interlard their main occupation, slaving, with a few acts of piracy, to give it zest."[86]

By no means was Trist exaggerating the situation. Time after time Cuban authorities enabled, even emboldened, slave traders, including those who had been accused of piracy. Some, like Juan José Zangroniz and the Blanco & Carvallo company, were well-known sponsors of piratical actions. Zangroniz was accused in 1831 by William Sharp Macleay, one of the judges of the Havana Mixed

Commission Court, of "being connected with pirates."[87] And in April 1835, his initials were linked by Consul Trist to the case of the *Panda*, suggesting that he might have been the vessel's real owner.[88] Ships owned by Pedro Blanco and Lino Carvallo were also considered to be regularly engaged in piratical actions at sea. Their vessel the *Escorpión* was accused, on at least one occasion, by Carvalho & Bastos of Rio de Janeiro, another slave-trading house, of attacking and violently plundering Carvalho & Bastos's barque *Rosa*.[89] In all these cases, without exception, Cuban authorities looked the other way or sided with those involved in illegal activities.

Surveillance was so lax in places like Cuba and Brazil that when piratical actions took place within their harbors, the authorities did little or nothing to protect those who were targeted. When notorious British slave trader Edward Jousiffe was found to be on board the *Preciosa*, a slave ship taken to the Havana Mixed Commission Court in 1836 by HMS *Pincher*, the slave-trading community there hatched a plan to break him out of the ship where he was being detained. In a letter to Lord Palmerston, written at the end of July, Edward Schenley, judge of the Anglo-Spanish Mixed Commission Court, referred to the slave trading community as "a mass of the blackest perjury," who had assembled "with the knowledge and assistance of some persons who pass for being of the highest respectability," in the city.[90]

When they failed to get an official release by providing fake papers to the governor of the island, the slave-trading community there assembled, according to Schenley, with the support of the city's Department of Marine, and prepared to attack the ship and free their colleague. Seeing the danger escalate quickly, Schenley sent a short note to Lieutenant George Byng at eleven o'clock that night, ordering him to leave at once for Jamaica and to do everything in his power not to surrender the prisoner, "unless such a force should be employed to gain possession of him as in your judgment as a British officer it would be a useless sacrifice of life to resist."[91]

Brazilian ports, where slave-trading communities also lived at large under the indifferent eyes of the local authorities, saw similar events occur time and again during the period. In 1840, the judge in the British Mixed Commission Court in Rio de Janeiro, George Jackson, wrote to London expressing his views on the regularity and consequences of these events. In Jackson's words, the "escape of prisoners" and the "abstraction of negroes, which have occurred in several cases of Prizes brought into this Port by British Cruizers," happened all too frequently.[92] Attacks on the hulk of the *Nova Piedade* and on the *Diligente*, which have been discussed by Beatriz Mamigonian and Jennifer Nelson, support Jackson's opinion.[93]

Probably the best-studied case of this kind occurred in late April 1848, in Salvador de Bahia, soon after HMS *Grecian* seized the Brazilian ship *Bella Miquelina*, which was on its way back to Bahia with more than five hundred enslaved men, women, and children on board. The officer placed in charge of the prize, Lieutenant T. J. D'Aguilar, was forced to stop for supplies at Salvador before continuing down the coast to Rio de Janeiro, where the vessel would be adjudicated by the Anglo-Brazilian Court of Mixed Commission. What was meant to be a short stop soon turned into a battle, as D'Aguilar and his men had to repel an attack organized by the local slave traders, who attempted to seize back the ship and the enslaved Africans.[94] A possible second attack may have taken place soon after, although the evidence is inconsistent. What is clear is that before the *Bella Miquelina* finally made it out of the Bay of All Saints harbor days later, in the company of the *Grecian*, its crew and captors had had to deal with repeated threats and straightforward instances of "violence and piracy," as the British vice-consul at Salvador, Edward Porter, labeled the attempts on the ship.[95]

Two similar incidents took place in 1850 south of Rio de Janeiro. The first involved a group of sailors from HMS *Rifleman*, who in late June were forced to disembark near Santos, in the state of São Paulo, after being in distress due to bad weather. Soon after landing, they were attacked by "a large number of persons, armed, who fired upon them," killing at least one of them and forcing the others to return to the boat and flee.[96] The second incident was even more remarkable and daring, and it happened barely less than a week later, on July 1. As HMS *Cormorant* was towing three vessels that had been found to be fully fitted for the slave trade out of the river Paraguaná, the slave traders affected by this seizure, and likely with the support of the local population, began bombarding the ship from a nearby fort. The attack did not have major consequences for the *Cormorant*, but the ship's commander, Herbert Schomberg, was forced to burn down two of the ships they had seized, after moving outside of the range of the fort's guns.[97]

In the Atlantic during the middle decades of the nineteenth century, Western imperialist powers did not hunt for pirates in the same way they pursued them elsewhere in the world. This singular approach is, arguably, one of the main differences to be observed when comparing the schemes of suppression of maritime raiding throughout this period across the globe. Most of the confrontations recorded in Atlantic waters speak of a policy of containment that, even in cases against peoples unequivocally defined as pirates by the Law of Nations and by their own national laws and international treaties, allowed those apprehended to be let off the hook.

Although the approach to pirates was different, the policies and patrolling practices in the Atlantic world shared, with other geographic areas, the goal of furthering imperialist interests. It just meant that within this realm, they refrained from using pirate imperialist approaches to pursue and suppress mostly white, Christian pirates. Equating slave trade with piracy allowed Western imperial powers to use abolition as a back door for imperial prospecting and expansion, land grabbing, and expropriation and exploitation of natural resources. A clear example of this sort of pirate imperialism occurred in 1851, when a British fleet bombarded and occupied Lagos under the guise of abolishing the slave trade practiced by the local ruler, Kosoko, who had refused to obey or even negotiate with the British.[98] Although enforcing the abolition of the slave trade at this Atlantic port was the main reason for this act of open warfare, it is worth noting that the British also justified their actions as a "duty owing to civilized nations" and as a "vindication of the law of nations." More to the point, to shore up their civilizing and legal argument, they argued that they had been forced to do so because Lagos was nothing but "a nest of piracy."[99] Within ten years of this arguably progressive action, the British had carved for themselves a rich colony, which they continued to expand over the following decades, taking lands of other peoples by force and using abolition as the justification for grabbing and colonizing of new territories.[100]

There is little doubt that while suppressing slave trade and piracy along the African coast, European and American cruisers engaged in serious prospecting and proto-colonial activities, scouting potential locations for colonial settlements, and enforcing yet more treaties on local rulers that eventually gave them the openings they needed to occupy and colonize these lands. Disguised by their anti-slave trade patrolling endeavors, the British repeatedly forced themselves on peoples along the African coast.[101] The bombardment and invasion of Lagos was hardly an isolated event. One of the vessels that led that attack, HMS *Teazer*, bombarded the town of Medina, near Sierra Leone, two years later.[102] In another glaring example of this sort of pirate imperialism, two decades earlier in 1823, at the beginning of the First Anglo-Asante War, the town of Sekondi was bombarded by two anti-slave trade patrol vessels, HMS *Bann* and HMS *Owen Glendower*.[103] In the late 1820s and early 1830s, British abolitionism also served as a cover for an unsuccessful attempt to snatch—either by a monetary transaction or by force—the island of Fernando Po from the Spanish crown.[104]

The French, too, took advantage of their anti-slave trade and anti-piracy operations along the African seaboard to scout and occupy new territories, especially after they increased the number of ships engaged in these activities in the 1840s. For example, in 1845, the commander of the brig *La Zebre*, Jérôme Félix de Monleón, was given confidential instructions to observe the stretch of coast between Cacheu and Seabar. These orders resulted in a detailed report of the region that shed light not only on the slave trade there but also on the most convenient places to start new colonies.[105] His compatriot Auguste Baudin, apparently also charged with a similar task, reported with concern from Gorée over a month later, that the British had settled in Badagry, near Whydah, and were planning to reoccupy their fort there.[106] A year earlier, Baudin had produced what was perhaps the most comprehensive report on potential sites for new French colonies on the African coast. In this exhaustive intelligence report he discussed the potential of numerous spots, including some like Whydah, Dahomey, and Gabon that eventually would be occupied by the French and turned into colonies a few decades later. The report even had a section "Colonization," in which Baudin offered his advice as to the best ways to take advantage of the presence of the anti-slave trade squadron in Africa to further French colonialism in the region.[107]

The American and the Portuguese also benefited from their anti-slave trade patrols in the region. The Americans, for example, coveted Fernando Po just as much as the British did, and as the Liberian colony expanded in the 1820s, they offered armed support against the local populations, referred to as "hostile natives," that opposed the new settlers.[108] The Portuguese, for their part, used the gunboats they had destined to chase slave traders to consolidate their colonial possessions along the Angolan coast by firing against numerous settlements there, settlements they frequently accused of being engaged in slave-trading activities.[109] From these examples, and many others discussed elsewhere in this book, it is clear that although abolition efforts did have a significant impact on the end of human trafficking in the Atlantic, they also served as a cover for an assortment of proto-colonial undertakings.

Beyond Atlantic waters abolition was also used and abused on a frequent basis to validate a wide array of hydrarchic imperialist behaviors, including the suppression of amphibious communities accused of being pirates. This situation was made worse by the hypocrisy shown by these same imperialist powers while engaging in such suppression activities. The Spanish, the Dutch, the Portuguese, and the French, all suppressed enslaving beyond the Atlantic, while they continued to allow, to varying degrees, the existence of slavery as an institution in their Atlantic colonies. The French, for example, did not abolish slavery until the proclamation of the Second Republic in 1848, while the Dutch (1863), the Americans (1865), the Portuguese (1869), and the Spanish (1886) took even longer to bring this obsolete institution to an end. In the cases of the Americans, the Portuguese, and the Spanish, they all continued to be heavily involved in the transatlantic slave trade until its final abolition in the late 1860s.

Arguably, even the British, who showed an unremitting commitment to abolishing the slave trade and slavery in the Atlantic during this period, occasionally overlooked the practice of both activities in places like Siam in the mid-1820s and the Straits Settlements as late as the mid-1840s, while simultaneously consolidating their strategic imperial goals in the region.[110] The journals of

Captain Henry Burney dating to his stay in Siam in the mid-1820s, when he was in charge of conducting negotiations with the Siamese king Rama III, leave very little doubt about the extent to which human trafficking and enslavement were practiced within the kingdom. In particular, Burney was keen to repeatedly mention in his correspondence with Calcutta and London how the Siamese had been carrying thousands of men, women, and children out of territories they had conquered, among them Burma, Kedah, and Patani. While negotiating a new treaty between Britain and Siam, Burney's main side activity was to lobby and threaten Siamese officials so that hundreds of Burmese captives could be released.[111] Among the notes to the first volume of his journals, there is a damning one accusing "the King, Wang-na and almost every Siamese Minister" of keeping thousands of enslaved Malays captured after the conquest of Kedah, in their possession.[112] Before concluding his paragraph, Burney made sure that the double standards of Britain in this situation would not be lost on future readers: he pointed out that there was "no question, that these conquests would never have been authorized, if the Court of Siam had been certain that the British Government would have interfered."[113]

There is little doubt that, even after Burney's remonstrations, the Siamese continued to carry out an extensive slave trade from the occupied territories. In May 1826, Burney wrote to Rama III's ministers, denouncing the carrying away of more than one thousand Pegu "from the districts of Mataban."[114] Only a couple of years later, John Crawfurd, who had also represented Britain before the king of Siam, described, in a book published in London, how the Siamese would always "indiscriminately carry off into captivity" the "unarmed men, women, and children" of any country they invaded.[115] More to the point, Crawfurd wrote that "the seizure of these unfortunate persons appears to be the principal object of the periodical incursions which are made into an enemy's territory."[116]

The lack of action, or what is worse, the support offered by the British to Siam during the years following the First Anglo-Burmese War (1824–1826) reveal a much more questionable British commitment to abolition in this region.[117] Desires to consolidate the territorials gains resulting from the war led the British to form an alliance with Siam that was eventually enshrined in the so-called

Burney Treaty of 1826, which guaranteed the British possession of Penang while sacrificing Kedah, Perlis, Kelantan, Terengganu, and Patani to the Siamese. Although Captain Burney in Bangkok led the negotiations, the quiet endorsement of the Siamese slave trade was done under instructions sent from Calcutta and, especially, London, at the time the epicenter of the crusade against the transatlantic slave trade. When Malaysian leaders Tunku Kudin and Tunku Mohamed Saad took arms against the Siamese in 1831 and 1838, respectively, the British did not hesitate to honor their commitments to the Siamese, offering their full support to suppress Malay insurgencies, in spite of knowing that such support would almost certainly lead to the deaths, enslavement, and trafficking of many more Malays, as in fact happened after each Malay defeat.

No wonder some of the participants in these events, men like Burney and Osborn, were highly critical of British decisions and proceedings. Burney himself not only attempted to free as many enslaved people as he could but often questioned the British decision-making in his journals, and he was clearly opposed to sacrificing Kedah in 1826.[118] Osborn, who was heavily involved in the British blockade of Kedah that resulted in the Siamese reoccupation of the territory in 1838, criticized British efforts to curb the slave trade in the region, which, although conducted at a smaller scale than in the Atlantic, was "still with all miseries of the middle passage."[119] Osborn also questioned the lack of action against the slave markets near the pepper plantations of Sumatra, where many of those captured were being sold, and against Dutch planters in Borneo, who were always ready to "take the slaves off the hands of the Malay slave-catcher, and work them to death in the plantations and gold or antimony mines of those countries."[120]

In an excellent article published a few years ago, Shawna Herzog demonstrated how British governors and officers in the Straits Settlements during the 1830s, 1840s, and 1850s not only refrained from suppressing known slave-trading activities but tacitly allowed them. Herzog pointed out that the Straits Settlements' first governor, Robert Fullerton, while critical of the slave trade in the region, failed to repress it, as he considered it to be "an alternate emigration policy" that could help solve the colony's gender imbalance.[121] In Herzog's words, "While there is no explicit evidence that officials consciously facilitated an illicit traffic of women and girls into their male dominated settlements, it seems clear that they were willing to 'turn a blind eye' to it in order to ensure the peace and stability of the colony."[122]

British double standards when it came to implementing abolition policies in the Atlantic and beyond were problematic and caused plenty of rifts between politicians, merchants, and those in charge of suppressing slave-trading and piratical activities. "Rescuing" captives or enslaved peoples from slave traders/pirates became a sort of casus belli to vindicate pirate imperialism, not just in the Atlantic, where tens of thousands of Africans were snatched from the hands of slave traders, but also in other corners of the world. Unfortunately, the needs and calls for rescuing enslaved peoples gave pirate imperial powers a pretext to displace, kidnap, and kill those they considered responsible, often making use of their superior fire power and deadly war strategies.

Many of the expeditions jointly carried out by James Brooke and the British navy against the amphibious peoples of the north coast of Borneo, who he determined to be pirates, were justified by the need to rescue enslaved peoples who had been seized during piratical raids. In fact, the supposed rescuing of captives was a cornerstone of Brooke's defense against the many accusations raised against him in Singapore and London after the Batang Marau massacre of 1849. Some of his supporters, including Straits Settlements' governor William John Butterworth, often referred to these as acts of kindness and praised Brooke for them.[123] Considering the level of violence associated with Brooke's expeditions against the northern Bornean peoples during the 1840s, it should not surprise anyone that his offers of freedom to those he had found in the hands of the Dayaks were not always accepted. In a story recounted by various witnesses to the 1849 events, a Dayak woman refused Brooke's offer of freedom and decided instead to go back into the Saribas River with a local chief, choosing to remain as a slave rather than falling under Brooke's so-called protection.[124]

Although the contrast between British implementation of abolitionist policies in the Atlantic and its actions in the rest of the world reveals a lack of consistency and zeal when dealing with slave-trading activities in places like the South China Sea and

James Brooke Esq., governor of Labuan. *The Illustrated London News* (October 9, 1847).

Southeast Asia, it is also clear that the British used the pretext of abolition to further their imperial goals whenever possible. In the Persian Gulf and along the East Coast of Africa, they were relentless in their pursuit of anyone involved in illegal activities that could affect British trade and territorial expansionism, which notably included both pirates and slave traders.

For example, in 1826, the British pressured Said bin Sultan, the imam of Muscat, questioning the close relationship between Oman and the French and implying that the imam had been enabling the French slave trade out of Mauritius for years.[125] Eventually, such pressures led the imam of Muscat to cooperate with the British in putting down the French slave trade in the region and to sign a bilateral treaty in 1845, by which he committed to end both the slave trade and piracy in the territories under his control.[126]

While British double standards are clear to anyone reading the documents produced by imperial officers in charge of putting down slave trade and piracy, the duplicity of the rest of their partners within this hydrarchic system was even more conspicuous. The Spanish are a clear case in question. As European and American countries began to cut their links with the transatlantic slave trade, the Spanish colony of Cuba kept this odious commerce alive until the late 1860s.[127] Slavery as an institution was defended by successive Spanish governments, and, ultimately, Spain was the second to last country to abolish slavery in the Western hemisphere, in 1886.

Such pro-slave trade and pro-slavery policies, however, were not part of the Spanish plan in the Philippines. There, against all the odds, the Spanish proclaimed both practices to be inhuman and illegal and became fervent in their opposition. Whereas slavery and the slave trade were part of the social, political, and economic fabric of places like Cuba and Puerto Rico, in the Asian colonies they simply were not tolerated. What is more, rescuing enslaved persons from the hands of so-called pirates who happened to control the southern parts of the archipelago, which were still out of the jurisdiction of Manila, was nothing short of a labor of humanity that needed to be carried out at any cost.

Calls for rescuing innocent captives from "pirate" hands were often accompanied by references to insults to the Spanish honor or the Spanish flag. In March 1851, Governor Antonio de Urbiztondo, a general with strong links to conservative groups that supported the continuation of both slavery and the slave trade in the Atlantic, wrote a line lamenting the "infamous trafficking of the human race," that had been carried in the Sulu Sea for over two hundred years.[128] In the same missive, Urbiztondo commented that for the Spanish government, repressing this traffic was a duty, necessary to "repair its honor and the good of humanity."[129] Barely three months later, Urbiztondo rejoiced in the rescue of ten captives, doing so soon after he had carried out a deadly operation against "some enemy embarkations that had been spotted in the most occult part of the coast."[130]

One of Urbiztondo's successors, Rafael de Echagüe, who was governor of the Philippines between 1862 and 1865 and who had had a history of supporting pro-slavery causes to the point of being accused of repressing dissent and persecuting abolitionists during his time as governor of Puerto Rico between 1860 and 1862, was just as keen on eliminating slavery and the slave trade in the Sulu Sea.[131] In a letter to Madrid, sent shortly after his arrival in Manila, Echagüe congratulated himself for the successful mission to rescue "from the tyrannical power of their oppressors," twenty-three subjects who had been "reduced to slavery by the pirates."[132]

Although there is no question that both slave trade and slavery were widely practiced in the region during these years—as numerous reports attest—it is critical to emphasize that colonial governors and officers took advantage of these practices to further their imperial objectives. In the late 1850s and early 1860s, Spanish authorities in Manila recorded numerous cases of former enslaved persons who had managed to escape their condition of servitude.[133] These events were also reported by local Spanish and even Joloan authorities. For example, in September 1849, the sultan of Joló forwarded to Manila, via Zamboanga, a number of "captives from the island of Negros," who had come into his territories.[134] In another similar case, in June 1859 the Spanish commander of the island of Burias wrote to Governor Norzagaray communicating "the abduction of 17 captives, during a pirate invasion" that had taken place days before.[135]

Spanish officers frequently shared their tactics with administrators of the neighboring Dutch territories, at times collaborating to free their subjects from the maritime raiders who inhabited the Sulu and Celebes Seas and nearby areas. One such example is Fernando de Norzagaray, governor of the Philippines from 1857 to 1860, who had close ties to politicians like Leopoldo O'Donnell and Ramón María Narváez, both of whom were staunch defenders of the slave trade and the slavery system in Cuba.[136] As we have already seen, during his time in Manila, Norzagaray was unswerving in his attempts to clear the southern islands of the archipelago of supposed pirates, while also taking every opportunity to expand Spanish control over these territories. In April 1857, more than a year before ordering the attack on the Balanguingui Samal and the kidnapping of their women and children, Norzagaray wrote a letter to his Dutch counterpart in Batavia, Charles Ferdinand Pahud, lamenting the capture of a number of Dutch subjects by the "moor pirates of Siocon" and informing him of the measures he had taken to punish them for their "criminal behavior."[137]

The Dutch, too, had conflicting policies regarding slavery. While they employed virtually all means available to hunt slave-trading "pirates" throughout the so-called Eastern Archipelago, also actively displacing and murdering maritime communities, they continued to hold tens of thousands of enslaved peoples in their Atlantic colonies. Until 1863, when the abolition edict was finally implemented, tens of thousands enslaved men, women, and children inhabited their Caribbean colonies; Suriname alone had a slave population of over 34,000 in that year.[138] For the Dutch, as for the Spanish and the British, "rescuing" captives became a convenient type of operation, that allowed them to expand their sphere of influence in the region, while restructuring it to their needs.

Time after time, Dutch cruisers engaged in the appropriation of new territories while their commanders and other Dutch authorities on shore praised themselves for freeing scores of enslaved men, women, and children from supposed pirates' strongholds. In 1831, the Dutch resident in Banten, Franciscus Henricus Smulders, described how slave raids had been taking place for a while in the vicinity of Serang, in Western Java, and commented on the ways that people were being bought and sold, and how some of them had escaped at the first opportunity they had.[139] In reality, Smulders's opinion was based on facts. As was the case in the British and Spanish East Indies, local amphibious peoples were often abducted by maritime raiders, who also engaged in human-trafficking activities.

These enslaving and piratical activities, which were often accompanied by acts of violence, were intensified as a result of European colonial encroachment and demands for cheap labor to supply expanding markets for products like trepang and birds' nests.[140] For example, between 1850 and 1851, a large number of formerly enslaved people who had found various ways of escaping their captors testified before the local authorities at Surabaya. Most of them described how they had been abducted from their homes, subjected to various levels of violence by their captors, and forced to carry out intensive work for them.[141] In fact, the situation was at times so desperate that businessmen were compelled to pay large amounts as ransoms to rescue their employees, as did Mr. W. Wijndham in Riau in 1847.[142]

In a government report written in Batavia four years later, an anonymous author commented that most of the population at the Indragiri River consisted of "Javanese who had been kidnapped by the Linganese."[143] In the same report it was stated that pirates from Lingga would snatch the people "from Java and Banka every year, plunging them into slavery."[144] The recommendations made by this author included "depriving the pirates of their vessels, weapons and other means in the waters of Linga" and subsequently forcing them to sign a treaty with the Dutch government, by which they would commit "to counteract all pirates and slave traders" in the region.[145]

As did the British and the Spanish, the Dutch justified many of their actions on the need to rescue captives, people who were exposed to the extreme violence of the neighboring maritime raiders. When in late 1860 Lieutenant W. G. Willinck led the steamship *Reinier Claeszen* into the Celebes Sea, he did so convinced that local pirates had been engaged in truly atrocious deeds against people they had violently abducted from various places in the Makassar Straits. Willinck's suspicions were soon confirmed by a second account, sent by the commander of the East Indies Maritime Forces, G. Vogelpot, to Dutch governor Pahud.[146] Willinck reported rescuing numerous captives during these operations. In a letter recounting his tour, he described how he had been struck by how happy three of them, named Akasa, J. Bagin, and Badju, had been after being liberated by his men.[147] All three confirmed to him that "another 80 women and nearly 40 men were still being kept in slavery, by about 30 to 40 robbers," who had escaped the initial attack.[148] Such news led Willinck to immediately order pursuit, with the intent of chastising those he referred to as "pirates from Maguindanao."[149]

The other pirate imperial powers still heavily involved with slavery in the Atlantic world behaved similarly when it came to using abolition as an excuse to attack, dispossess, and displace amphibious communities, irrespective of whether they were engaged in maritime raiding activities. The Portuguese, for example, repeatedly named as governor for their colony in Macau men who had previously been in charge of one of the main regions for slave exports in the Atlantic world: Angola.[150] As the Spanish and the Dutch had

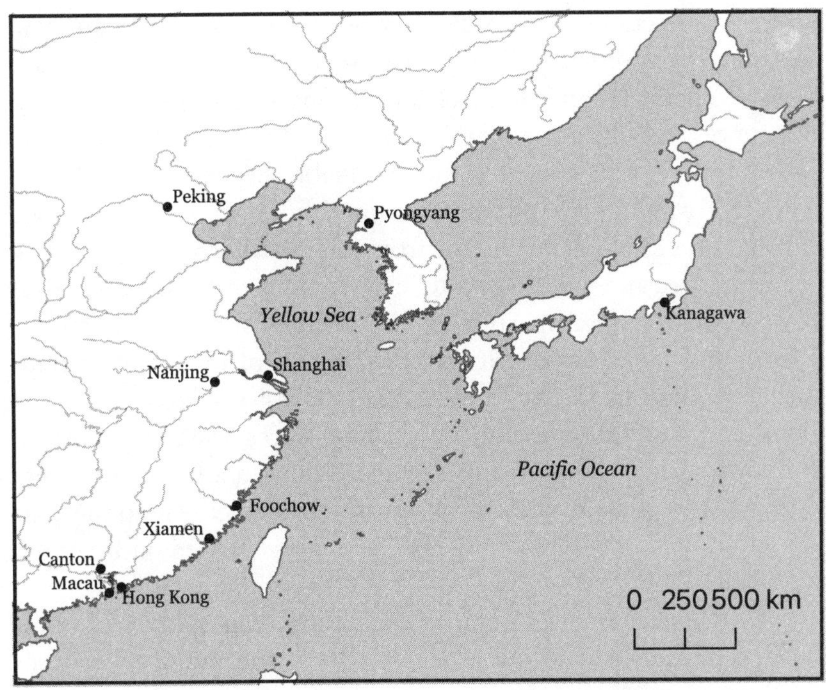

East Asia

done, in Macau the authorities proclaimed the kidnapping of people for ransom or for selling them as enslaved peoples a crime, a circumstance that allowed them to devise new repressive means against neighboring maritime communities.[151] Throughout the 1840s in the eastern part of the island of Timor, the Portuguese also complained of and attempted to stop an extensive slave trade being carried out by Makassan ships, occasionally under the Dutch flag.[152] The French and the Americans also engaged in naval operations against various peoples around the world, under the premise of rescuing captives, which in some cases, as those concerning Christian missionaries in Vietnam in the late 1850s, resulted in full-blown armed conflicts.

In 1847, Montagu Burrows, who would eventually become the inaugural Chichele Professor of Modern History at Oxford University and who at the time was gunnery instructor on HMS *Excellent*, wrote recollections of his time serving in the Indian Ocean from the mid-1830s onward. Burrows had served on HMS *Andromache*, under Captain Henry Ducie Chads, during the heightened period of suppression of piracy organized from Calcutta and Singapore in 1836, and he had gained some invaluable experience about the ways in which slave trade and maritime raiding overlapped throughout the Indian Ocean, from the southern Philippines to the East African coast.[153] In a telling segment of these notes, Burrows lamented that, in spite of the treaties signed between the British and the imam of Muscat, the "dhows of the Moorish traders" had continued to be "always ready to assist in slavery transactions and not infrequently . . . making slaves themselves."[154] To Burrows, British pressures to bring the final abolition of slavery and the slave trade to the Omani Empire had failed due to the continuation of "both legal and illegal" activities "carried on by Arabs, or Moors."[155]

To Western empires bent on expanding their spheres of influence, self-imposed and questionably ethical and moral obligations to abolish real or imagined piracy-related slavery and slave trade activities served as a cover to a varied assortment of imperialist endeavors. In the Atlantic, where maritime raiding had peculiar characteristics that made it different from most of the rest of the world, strong links with the transatlantic slave trade provoked distinctive suppression approaches. Slave traders who moonlighted as pirates, and who were mostly white, were hardly ever treated as such. Only when they offered armed resistance were they seized and formally indicted. Even then, almost universally, verdicts based on the Law of Nations, which applied only to states that formed part of the "civilized" family of nations, saw them escape any sort of serious punishment.

On a day-to-day basis, slave traders who were deemed to be pirates were still cut slack, allowed to flee, or to disembark with just a slap on the wrist, even when they actually retaliated against anti-slave trade patrol ships. In some extraordinary cases, like that of the Portuguese schooner *Arrogante* in 1838, their captains were praised by the prize officers after they spent time together and got to know each other.[156] Such leniency against those considered as pirates was, of course, unheard of anywhere else in the world. In these other regions, regardless of whether they were engaged in piracy or slave-trading activities, amphibious communities found themselves almost always under the relentless and superior firepower of their Western counterparts, who did not hesitate to use questionable legal means, even extreme force, to stop them from engaging in any activities they perceived as against their interests.

Their towns and villages were frequently attacked and their peoples kidnapped, displaced, and massacred. It is, therefore, hard to ignore the racial dynamics behind such differing approaches—between white pirates and slave traders, on one hand, and nonwhite seafaring peoples who may or may not have been engaging in piracy and slave trading, on the other. Linking abolition to the suppression of piracy was, in fact, a fitting move that reflected the true aims of each of the pirate imperialist powers. In most parts of the world, abolition and suppression allowed them to perform the prospecting of territories that could and would be turned into colonies in years to come, while portraying these activities as a burden that only civilized and humane saviors ready to sacrifice themselves could carry.

Ultimately, there is little doubt that pirates and enslaved peoples meant different things to the same Western powers within the Atlantic realm when compared with other corners of the globe. In fact, while some of them continued to hold sizable enslaved populations in their colonies and to protect the transatlantic slave trade, they concluded that "rescuing" enslaved peoples from "pirates" in places like the Persian Gulf or Southeast Asia was nothing short of a labor of humanity that needed to be done at any cost. The conflict between having and trafficking enslaved human beings in one part of the world and suppressing slavery and slave trade in another added to the sociopolitical context of each area, giving lie to the fact that the true reason for implementing abolition, alongside the suppression of piracy, was that they considered it to be an act of humanity.

CHAPTER THREE
Commerce and the Suppression of Maritime Raiding

On the morning of August 7, 1856, Prince Adalbert of Prussia, who had recently been named admiral of the Prussian fleet, took the paddle corvette SMS *Danzig* on a cruising mission off the northern coast of Morocco. The alleged reason behind his visit to these waters was to scrutinize the coastline of Cape Tres Forcas, where the Prussian vessel *La Flore* had been attacked by "Riff pirates" four years earlier. Once there, in what would become a very costly blunder, Prince Adalbert decided to "sail peacefully along the shore on the [*Danzig*] boats."[1] As the prince and his men got closer and closer to the land, they spotted a group of armed men waving "a white handkerchief as a sign of peace," but soon after, as they got even closer, at a distance of about 150 paces from the shore, they were fired upon. Even though the only shot discharged was almost certainly just a warning, as it fell on the water well away from their boats, Prince Adalbert and his men saw this action as an affront to the Prussian flag, "which together with the plunder of 'La Flore,' imperatively and without delay demanded decisive and energetic measures."[2]

In an unsigned account of the events left by a sailor who participated in the action, it was made clear that Prince Adalbert was not

The corvette *Danzig* at the battle of Tres Forcas. Alexander Kircher.

content with just bombarding the heights of Cape Tres Forcas, as many other European navies had done in years past, following similar attacks. Instead, a pumped-up prince returned to the *Danzig* and hastily prepared an armed expedition of three long boats, with the ultimate goal of making himself "master of the hill" and of flying the "Prussian colors again, if only for a short time, on African soil."[3] As their assault unfolded, the *Danzig*, under the command of Prince William of Hesse, followed closely, providing supporting fire. Their enthusiasm to chastise these "mountain people" was, however, short lived.[4] As Prince Adalbert's men climbed the steep cliffs, some fell to their death and others were wounded by the heavy fire coming from above. Ultimately, the Prussians managed to reach the top and to plant their ensign on the hill for a few minutes before reinforcements received from the interior threatened to surround them and to cut off their retreat route to the coast.

By this time, it was clear that Prince Adalbert's plan had been a stunning piece of miscalculation. In a precipitated retreat and still under heavy fire, the Prussians ran downhill and jumped into their boats, hoping to make it back to the *Danzig*. As they began rowing for their lives, Prince Adalbert's aide-de-camp was shot dead in front of him, and the prince himself received what British captain Edward George Hore described a few hours later, upon the *Danzig*'s arrival at Gibraltar, as a "severe flesh wound to the thigh."[5] Seven men lost their lives and many more were injured, all to satisfy the royal prince's whimsy and need for revenge.[6] No wonder the *Illustrated London News*, when reporting the events weeks later, compared Adalbert with none other than James Brooke and subtly suggested that his attempts of castigating and rooting out those referred to as "water-rats," had perhaps been inspired by the British adventurer.[7]

The assault led by Prince Adalbert on the maritime people of the Tres Forcas region was an archetypical case of pirate imperialism inspired by the "need" to protect Prussian supposed rights to trade in northern African seas; a heavily armed iron-plated steam vessel, for no reason other than showing off, decided to enter waters where the Riff people had navigated and fished for generations. In spite of the initial peaceful gesture, as the white handkerchief reported by the anonymous sailor suggests, Prussian pride led the prince and his sailors to get closer to the coast, provoking the locals to shoot a warning shot, which they then used as a propitious pretext for bombing and assaulting them.

To be sure, the region of the Riff in northern Morocco had been an area of contention for years, and European vessels that ventured too close to the coast had been frequently attacked and ransacked.[8] Contrary to what the press and European politicians of the time implied in their reports of Riff piracy, however, these attacks on foreign ships had become more frequent as Western intrusions across the region increased in the years and decades that followed the occupation of Algiers by the French in 1830.[9] As the late 1840s correspondence between Consul Edme de Chasteau and General Louis Juchault de Lamoricière indicates, the French had intensified their attempts to add eastern Moroccan territories, including the Riff Coast, to their northern African colony, making native fears of an invasion even more plausible.[10]

These attempts reached their apex during the Franco-Moroccan war of 1844, when French troops entered Moroccan territory and

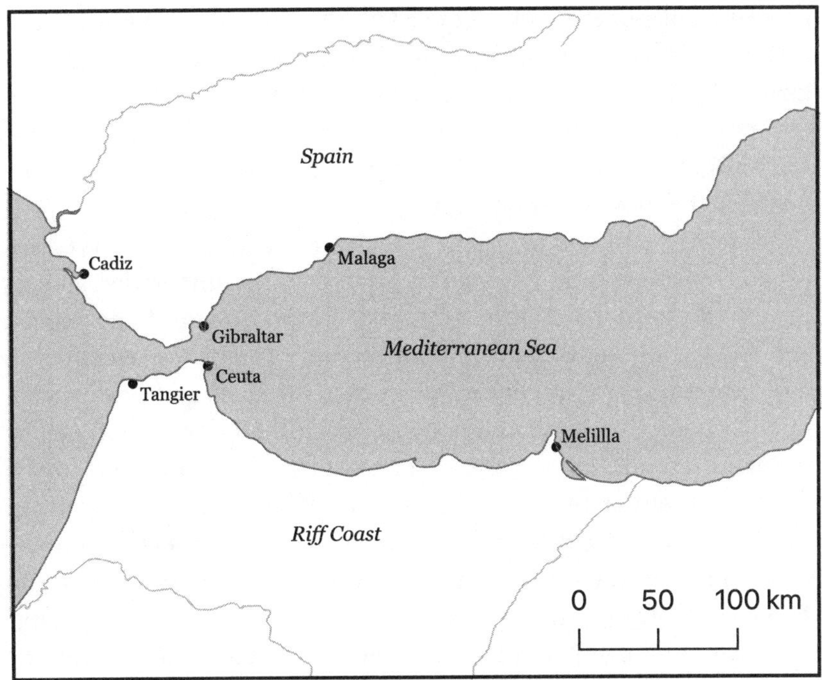

Western Mediterranean

their vessels bombarded the ports of Tangier and Mogador.[11] The Spanish settlements of Melilla and Peñón de Vélez de la Gomera had aggrieved the French for generations, often leading to renewed instances of confrontation.[12] Put in other words, Riff amphibious peoples, unlike the famous corsairs of Algiers in years past, had mostly engaged those they had perceived as threats or whom they saw as trespassers. For the Europeans at the time, however, these cases of maritime violence were seen as inadmissible aggressions, as they disturbed the ordinary flow of international trade in the Western Mediterranean Sea.

Pirate imperialist actions during these years were habitually justified by comparable threats to international and domestic commercial activities conducted, overwhelmingly, by Western imperial powers. Arguably, such threats were the most frequent and persuasive reason given for attacking non-Western amphibious peoples, even more than the repeated tropes reflecting empty civilizational pretexts and hopeful, self-imposed abolitionist obligations. In fact, it is worth stressing this difference in even clearer terms. Both civilization and abolition were indeed frequently used justifications to cover up pirate imperialism, but the protection of commerce was not simply another pretext but an actual reason, underpinned by possibly the most vital concerns.[13]

International and domestic trade were at the heart of Western expansionism, and they were also central to the imperialist actions of non-Western states—the Ottoman Empire, Siam, Qing China, and Russia, among others. The protection of trade was essential in multiple ways, as in reality it meant that revenues and profits were safeguarded. To each of these states, maritime raids carried out by seafaring communities were a source of concern that had to be dealt with, either by diplomatic pressures or by armed means. In this sense, Prince Adalbert's ill-informed decision to take on the Riff people on their own turf was not out of line with what would be expected from any imperialist power at the time. In Prussians' eyes, these people had attacked multiple merchant ships over the years, including one of their own, and such offenses merited the sort of punishment that, they hoped, would dissuade them in the future from unsettling foreign trade carried out in their waters.

Yet, when it came to commerce, the imperial hydrarchy of the period was not always in synchronicity. Whereas some imperial powers, like the British, the Americans, and to a lesser extent the French and the Dutch, began to practice and force free trade on to others around the world, virtually all other imperialist powers at the time continued to rely on protectionist practices that were perceived as an anathema by the champions of free trade.[14] Maritime plundering, however, affected them all equally, and thus, in spite of their differences they often resorted to similar methods of suppression to protect the continuation of their commercial activities worldwide.

The role of free trade—and its protection—in many of the imperialist endeavors of the middle decades of the nineteenth century is undeniable. John Gallagher and Ronald Robinson established the link between free trade and imperialism beyond any doubt in a widely cited article entitled "The Imperialism of Free Trade," first published in 1953.[15] This connection had been discussed by earlier authors—John A. Hobson and Vladimir I. Lenin, among others—and, notably, by many contemporary witnesses who observed, condemned, and questioned the ethics of the dissemination of free trade.[16] Alongside various other forms of resistance against the enforcement of new commercial practices on other peoples, maritime raiding increasingly became a crucial nuisance for these imperial powers during this period. The repeated attacks and plundering of their merchant ships meant unceasing and often significant losses. Not surprisingly, when it came to commerce and profits, the many heads of hydrarchic imperialism acted in unison to suppress those responsible for these losses. As Patricia Risso has argued with regard to British interests in the Western Indian Ocean, "The suppression of what they considered piracy was a tool in commercial competition and in the building of empire—bad means to a bad end."[17] This statement could be confidently applied more widely, even to include those who continued to trade under protectionist systems.

Free trade was, of course, a euphemism, as it was "free" only to those who imposed it on others. Its very imposition brings into question any alleged "free" character drummed up by the imperialists of the time, and by some that until today continue to champion such a coerced variety of commercial relations. This is especially the case if we consider that in many situations, weaker states agreed to partake only after various sorts of bullying and manipulation schemes had been employed. There were plenty of examples of this kind: some that employed coercion by diplomatic means, like those in Siam and Japan in the 1850s, and others where blood was spilled during pirate imperialist incursions, as it happened during the two Opium Wars (1839–42 and 1856–60) in China.

The "free" aspect of free trade was probed almost from its onset. Already in 1826, British MP William Huskisson brought it into question when he highlighted that the proponents of free trade relied on inequality and on the use of their superior fire power to force others to be part of it. In Huskisson's words, there was "one rule of independence and sovereignty for the strong, and another for the weak;—when, abusing its naval superiority, England shall claim for herself, either in peace or war, maritime rights which she refuses to acknowledge in other States."[18]

Those who persevered with protectionist schemes were also quick to resort to diplomatic or armed means, whenever necessary, to protect their trading privileges around the world. Not surprisingly, when discussing protectionism in the second part of the nineteenth century after having observed its effects for decades, Frederick Engels did not mince his words when he stated that protection was "at best an endless screw."[19] While British, Americans, and French attempted to "open" others to their commerce under false pretenses of equality and by the use of force, most other empires persisted in controlling and regulating trade in order to guarantee and maximize their own profits.[20] While doing so, each of them hunted down any seafaring communities, whether engaged in maritime raiding or not, that dared to interfere in the advancement of their grand commercial schemes.

Although diplomatic means were at times used by pirate imperialist powers to protect international and domestic trade, these means were usually accompanied or preceded by armed violent actions: armed violence was the centerpiece behind many of the strategies to protect commerce from maritime raiding. The examples are numerous. The British, fully imbued by utilitarian ideas, were perhaps the most active empire—although hardly the only one—to use armed violence to protect trade and, in their particular case, so-called free trade. Before resorting to armed violent means, however, pirate imperialism occasionally made use of a variety of measures that included diplomatic pressures and threats as well as coercion and deception in order to achieve their goals.

Pressures and threats against those who dared to disrupt trade were essential weapons among the vast arsenal available to pirate imperialist representatives around the world. Pointedly, these tools were not brandished solely by those who were trying to stop maritime raiding, or even against those who tolerated predatory activities. At times they were used internally, among those scions of empire who disagreed with each other as to the best ways to protect commerce and to suppress those who dared threatening it. Merchants engaged in commercial endeavors overseas often exerted pressure on their local or imperial officers so that they would turn the screws on those who were damaging trading prospects. Lauren Benton has referred to such events as "protection emergencies."[21] While discussing the role played by British merchants in imperial endeavors, Benton noted how protection emergencies "became increasingly frequent in the mid-nineteenth century as British merchants reached farther into distant markets."[22] A case in question took place in 1850, when three traders based in Thessaloniki addressed a letter to the British consul in that port, warning him about possible attacks on British vessels by a pirate named Jean Valença, who had been terrorizing the waters near Volos for some time. Among other appeals, they demanded that the British consul send a war vessel to the Gulf of Volos—the Pegasetic Gulf—as soon as possible, where its presence was "very necessary."[23]

The British, in particular, excelled at exercising such internal and external pressures all around the world. Requests similar to the one by the three Thessaloniki-based traders were made on various occasions during this period by merchants residing in the Straits Settlements. Arguably one of the most consequential was a memorial sent by a group of merchants from Singapore to the governor of India in 1835. The signatories to this document complained extensively about the "piracies and murders" that had "for a long time past been of frequent occurrence" in the vicinity of Singapore.[24] Commenting that trade there was threatened with "total annihilation," they gave a stern warning to the government about the dire consequences should it fail to act upon the issues raised in the memorial.[25] For good measure, the signatories made sure to gain the support of the Straits Settlements' governor, George Bonham, who had been raising the issue for years with both Calcutta and London. Forced by the combined action of the merchants in Singapore and their governor, a number of measures were taken in Calcutta to satisfy their wishes. Within a short period of time Captain Henry Ducie Chads was sent to the Straits Settlements, where he was named as "Commissioner for the suppression of Piracy" in the region, sharing the title and responsibilities with none other than Bonham himself.[26]

Twenty years later, another group of merchants from Singapore wrote to Calcutta with very similar demands and gloomy predictions should their repeated requests for the steam-powered warships needed to pursue and overpower pirates in their waters fail to be fulfilled. This time they pointed out the "almost total cessation of trade with some states, such as Cochin China and Cambodia," and blamed "Chinese pirates in the Gulf of Siam" for all their commercial losses.[27] As they expanded on their complaints, they called the support they had received from the Royal Navy "inadequate" and lamented the nature of the instructions under which Royal Navy commanders were being forced to operate. These, they argued, prevented them "from acting with that vigour which would alone prove effectual in putting down" maritime raiding in the area.[28]

In Morocco, the British consul John Hay Drummond Hay repeatedly pressured his government to take various types of actions to protect British commerce and other interests in this part of the world. Throughout the 1840s and 1850s, Drummond Hay was constantly mortified by the lack of a belligerent desire shown by the British government when it came to looking after the interests of British merchants and their ships in the region. Time after time he criticized both the government in London and the Royal Navy admirals in the Mediterranean for failing to respond appropriately to the many attacks carried out by the people of the Riff against British vessels. On one such occasion, in 1856, he wrote to the foreign secretary, the Earl of Clarendon, urging that "everything should be done to leave such an impression of terror of the British power upon these lawless people" in order to deter from further piratical attacks.[29] As we will see in chapter 4, Drummond Hay went as far as devising plans to conquer and colonize the Riff Coast, as he believed it was the best way of stopping both the attacks against British ships and a French expansion westward from Algiers into Morocco.

Likewise, barely three years earlier and on the other side of the world, William Jervois, acting governor of Hong Kong, wrote to the secretary of state for war and the colonies, the Duke of Newcastle, regretting the immense losses suffered by Hong Kong vessels due to the prevalence of maritime raiding in the surrounding seas. Jervois demanded that the government should take "efficient measures" to check "this enormous evil," and highlighted as "a matter of grave consideration, whether the colony should not have the means of defending the lives and property of Her Majesty's subjects."[30]

A few years after Jervois's demands, in 1865, Captain Matthew Stainton Nolloth echoed his pleadings, when he wrote to William Thomas Mercer, the acting governor of Hong Kong, pressuring him to demand "active measures" from their Chinese counterparts against the population of Mirs Bay and Deep Bay.[31] According to Nolloth, the seafaring inhabitants of these places had "little other occupation than piracy."[32] Such criminals, he argued, should be brought to justice by the British and their houses and other property should be dealt with summarily. In Nolloth's opinion, should the Chinese decline to cooperate, the British governor should seek their permission to allow British "gunboat crews" to land in these places in order to dispense the appropriate punishment to those he considered to be a threat to his country's trade in the region.[33]

Similar internal demands plagued all empires invested in defending their own trading interests, whether these were linked to free trade initiatives or carried out under protectionist rules. The Dutch are a case in question. In the middle decades of the nineteenth century, Dutch residents at various locations in Southeast Asia often wrote to Batavia, exerting pressure to protect the commercial activities of those living under their respective jurisdictions. In March 1846, for example, the resident at Manado messaged the governor of the Moluccas Islands, Johannes B. Cleerens, lamenting the insecurity of the coast of his residence and demanding that new efficient measures be immediately taken to stop what he referred to as a "new mare [*sic*] of the boldness of the pirates."[34]

These demands increased in the years to come. In 1848, for example, the US consul in Batavia, Owen M. Roberts wrote to Washington lamenting that "the greater part of the produce" of the island of Java was being "monopolized and sent to the Mother Country in national ships" freighted by the Dutch government.[35] Roberts also noticed how Dutch merchants had complained for years about this monopoly, while also admitting that they were acutely aware that should the Dutch liberalize their commerce, "the whole trade would fall into the hands of strangers," thus concluding that "nothing but a monopoly" would guarantee their trading interests.[36]

In a parallel case, the Spanish government of the Philippines was made aware in November 1863 of a strong grievance presented by the governor of Mindanao, who lamented the constant attacks carried out against the local trade in the waters near his town. Keeping with what other officers from contemporary empires had done, the governor begged Manila to "assign to that territory a steamer or a gunboat on a permanent basis," in order to stop these depredations.[37] In response, Captain General Rafael de Echagüe sent a steamer and two gunboats his way, but only temporarily as they were destined to Zamboanga and Balanguingui, where their maritime raiding suppression services were required.[38]

Although internal appeals and disagreements were a common occurrence among the representatives of pirate imperialism during this period, external ones were even more common. External pressures, which often came accompanied by threats, demands, and various kinds of accusations, were wielded both against other empires and against the leaders and members of amphibious communities that were identified as piratical. Time and again, all over the world, representatives of pirate imperialism exerted their influence, usually shielded by their diplomatic immunity or supported by their gunboats, in order to protect whatever commercial interests they considered to be at risk.

In late November 1854, Baron Alexandre de Forth-Rouen, a career diplomat who had held important posts at the French legations in Britain, Portugal, and China, and who was now his nation's representative before the government of Greece, wrote to Prime Minister Alexandros Mavrokordatos, complaining about the noticeable increase of piracy, especially around the town of Chalcis, in Euboea. In the same letter, Forth-Rouen demanded to know what measures had been taken by the Greek minister of navy, Konstantinos Kanaris, to put an end to these commercial disruptions.[39] A few days later, Mavrokordatos replied to Forth-Rouen, informing him that Kanaris had sent the royal corvette *Le Ludovic* "to go in search of the pirates of Naxos and of the deserted island of Stoura."[40]

Far from satisfied, an entitled Forth-Rouen responded almost immediately criticizing the choice of the ship made by the Greeks, noting that *Le Ludovic* was "a very heavy vessel," which, in his opinion, "would not be able to keep much lighter ships in check."[41] Evidently disappointed by Mavrokordatos's response, Forth-Rouen decided to send "two steam-powered vessels from the Naval Division, under the orders of Admiral de Vinan" to search for "these brigands." Even after acting independently within the jurisdiction of a foreign nation, Forth-Rouen found a way to protest the lack of cooperation from Greek officers wherever French ships went. In a letter sent to Mavrokordatos on December 22, he openly accused Greek officials of cowardice for failing to provide any information to Admiral de Vinan during his cruise against Greek sea raiders.[42]

By the time Mavrokordatos was forced to contend with Forth-Rouen's demands and accusations, he had already received a series of belittling attacks on the Greek government and officers from Thomas Wise, the British consul in Athens. Wise repeatedly lambasted the Greeks for failing to capture and put to trial a group of sailors whom the British had unilaterally decided to declare as pirates. This case, which revealed perhaps better than any other how foreign officers could make use of their influence to bend the laws and procedures of an independent nation, began in late June 1854, when Lieutenant Henry Lloyd, commanding HMS *Triton*, saw a ship sailing to the northeast of Negroponte. For months, several "proprietors of farms in the vicinity," most of whom happened to be English, French, and Swiss, had been complaining about a "horde of pirates" that had been "infecting the adjacent creeks" and demanding that immediate action should be taken against them.[43]

Likely under the effect of such repeated complaints, Lieutenant Lloyd decided to pursue this particular vessel because it was "observed to shorten sail and pull in for land."[44] Although that was hardly a reason to consider another ship as a pirate one, Lieutenant Lloyd somehow convinced himself that he was following the bandit ship that the English, French, and Swiss farmers had been concerned about. What happened afterward is not clear, as two distinct versions of the events that unfolded were given—one by Lieutenant Lloyd and one by the Greek sailors.

According to the British, after being boarded once without any incidence, the Greeks threatened them when they attempted to board them for a second time, and then, for no apparent reason, began shooting at them. The *Triton* returned fire, forcing the Greeks to escape into the bush, where fifteen of them were seized soon after and delivered to the Greek police at Oreoi. The Greek sailors told a very different story. They did admit having "been

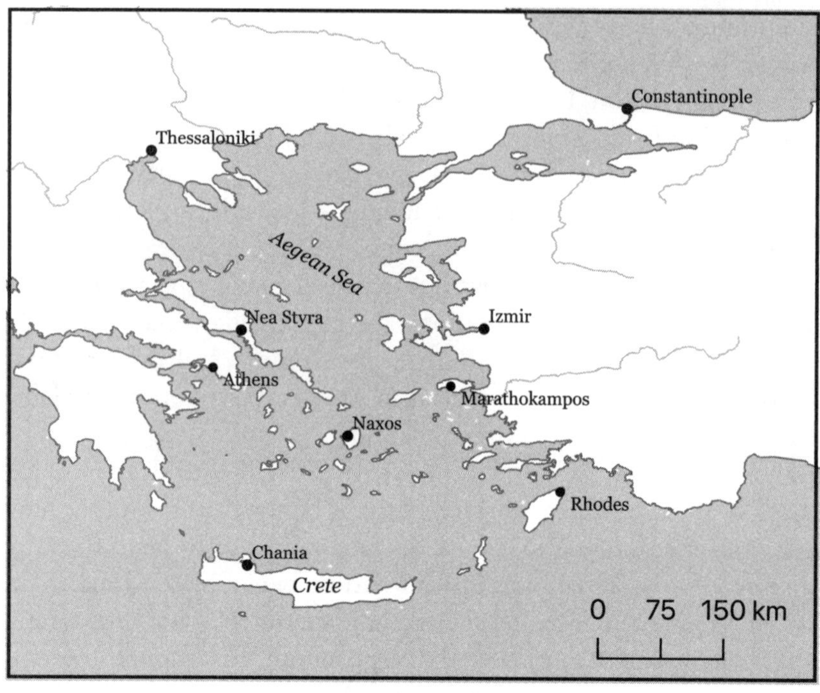

Eastern Mediterranean

chased by an English ship, and compelled to land," but when questioned by the police, they all denied "having fired upon the English."[45] Instead, they told of how they had complied and shown their papers to the English officer who had boarded their ship, and how they had explained to him that they were from Macedonia and had come on a trading voyage. When, sometime after the authorities at Kotsoubri asked them whether they had resisted the British, one of them replied, "No Brother, if we had wished to offer any resistance and especially to the English, we should not have come here."[46]

After examining all the evidence presented to them, the Greek authorities concluded that there was not enough evidence to charge the men. In their eyes, the Greek sailors had complied with the request of a foreign armed ship and had been forced to run away from what they considered to be an uncalled-for confrontation. The fact that the attack was carried out against Greek nationals by a foreign vessel operating within Greek waters seems to have weighed on the decision taken by the Greek magistrates who interrogated the sailors in the aftermath.

Such an adverse decision enraged Wise, who, from Athens, was resolved to make the Greeks pay for their alleged attack on a Royal Navy ship. In a letter sent to Mavrokordatos at the end of August, he again pressured the prime minister and accused the Greek police of not following procedure and of not having any interest "to elicit the truth," while also sniggering at those who had been in charge for not knowing how to read and write.[47] Perhaps nothing bothered him and Lieutenant Lloyd more than finding out that the Greek police commissary that had overseen the case in Kotsoubri and Agriovotano, where the fifteen Greek sailors had been taken, had recognized these Greek sailors "as Patriots and not as Pirates" for daring to resist the British within their own territorial waters.[48]

Several months later, seeing that his insolent tone had not worked on the Greek prime minister, Wise went on the offensive again. This time, again without substantial proof, he blamed the same Greek "pirates" for an attack on the British ship *Harriet*, near Andros, and reminded Mavrokordatos about his reservations regarding the conduct shown by the Greek officials who had overseen the case.[49] Wise was also at pains to point out to Mavrokordatos how for months he had continued to protest, receiving multiple assurances "without any other result," finally insisting that the "pirates" should be arrested again and put to trial.[50] As the months went by, and seeing an entire year pass without any further progress in his demands from Mavrokordatos, Wise changed strategy and sent an incendiary communique to the Greek foreign minister, Periklis Argyropoulos, in which he did not mince words, revealing the extent to which the British considered themselves entitled to intervene in the internal affairs of another state in order to protect their commercial interests. In his letter, Wise demanded the immediate dismissal of the magistrates who had originally "acted with culpable negligence, if not connivance, permitting the offenders to be liberated," and he argued that "for such dereliction of public duty they ought to be dismissed as an example to others."[51] More to the point, Wise was keen to impress on Argyropoulos that this was not his opinion alone; the British foreign secretary, the Earl of

Clarendon, was in full agreement as to what Mavrokordatos and the Greek authorities were expected to do to satisfy their demands.[52]

For countries that found themselves under various forms of foreign protection, whether requested by or imposed on them, demands of this sort were common. For a young independent nation, such as Greece was during the middle decades of the nineteenth century, the diplomatic demands exerted by allies like France and Britain were constant. The intrinsic fragility of the new nation, however, also encouraged other nations to make similar requests. The threats presented by maritime raiding against commercial activities in Greek seas were often the subject of demands from other foreign states. In the early 1840s, for example, diplomatic representatives from Austria and Sweden complained and required restitution from the Greek government with respect to the attacks to which their merchant vessels had been subjected while trading in the region.[53]

Similar demands, based on the protection of commerce, were made at the time to the Sublime Porte by a host of imperial powers. In 1862, seeing that Confederate ships were trading freely in Turkish ports, the US minister resident at Constantinople, Edward Joy Morris, requested an explanation from the Ottoman foreign minister, as, in his words, "the sole purpose of such vessels was to plunder the ships of the United States and to join a war of piracy against its merchant navy."[54] This remonstration from an allied nation prompted the Sublime Porte to ban all Confederate ships from trading in "the waters and ports of Turkey."[55] The news was received by Morris "with the greatest satisfaction." In a letter thanking Ali Pacha for the speedy resolution of this matter, he mentioned that President Abraham Lincoln regarded the measure "as a recognition of the principles of the Law of Nations" and as a "sincere proof of friendship."[56]

In the Western Mediterranean, the Spanish, the French, and the British used diplomatic pressures and threats to consolidate their trading interests. The French, for example, regularly threatened an invasion of the Riff from Algiers, presenting themselves as the only real power able "to repress vigorously piracy in these parts" in order to protect their "merchant navy."[57] The Spanish, for their part, often called for revenge for "the repeated acts of piracy" committed against their vessels, and the British engaged in a long-term passive-aggressive strategy, led by Consul Drummond Hay, against the sultan of Morocco and his government's officers.[58]

To be sure, for many years Drummond Hay excelled at making demands and extracting privileges from the sultan of Morocco, Abd al-Rahman, and many of his officials, in favor of his government. Requesting compensation for merchandise lost during attacks in the coastal waters of the Riff was perhaps the main reason for his recurrent interaction with the sultan during the 1840s and 1850s.[59] These demands often involved protracted negotiations, as Abd al-Rahman did everything he could to convince the British that he had no power or responsibility regarding the attacks. In 1856, after finally getting sixteen thousand dollars from the sultan, Drummond Hay commented to the Earl of Clarendon that even though the sultan had paid for one of the robberies at sea, he continued to refuse to accept responsibility for this or any future "acts of the people of the Riff."[60]

Although the restitution of property or money relating to British merchant vessels attacked along the Riff Coast was central to Drummond Hay's work, the consul also pressured the sultan to open "a port, or ports, on the Reef coast."[61] In his mind, this step would allow the British to trade freely in the region and would, he hoped, diminish the attacks that were taking so much of his time. Once the sultan showed some disposition to "build a town on the sea coast of the Reef, which [was] to be opened to traffic with Europeans," Drummond Hay attempted to persuade him to build this port at Ras Kebdana, opposite of the Chafarinas Islands.[62] The sultan, however, disagreed about the location, as he considered this place to be near "the Eastern confines of His Empire" and very close to the territories that had been taken by the French decades earlier.[63] Not to be discouraged by Abd al-Rahman's apprehensions, Drummond Hay wrote a secret letter to his foreign minister subtly attempting to convince him that this location was convenient for the English and requesting his help to induce the sultan to do as the British requested.[64]

Elsewhere, other empires similarly exerted every diplomatic pressure to protect their commercial interests, often resorting to coercion and extortion in their attempts to expand their commercial orbits. The Dutch, for example, employed different strategies to persuade the many local rulers in their Southeast Asian territories to protect trade and pursue maritime raiding. A system of residencies allowed the central government of Batavia to keep an eye on any developments and to almost always have someone on site to pressure these local rulers and their officers. Dutch navy vessels also patrolled their seas, frequently delivering letters and orders originating in Batavia or Amsterdam.

In a dispatch sent in late 1830 to the governor general of the Dutch East Indies, Johannes van den Bosch, the sultan of Sumenep, Paku Nataningrat, endeavored to convince his Dutch counterpart of his efforts to follow the instructions he had been given during a recent visit. In this letter, Paku Nataningrat wrote of the progress he had made tracking down persons who had been imprisoned by pirates and who were able to offer information about the pirates' whereabouts.[65] The sultan also provided intelligence about the movement of pirate fleets from Maguindanao, which had been coming down to his realm from the Sulu Sea. These pirates, he noted, had found a way to collaborate with local raiders, like the Tabiloo, to carry out larger attacks on trading vessels.[66]

Likewise, a long letter sent in 1837 by Jean Pierre Cornets de Groot to the Dutch resident at Riau, C. F. Goldman, featured multiple examples of pressures exerted on local princes, especially upon those who were not "restrained by the steady presence of any European supply, and militaries."[67] To Cornets de Groot, a case illustrating how efficient Dutch pressures had been was that of the sultanate of Sambas, on the western coast of Borneo. In his own words, Dutch actions, including the "renewal of the former relationship . . . and the restored Dutch government" there, had all "been done with a view to the interests of the trade, for which the possession of the ports of Pontianak, Maupawa and Sambas was necessary."[68]

In subsequent decades, the Dutch steadily increased their coercive demands on the territories under their rule or influence. Throughout the 1840s, 1850s, and 1860s, they continued to apply all sort of pressures, often accompanying their demands with gifts to sweeten their relationship with those rulers willing to cooperate. In 1860, for example, the assistant resident in Siak asked the resident at Riau to send some gifts to the sultan of Siak. These gifts, he said, had been promised to the sultan two years before, and because they had not arrived the sultan was in a "less favorable mood" toward any possible Dutch requests.[69] In another letter sent to the resident of Riau that same year by the director of products and civil warehouses, there was a discussion about sending a lithographic device to the local rajah, as it had been promised to him years before and failing to deliver it was not desirable.[70]

Gifts were, of course, a way to gain access to new ports and markets, a means of expanding the Dutch commercial sphere of influence in the East Indies. For a protectionist empire like the Dutch, pressures and demands on local rulers and populations—independent of Batavia or not—were accompanied by new laws and measures that had to be obeyed. One momentous measure highlighting such policies occurred in 1828 when the government of Batavia decided to ban the use of any currency that had not been issued by the Dutch themselves. The consequences for those who violated this law were dire and included fines of "four times the amount" of any counterfeit money confiscated.[71] These strict regulations were published in Dutch, Chinese, and local languages and posted in public places for all to see; they were republished in various times and places in the years to come.

Another protectionist empire, the Portuguese, operated in a similar way when it came to employing diplomatic pressures on those who threatened their commerce throughout Asian seas. By the mid-1850s, the Portuguese navy in the Far East had assembled a registry of vessels of different sizes and types, so that they could determine without delay who was engaged in licit commerce and who was not.[72] Faced with numerous attacks on vessels that were trading out of Macau, Portuguese authorities there continuously pressed both the people living in Macau, and their Cantonese counterparts, to bring them to an end. Throughout the 1850s, for example, they repeatedly asked for a man-of-war, permanently attached to the colony, that could patrol its waters and pursue those suspected of carrying out these attacks.[73] In 1858, following the capture of some Portuguese lorchas, the commander of the ship *Mondego*, which had temporarily been detached to Macau precisely as a response to the requests discussed above, visited Canton and attempted to extract an indemnification from the local authorities. In a letter to the secretary of marine and overseas colonies, Captain

José Severo Tavares confessed that the "negotiation did not succeed, even though the original proposal had come from the Cantonese chiefs themselves."[74]

The Spanish, too, made use of a vast range of strategies to place requests and extract commercial concessions from different nations. Until the second decade of the nineteenth century, Spain had a strict monopoly on trade with its colonies. It was only after the Napoleonic invasion of the Iberian Peninsula that Spanish colonial ports began to trade with neutral nations.[75] In the Philippines, in addition to deceiving schemes, like the one used by Norzagaray against the Balanguingui Samal in the late 1850s, Spanish officers never hesitated to intimidate those they considered a threat to their trade in the region.

One example is Agustín Bocalán, outgoing commander of the Spanish navy in the Philippines, who just before leaving for Spain wrote to the sultan of Joló, accusing him of not being honest and of failing to honor the treaties that his father had signed with the Spanish government.[76] In his letter, Bocalán reproached the sultan for signing treaties with foreign powers, for failing to suppress the pirates that operated within his territorial waters, for benefiting from their plundering, and for declining to give Spanish vessels better rights and tariffs than those given to other nations. In short, and revealing some audacity in his claims, Bocalán criticized the sultan for not having "behaved as a brother or a good friend" to the Spanish.[77]

The numerous accusations and recriminations carried out by the Spanish consul in Morocco during his negotiations with the sultan's representative, Mohamed El-Khateeb, reveal the extent to which the Spanish attempted to use questionable means to extricate more favorable trading rights from the emperor of Morocco.[78] Of course, when these allegations and the ensuing threats failed to work, the Spanish invaded Morocco in an attempt to emulate what France had done decades earlier in neighboring Algiers.

Diplomatic pressures and demands around the protection of commerce, effective as they could be, often failed to produce the results that the representatives of pirate imperialism longed for. Always relying on the superior weaponry of their nations, imperial agents rarely hesitated to use a large assortment of threats when their diplomatic demands were not satisfied. Once again, the British can provide plenty of examples that illustrate such behavior.

Faced with constant maritime plundering against traders based at their Sierra Leone colony between the 1810s and 1840s, colonial authorities there regularly resorted to various kinds of threats to dissuade their African neighbors from causing further interruptions to the colony's trade. The letter books of the Liberated African Department and colonial secretary for this period feature numerous examples. The situation became so serious by the early 1830s, that Governor Alexander Findlay was forced to create a "water police" force to deal with the frequent instances of robbery and kidnapping that were taking place within the colony's jurisdictional waters.[79]

Sierra Leone traders faced similar threats in neighboring countries. Whenever news of one of these cases reached the authorities of this British colony, the reply almost always came as a belligerent threat. In 1844, for example, Governor Norman William Macdonald took issue with the reported depredations to the colony's commerce carried out under the auspices of a neighboring chief, identified in the sources as Bocarree Sillee. In a menacing letter to this chief, sent on the last day of December 1844, Governor Macdonald warned him that should he fail to put a stop to these piracies, the British would be forced to resort "to severe measures" to compel him to "respect the persons and properties of British subjects."[80] Not satisfied with this clear line of intimidation, Macdonald warned the neighboring chief that should he "molest, illtreat or rob them" he would "most assuredly be punished" by the men under his command at Sierra Leone.[81]

In their relations with another imperialist state of the time, the Siamese Empire, the British were often forced to make allowances in order to secure limited trade rights. In the mid-1820s, and despite Captain Burney's genuine efforts to avoid such a concession, the British found themselves with little choice but to agree to Siam's occupation of Kedah. Before this compromise was reached, Burney had alerted his superiors that the Siamese had "no idea of a free and unrestricted trade," and that any negotiations around this issue would likely linger for a long period of time and would involve discussing every "minutest detail" about common rules, duties, and charges.[82] Before him, John Crawfurd had pointed out that British traders could not "trade to Siam with advantage," justifying British demands by the fact that the Siamese had "permitted the Portuguese to establish a commercial house at Siam" and that they had "promised the same thing to the Americans."[83] Ultimately, the Anglo-Siamese Treaty of 1826 incorporated some commercial provisions, but it left the British with much to be desired when it came to trading freely within the Siamese Empire.[84]

That situation was solved just under three decades later, in 1855, when John Bowring, following Burney's steps, arrived in Bangkok with the intention of opening Siam's ports to international trade. As David Todd has pointed out, undeterred by the resistance presented by the Siamese to such measures, Bowring made it clear to them that should they fail to agree with his demands to abolish a number of commercial restrictions, he would leave one of his steamers, the *Rattler*, permanently stationed in front of Bangkok.[85] Before long, King Rama IV saw no other choice but to agree with the demands presented by Bowring and signed the treaty that abolished Siam's Royal Storage and opened its the ports to foreign trade.[86]

The use of gunboats, particularly steamers, to impose pirate imperialist demands was a trademark way of threatening during the period. In the Persian Gulf, British residents often instructed navy commanders to take their menacing gunboats to places where it was necessary to remind local chiefs of Britain's might so that these chiefs would not resort to piracy and harm British trade with India. David Alexander Blane, one of these British residents, made it clear in 1833 to the commander and senior officer of the Royal Navy in the Persian Gulf that "the suppression of Piracy in the Gulf of Persia and the protection of the trade to Bushire" were arguably "a most important part of the service required of the Indian Navy."[87] Blane's opinion was soon backed by the chief secretary to the British government in Bombay, Charles Norris, when barely a few months later he wrote that "Britain's only concern was the maintenance of the maritime commerce in the Gulf" and that "British maritime superiority would deter from piracy whoever controlled the harbor of Muscat."[88]

Such a strategy had been in place as soon as the treaty of 1820 was signed between Britain and a number of Gulf States. British residents had been resorting to coercion and threats against various Gulf chiefs whenever they thought it was prudent to do so. David Wilson, Blane's predecessor in Bushehr, did just as much when, in January 1829, he ordered the senior naval officer in the region to take his war vessel to Bahrain, Abu Dhabi, Sharjah, and Ras Al-Khaimah in an exercise that was a pure show of strength.[89]

In 1841, another British resident in the Gulf, Samuel Hennell, wrote to Commander George Barnes Brucks, ordering him that on his way to Qatar, he should take his entire squadron to Bahrain, "being the object that the Steam Frigate should be seen at all principal ports."[90] Over two years later, echoing Hennell's instructions almost word by word, Commander J. P. Porter ordered the captain of the East India Company vessel *Coote* to proceed to Abu Dhabi, "showing [his] ship off that port."[91]

Other empires also paraded their ships in front of those they saw as threats to their commercial interests. The story of Prince Adalbert and the *Danzig* is one example. From the various accounts of the so-called battle of Tres Forcas, between the Prussians and the maritime people of the Riff, it is clear that the Prussians used their steamship to display their superior power. On numerous occasions, the Spanish, too, paraded their steamships and gunboats along the coastlines and harbors of the peoples they considered a menace to their interests, just as their warmongers clamored for the extermination of the people of the Riff. In early 1859, and following the requests of Spanish consul in Tangier, Juan Blanco del Valle, a Spanish fleet carried out a "naval demonstration" off the coast of Morocco with the goal of intimidating the sultan in order to extract yet more trading concessions from him.[92]

A similar situation unfolded in the Dutch East Indies throughout this period, where threats against local amphibious populations were quite frequent.[93] In 1827, the British resident councilor in Singapore, John Prince, who had stopped at Batavia on his way back to London, reported that the Dutch had sent the war vessel *Bellona* to the eastern coast of Sumatra to induce "the natives to discontinue the purchase of salt" from the British.[94] In this missive, Prince also suggested that the appearance of such a ship at places like Siak, Kumpar, and Jambi could intimidate inhabitants into compliance with the Dutch "through fear."[95]

Emerging American imperialist incursions, supported by notions connected to the Monroe Doctrine and the idea of Manifest Destiny, and following recent gains in its expansion to the west and, later on, in the Mexican-American War, were also patent overseas. Already in the second decade of the century, United States consuls and navy commanders saw themselves as powerful enough to make all sorts of demands, following up with threats and violent actions when needed. This was particularly the case when suppressing piracy or, as happened with Japan in the mid-1850s, when forcing another country to open its ports to foreign trade. In his two visits to Japan, in 1853 and 1854, Commodore Matthew Perry made sure to parade his large squadron in front of numerous Japanese ports, conciously generating high levels of apprehension and fear among anyone who observed the steamers operating against high winds.[96]

The exhibition of overwhelming strength shown by Perry's heavily armed and threatening squadron eventually led to the signing in Yokohama, still under the menacing presence of his ships' guns, of a so-called treaty of peace and amity, better known as the Treaty of Kanagawa, at the end of March 1854.[97] By this treaty, the Americans were guaranteed the opening of the ports of Shimoda and Hakodake to foreign trade and secured the approval from the shogunate to appoint a US consul in Japan, who would be based at the former location. Almost simultaneously, a Russian fleet commanded by Admiral Yevfimiy Putyatin arrived in Nagasaki, also exhibiting a superior firepower and displaying its ships in a menacing manner. Not surprisingly, the Russian expedition had as its core mission the opening of Japanese ports to Russian commerce. These rights were granted after a series of protracted negotiations that only concluded with the Treaty of Shimoda in February 1855.[98]

Along the African coast and in the Caribbean, the French also used their gunboats to threaten and intimidate those who stood in the way of their securing new trading privileges. For example, at the height of the French Anti-Slave Trade Squadron actions in West and West Central Africa in the 1840s, their ships frequently visited slave-trading ports and threatened their inhabitants, regardless of whether they were Africans, Americans, or Europeans, with reprisals of various kinds should they continue to hamper French commerce in the region.[99] In some extreme cases, they went so far as to concoct plans to occupy forts and towns along the coast, one example being Captain Charles Baudin's suggestion in 1845 of taking possession of the former slave-trading fort at Dahomey.[100]

In 1825, in an even clearer display of strength, the French sent a war fleet of fourteen ships, commanded by the Baron de Mackau, to Haiti, to enforce the Ordonnance of April 17.[101] While acknowledging the independence of Haiti for the first time, this document conditioned such recognition to three concessions. Of these the indemnity payment of a very large sum of money has been the best known and more often discussed.[102] Two other commerce-related concessions, however, were also integral parts of this ordonnance. The first one was that the Haitian ports should be open to trade with all nations, and the second, that French vessels should pay only half duties for any export and import transactions carried out at these ports.

In order to persuade the Haitians to accept, Mackau paraded his ships in front of the capital, Port-au-Prince, threatening an indefinite blockade should they fail to agree to his demands. To be clear, this strategy had been a central part of the instructions given to Mackau before he departed for the Caribbean a few months earlier.[103] In a "very secret" letter sent to Commander Jurien de la Gravière, dated on the same day the ordonnance was signed, the Count of Chabrol made it clear that should Haiti refuse their terms, a blockade of their main ports, especially those of "Port-au-Prince, Cap Français, and Les Cayes St Louis," should be immediately implemented.[104]

From the early part of the century, the French and other European nations had come to consider the Haitians, especially those from the north of the country, as pirates, a circumstance that allowed France to display whatever threats were considered necessary, so that this "hydra [could be] be promptly crushed."[105] Forcing them to trade in a way that suited the French, through menaces and intimidation, was seen as an acceptable and convenient way to stop Haiti's supposed piratical activities and to boost French trade, through the opening of ports and the halving of taxes paid by France.

Across the world, as Western empires attempted to expand their informal commercial networks, they found, time and again, that not everyone welcomed them. More to the point, despite pressures and threats, many countries refused to comply while others challenged efforts to dominate them. When pressures and threats did not suffice, pirate imperialist agents resorted to violence, often using their overwhelmingly superior firepower and disproportionately forceful measures to achieve whatever goals they had. The protection and support of commerce, even against the wishes of those that opposed them, were frequently at the center of pirate imperial armed violence in virtually every maritime region of the world during the middle decades of the nineteenth century.

Armed suppression was carried out, more often than not, through punitive actions against those who had disturbed or compromised trading operations. Failing to comply with treaties that had been signed under the menacing presence of gunships, for example, led to accusations of uncivilized behavior and piracy, which were seen as justification for a disproportionate military and naval response. As most of the historical sources describing these actions were bequeathed to us by these pirate imperialist agents, they almost universally present themselves as saviors or, at the very least, as legally obliged to resort to violence to protect their trading interests. In many cases, they claimed to have used force only as a last resort, after being attacked by pirates, savages, cannibals, and the like. Put in other words, those at the bloody end of punitive expeditions were almost always blamed for provoking Western powers into action.

Blaming their victims was a common argument presented by representatives of pirate imperialism, who did not hesitate to paint themselves as agents of peace and commerce, who had almost always been attacked first. Some, like John Bowring, took these supposed grievances so far that they unleashed bloody wars; others used them as excuses to colonize new territories, as we will see in the next chapter. Surprisingly, especially if we consider their self-proclaimed pacific and commercial interests, they all reached these distant regions on heavily armed gunships, and most forced themselves on alien peoples, appearing before them uninvited and seemingly out of thin air.

There is little doubt that amphibious communities did disrupt trade. They did so for multiple reasons, as J. L. Anderson has concluded. Many had been engaged in maritime raiding for many years and were rightly referred to as pirates by both imperialist agents and the local amphibious communities they had repeatedly ravaged. Another chief reason seems to have been their dissatisfaction with the disadvantageous commercial agreements often imposed on them. Their unwillingness to trade with foreigners, or to trade in the ways these foreigners claimed was best for them, was undoubtedly another powerful motivation behind their role in disrupting the trade of newcomers.

During this period, Western navies carried out numerous attacks, both at sea and on land, against parties they considered to be piratical and had disrupted, in one way or another, their trading rights. Even in some of the most isolated aquatic regions of the planet, empires and maritime communities accused of piracy found themselves at war. The Caspian Sea is one such place. During the 1830s and 1840s, Turkmen, or Turcoman, seafarers were frequently reported to have raided merchant vessels belonging to the Persian and Russian empires.[106] Russian navy vessels had repeatedly attacked the Turkmen throughout the Caspian Sea, at least since 1828 when the sea became in effect a mare nostrum for the Russians after the signing of the Treaty of Torkmenchay with Persia, which granted them free roaming across it.[107]

In the late 1830s various expeditions were sent to pursue the Turkmen, and new British-built steel gunboats, purposedly constructed to draw less water, were employed, thus allowing them to chase the "pirates" into their homes.[108] In 1842, a new naval force, led by Yefmimiy Putyatin, the same officer who years later would force the Treaty of Shimoda on the Japanese, brought maritime raiding in the Caspian Sea to a halt, and also secured the lifting of restrictions in Persian ports to Russian trade.[109] Ashooradeh Island, off the coast of Persia and where the Russians had built a fort, was used as a base for these operations. In spite of Putyatin's success, however, these attacks resumed only a few years later. In late December 1856, for example, Russian navy vessels were reported to have destroyed the "Starpa pirates" in these same waters, making "great havoc among them."[110]

From the mid-1820s, another empire, the Spanish, began to intensify their efforts to suppress, through armed means, any resistance to their relentless efforts to expand both their colonial possessions and trading privileges in the Philippines. Already in 1827, Captain General Mariano Ricafort had dispatched an expeditionary force of twenty warships and 500 men to Joló. Although their planned assault on the city did not materialize, they navigated up and down the nearby coastline, "burning many towns, and causing the biggest damage possible."[111]

Repeated attacks on Joló, Balanguingui, and other supposed nests of pirates were ever more frequent thereafter, with particularly noteworthy expeditions in the years 1848, 1851, and 1857. In 1862, the recently appointed captain general, Rafael de Echagüe, who had served in the Spanish invasion of Morocco a few years earlier, sent a new armed force to the Samal Islands. This expedition, once again, resulted in heavy losses for the inhabitants of the islands of Carongdong and Patián. In a letter to Madrid, Echagüe boasted of the "new triumph obtained over the bloodthirsty and warring races" living in the south of the archipelago. Dong Dong, he noted, had been taken after killing twenty-three of its inhabitants and then "reduced to ashes," and Patián had been "destroyed by the flames."[112]

For the sake of protecting commerce, the Dutch, too, carried numerous armed incursions throughout Southeast Asia. It was especially so after the Treaty of London, signed in 1824, when various colonial territories were exchanged with the British. The detailed description of many of these armed, heavy-handed expeditions can be found in Cornets de Groot's book *Notices historiques sur les pirateries*, published in 1847. In 1834, a naval force was sent against Batu Putih and Berou, and numerous villages were destroyed and set on fire.[113] Five years later, another force, under the command of Lieutenant J. W. F. Frucht, was dispatched to put down supposed pirates who had been damaging Dutch trade around Lingga, in eastern Sumatra. This expedition, too, burned villages, while also rescuing some captives along the way.[114]

As colonial and trading rivalries were exacerbated around the world from the 1820s onward, other empires began to engage in violent expeditions of this kind. More than twenty years after invading and occupying Algiers, the French continued to have ambitions over its neighbor, Morocco. British and Spanish diplomats and navy officers frequently reported about French not-so-secret desires of expanding westward. This expansion never materialized, in spite of a real attempt that led to the Franco-Moroccan War of 1844, when the French bombarded various Moroccan ports, including Tangier and Mogador.[115] In 1851, around the same time the British and the Spanish were considering a punitive expedition against the Riff, a French vessel wrecked off the Atlantic coast of Morocco, leading to another well-known incident of pirate imperialism, the bombardment of Salé.[116]

This incident was justified, as was customary at the time, by what the French considered to be the illegal pillaging of the ship's cargo by the local populations of Salé and Rabat. After the French attempted, unsuccessfully, to get retribution for the cargo, they sent a squad commanded by Rear Admiral Louis Dubordieu to chastise the Moroccans for daring to defy the French supremacy in the region.[117] The ships had been dispatched shortly after the French chargé d'affaires in Morocco, Nicolas Bourée, had written to Paris suggesting the need "to teach" the inhabitants of these two towns "a lesson."[118] The French war vessels, which had more than one hundred guns to their disposition, opened fire on Salé mid-morning on November 26. Within a few hours they had destroyed the city's defenses, with large sections of the Almohad walls collapsing under fire; the main mosque was also a target of multiple projectiles, with eighty guns firing in its direction. As a result of this attack, many houses in the mosque's neighborhood caught fire, and between twelve and fifteen civilians and close to ten soldiers were reported to have been killed.[119]

Punitive expeditions, often justified by the need to protect trade, were not the sole monopoly of European empires with colonial stakes around the world. The United States was also a major participant in retaliatory pirate imperialist endeavors, at least after 1832 when President Andrew Jackson sent the USS *Potomac* to take revenge against the residents of Kuala Batee for an attack of the merchant vessel *Friendship*, which had resulted in the death of some of its crew.[120] According to Lieutenant Irvine Shubrick, who led the expedition, the Americans killed over 150 people and bombarded and set the town on fire.[121] Barely six years later, when another American ship, the *Eclipse*, was attacked off the west coast of Sumatra, a second expedition was organized and sent against the inhabitants of the same region.[122] This time, two war vessels, under the command of Commodore George C. Reed, attacked Kuala Batee and Muckie in what one of his crew considered an "act of vengeance," again destroying and burning them to the ground and killing any inhabitants who chose to resist their attack.[123]

It is worth noting here that in both of these cases, the only existing accounts and explanations of what transpired between the crews of the *Friendship* and the *Eclipse* and the inhabitants of Kuala Batee were written by Western actors who were involved in the events in one way or another. In both cases, as it would happen again a year later with the French ship *Denise*, Malay amphibious communities were accused of attacking, suddenly and without a reason, peaceful foreign traders.[124] The Kuala Batee inhabitants' version of the events, if it was ever given, did not reach us, which leaves us with potentially compromised narratives that presented, from the start, a massacre of noble Western white men by non-white, uncivilized pirates.

During the following years, and in spite of these punitive actions, alleged attacks against foreign ships off the coast of Sumatra continued. In 1851, soon after replacing Joseph Balestier as US consul to Singapore, W. W. Shaw wrote to Washington mentioning the "excesses lately committed on the West Coast of Sumatra" by the local populations against foreign merchant vessels.[125] According to Shaw, the USS *Missouri* had been attacked and its captain and officers murdered. In this same missive, he referred to two Sicilian and French vessels that had been plundered as well. In Shaw's opinion, the most beneficial measure that the US could take to protect "the large trade carried on there" was to assign a steamer to the region.[126] In addition to this suggestion, he emphasized that no time should be lost in sending instructions to the commanders of the ships on the East India Station in order to "let the natives again know that retribution will follow their outrages on American lives and property."[127]

American armed attempts to force others to trade with them during this period saw a last episode of note in 1866, when the heavily armed steamer *General Sherman* went up the Taedong River, defying various orders from Korean authorities to turn around. Instead, and relying on its supposedly superior firepower, the steamer reached Pyongyang, where, frustrated with the ongoing refusal of the authorities to negotiate and now inconveniently beached at Yang-Gak Island, its sailors abducted some local officials and demanded a ransom.[128] As things got heated between the sailors and the inhabitants of Pyongyang, they fired their guns upon a group of civilians who were standing at the riverside, killing at least seven. Probably tired of indulging the excesses of the Americans, Korean troops set the *General Sherman* on fire. As they tried to run away, crew members were murdered by the people on the shore.[129]

Although most surviving accounts of this event were, once again, recorded by westerners, even their authors were forced to admit that the *General Sherman*'s captain and crew had been responsible for their own demise, by resorting to what can only be described as a piratical behavior. The secretary to the US legation in Peking in 1867, Dr. S. Wells Williams, commented that the evidence he had managed to gather pointed to "the presumption that they invoked their sad fate by some rash or violent act towards the natives."[130] Even so, within months of finding out about the attack, the US dispatched the USS *Shenandoah* to chastise the inhabitants of Pyongyang for daring to defend themselves.[131]

The civilian onlookers who lost their lives on the banks of the Taedong River, just as those who were killed by French projectiles in Salé in 1851, were not, in fact, a rarity. Pirate imperialism claimed numerous innocent lives as its agents tussled for new markets and spheres of influence. Collateral victims were recorded in virtually every corner of the world where pirate imperialist powers displayed their gunships with the aim of eliminating threats to their trading interests. In some notable exceptions, though, civilians and their property were specifically targeted by these agents of empire.

In May 1843, HMS *Dido*, commanded by Henry Keppel, a trigger-happy officer who also happened to be a personal friend of James Brooke, came under attack from a group of natives of Sarawak, who likely perceived Keppel's ship as the invading element it was and decided to repel it from their waters. Keppel confirmed as much when he observed that they had likely mistaken the British for pirates. Even though the *Dido*'s significantly superior fire power and speed meant that the British were never really under a serious threat, Lieutenant Wilmot Horton decided to fire upon the natives, killing "no less than 10" and wounding at least 11 more.[132] Soon after this needless slaughter, Keppel was compelled to admit that these men were not pirates and that Horton and his men had killed many "by mistake."[133]

In spite of the apparent fact that Horton and his men needlessly attacked and killed innocent people who, at most, were defending their homes, they were widely praised by numerous British officers. In fact, Horton received a promotion to commander, bizarrely, for fighting against pirates. In a letter sent by the Admiralty to Vice Admiral William Parker in early January 1844, Horton's conduct was praised as "gallant" for fighting "against a piratical force."[134] In his reply to the Admiralty a few months later, Parker once again repeated the claim that Horton's "spirited" actions against pirates had been rightly rewarded with this promotion.[135]

Another event where civilians were targeted with premeditation occurred in the Persian Gulf, in 1855. In this case, property rather than lives was claimed by a British vessel commanded by Commodore Richard Ethersay. Following instructions of Arnold Burrowes Kemball, the British resident in the Gulf at this time, Ethersay led the ships *Tigris* and *Constance* to Abu Dhabi, with the clear intention of demanding a monetary restitution from Sheik Saeed bin Tahnun for the pillaging of the boat belonging to a man named Abdul Kareem. Although the sheik refused to take responsibility for the actions of men who were no longer under his jurisdiction, he agreed to pay the money demanded by Ethersay. The money alone, however, was not enough, as Ethersay had clear instructions from Kemball to make a "demonstration of force" to "any extremity" if he thought it necessary.[136]

Kemball had insisted that once the pecuniary reparation had been obtained, the two piratical boats involved in the attack should be seized and "burnt on the spot as a warning to other evil doers."[137] Notwithstanding Ethersay's repeated attempts to convince Sheik bin Tahnun to deliver these boats to him, the request was denied;

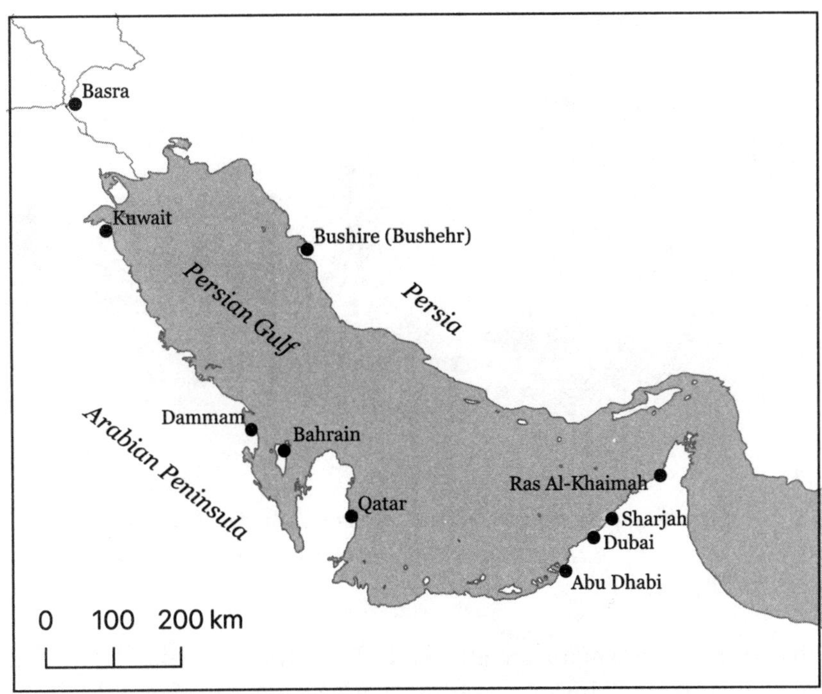

Persian Gulf

the sheik explained that "they were not at Aboothabee and that neither himself nor any person at the place knew where they had gone to."[138] Faced with a challenging situation, as the two boats were not likely to be given up, Ethersay decided to threaten bin Tahnun by going to the Pearl Banks, where he would take two random boats and set them on fire and "by creating such a panic among the men of his tribe who were fishing as would cause them all to leave the banks."[139] Ultimately, bin Tahnun was left with no option but to sacrifice two boats he chose among those found in the harbor at the time, which Ethersay duly burned and sank immediately.[140] This arguably excessive action was, however, applauded by Kemball's deputy, Herbert J. Disbrowe, who praised the "firm, forbearing, and at the same time, judicious manner" in which Ethersay had taught "a severe lesson" against any would-be pirates in the Gulf.[141]

A few years later, in 1867, the British once again accused the chiefs of Abu Dhabi and Bahrain of violating the provisions of the

Burning pirate dhows in the Persian Gulf. *The Illustrated London News* (November 28, 1868).

maritime truce when they attacked Qatar and, accordingly, moved to punish them. Almost a year later, in the autumn, HMS *Vigilant*, accompanied by the steamer *Sind* and the gunboats *Hugh Rose* and *Clyde*, appeared before Bahrain.[142] Once they ascertained that the local chief, Muhammad Al Khalifa, had fled, they tracked down his men and dhows to a fort in the vicinity of Bahrain. Pounding the fort with shell and rockets for a few hours, they left it in ruins. Before departing, they set alight the few boats that had been kept nearby.[143] Immediately after, the fleet sailed for Abu Dhabi, where the local ruler was given the option of accepting the terms put forward by the British—which included a monetary fine as well as giving up all his guns—or, alternatively, having his fort bombarded by the gunboats.[144]

On occasion, punitive expeditions aimed at protecting commercial interests against supposed piratical attacks descended into uncontrolled violence, leading to unnecessary massacres, which also involved scores of innocent peoples. Edward H. Cree, during his cruise off the coast of China during and after the First Opium War, left both written and graphic testimony to the lengths the British could go to safeguard their privilege to keep exporting drugs into Qing China. Already in the midst of the war, and certainly for years

Street in Ching Kiang Foo, by Edward H. Cree. © National Maritime Museum, Greenwich, London.

to come and as a direct result of it, an increment of maritime raiding on both sides became apparent. In March 1841, Cree mentioned the "many dead bodies floating down the [Canton] river, naked and blown out, some of them mutilated by our shot from the ships' broadsides."[145] Cree's watercolors, especially those showing slaughtered civilians, including many women and children, after the attack to Chinkiang, expose the vicious nature of the invasion. Invariably, each sketch shows scores of Chinese soldiers and civilians who lost their lives during the British bombardment and subsequent landing at this place, shortly before the signing of the Treaty of Nanjing in 1842.[146]

It is well known that British traders had been defying Chinese authorities and the East India Company for years in the period leading to the breakout of hostilities, attempting to force their own brand of free trade upon China by any means necessary. As Ting Man Tsao has demonstrated, already in 1832 the president of the East India Company at Canton, Charles Marjoribanks, had dispatched an illegal scouting party on a secret mission to the ports located north of Canton, with the objective of ascertaining whether they could be persuaded to open up to British trade.[147] In the years to come, after the island of Hong Kong had been annexed and five of the kingdom's ports had been forcefully opened to foreign trade, the British were faced with ever increasing levels of maritime raiding, which as Chappell has noted, were nothing but a direct consequence of their war of subjugation, which contributed to a "wider dispersal of existing trade" and to an increase in unemployment that drove many into maritime raiding.[148]

Perhaps the most well-known names associated with maritime raiding in the seas of China during this period were those of Shap-ng-tsai and Chui-a-poo. The former seems to have been not a single individual but an association of maritime raiders, and the latter was likely the best-known lieutenant within its ranks.[149] After years of attacks across the South China Sea, a combined British and Qing Chinese expedition was sent to punish their deeds in the early autumn of 1849. The attack on the "Chinese pirates," as narrated by various British witnesses, including Cree, was relentless and exceedingly vindictive.

Already by September 30, soon after the naval operations had begun, John C. Dalrymple-Hay communicated the destruction of "at least 250 pirates" in a letter to his superior officer.[150] A few days later, in another letter cited by the *China Mail*, Dalrymple-Hay informed that the number of dead people in a new action against the fleet commanded by Chui-a-poo in Mirs Bay had risen to over four hundred.[151] Although Chui-a-poo initially managed to escape, he was eventually captured; he later took his own life, while waiting to be deported to Van Diemen's Island.

A few days later, on October 21, the combined British-Qing naval force engaged the Shap-ng-tsai vessels in the Tonkin River. Boasting a much superior fire power, the British steamers *Columbine*, *Phlegethon*, and *Fury*, in particular, wreaked havoc among the Chinese, who, according to Cree, were decimated in the thousands.[152] Those who escaped this bloodbath, swimming to shore, seem to have been speared by the people who lived along the Tonkin River.[153] Again noticing the likely high number of civilian casualties, Cree mentioned that he feared that many women had perished during the bombardment of these ships.[154]

The suppression of piracy in the seas of China continued for at least another decade. As the Taiping Rebellion (1850–64) gathered momentum, and particularly during and after the Second Opium War (1856–60), maritime raiding became, once more, an economic activity practiced widely in the region. The violence associated with armed suppression, although not reaching the levels of the late 1840s, was significant, as the testimonies of Western agents in the region suggest. For instance, a few months after the Second Opium War came to an end, the commander of HMS *Nimrod*, William Arthur, described an armed operation against a group of supposed pirates, who upon their arrival had disembarked along the coast. The ensuing battle lasted for thirty uninterrupted hours and, according to Arthur, resulted in great losses for the pirates, based on his assessment of "the number of bodies" his men had found in its aftermath.[155]

Similar, or arguably worse, massacres were committed by the British while attempting to protect their commercial interests in the East Indies. Soon after Calcutta agreed to support the requests made by Singapore-based traders in 1835, a new, significantly more violent and repressive approach was taken by the British in the region. Essential to this new policy were Straits Settlements governor Bonham and the Royal Navy commander tasked with providing the necessary muscle to subdue all maritime raiding activities in their neighborhood, Henry Ducie Chads. Both Bonham and Chads, now under the titles of joint commissioners for the suppression of piracy, began working on a new strategy in early 1836, which would rely heavily on the introduction of passes or licenses issued by local rulers from across Southeast Asia. The idea was problematic, of course, as many of these rulers had no obligation to cooperate with the British, or, as Bonham himself pointed out, were not likely to ever receive the news of these dispositions.

To go along with the passes, Bonham proposed to be swift in applying violent means to stop piracy, even when there was no proof against paperless vessels. In some notes written in June, Bonham

Destruction of Shap-ng-tsai fleet, by Edward H. Cree. © National Maritime Museum, Greenwich, London.

reasserted British extraterritorial searching rights against boats and ships owned and crewed by Asians—rights that did not apply to Western vessels. Bonham also recommended destroying any ships found carrying "a superabundance of arms."[156] Even in instances when the naval commander in charge of searching the vessels was not sure that they were engaged in piratical activities, he added, "they should be destroyed."[157] Bonham was well aware of the despotic character of these measures, which themselves amounted to nothing short of openly fighting piracy with piracy. In fact, he predicted a push back from potential critics in Singapore, Calcutta, and London, confessing, "I am not unaware that this plan is open to many and serious objections," but he still doubled down on the need of its implementation, as he knew "of no better" way to fix the problem.[158]

Ready to act upon suspected vessels, then, Commander Chads went to sea on HMS *Andromache* in search of pirates, real or imaginary, to suppress and kill. In the middle months of 1836, the *Andromache* stopped, attacked, and destroyed various vessels suspected of being engaged in piratical activities. In one of these attacks, off the coast of Borneo in late May, the crew indulged in what was nothing short of a carnage. Colin Mackenzie, one of the members of the *Andromache*'s crew, recorded some impressions about the violence he observed firsthand with horror. Once the enemy's ships had been chased and destroyed near the coastline, their crews had no option but to start jumping into the water, in an effort to escape the British.

In Mackenzie's words, it was then that "the work of slaughter began, with muskets, pikes, pistols, and cutlasses."[159] As he "sickened" at the scene unfolding in front of his eyes, he still felt the need to excuse this massacre as an obligation. However, he described how plenty of men were murdered while they tried to stay afloat, now defenseless. Mackenzie recalled the case of one of them, who received "four shots and three thrusts from a pike."[160] In spite of his wounds, this "most muscular-looking savage" still tried to swim away to safety, but instead, in an apparent case of needless overkill, he was wounded again by the "blow from a cutlass," which cut his head open, and then "he was finished with a pistol."[161] Unsurprisingly, the excessive violence used in this action was praised by British authorities. In a letter sent to the Dutch governor in Batavia a few months later, Lord Auckland, governor of India, referred to the action as a success that had resulted in the death of many pirates, "generally after resistance and a severe conflict."[162]

Bonham's and Chads's violent attempts to gain control over all ships passing through the seas near the Straits Settlements continued in years to come. Two years later, two other British ships, the sloop *Wolf* and the steamer *Diana,* carried out a series of similar operations against an Iranun fleet, north of the island of Borneo. While the *Wolf* had been in service, pursuing pirates since at least 1836, the *Diana* was a new arrival, having been built in India and launched precisely in that year.[163] This new retaliatory expedition engaged six well-armed Iranun vessels, carrying a crew of approximately 360. Of these, according to Captain Edward Stanley, the commander of the *Wolf,* "about 90" were killed, while 15 more were wounded "and 30 taken prisoners."[164]

Captain Samuel Congalton, commander of the *Diana,* was more specific in his description of the armed action against these six vessels. The *Diana*'s guns, he confessed, opened fire on them "with dreadful effect," shooting them "through and through" until "not a man [was] to be seen above the bulwarks."[165] Once the ships had been left in an unseaworthy state, he observed, they continued to shoot at the pirates until "nothing but blood and water" could be bailed out of them. For what it is worth, other pirate imperialist powers engaged in armed suppression expeditions that resulted in similar levels of violence and goriness. In one such case, Spanish officer Antonio de Mora congratulated himself and his men for having killed no less than fifty men and for having set more than two hundred houses on fire on the island of Buan, south of Tawi-Tawi, in 1862.[166] All this violence, all this unnecessary loss of human lives, just so they could, to borrow Warren's words, "enforce the Spanish claim of sovereignty over the [Joló] Sultanate and to take control over its trade."[167]

In April 1835, two months after his arrival in Nassau, where he took up the position of lieutenant governor of the Bahamas, William Colebrook wrote an anxious letter to Lord Aberdeen, apprising him about one of the main issues he was already facing, namely, the problem of piracy.[168] To Colebrook, a seasoned colonial functionary who had been instrumental during the investigation and publication of the famous Commission of Eastern Enquiry in Ceylon, this new appointment to a relatively peaceful colony must have felt like a promotion.[169]

Colebrook was familiar with maritime raiding and the likely ways to suppress it, as well as the impact it could have on commercial interests. He had served in two regions of the world where it was a regular concern for imperial powers like Britain; he had fought against amphibious peoples in Java and had served both as a soldier and an administrator in Palembang, Bengal, and the Persian Gulf. In this early letter to Lord Aberdeen, Colebrook referred to the frequent attacks that had been occurring against British vessels in the Atlantic waters near the Bahamas, disrupting their business dealings. Significantly, before concluding, he made sure to let his boss know that the reduction in the number of British cruisers in the region was almost certainly the main reason why British traders were being targeted.[170]

The empires discussed here followed a very similar script whenever their commercial interests were threatened by maritime raiding—or by what they perceived to be maritime raiding. As they reached the most remote regions of the planet, they brought with them laws and characterizations that allowed them to pigeonhole and label amphibious peoples as pirates who threatened their commercial self-given rights. Whether they were attempting to support the spreading of free trade or the perseverance of protectionism, pirate imperial powers and their agents resorted to various means of diplomatic and armed suppression to guarantee their continuation and development.

The role played by merchants and other pirate imperialist representatives in these regions was also critical. Merchants and consuls often disagreed and challenged metropolitan authorities, querying their decisions and questioning the rationale behind their orders. During this period, they found ways of lobbying their regional superiors and the authorities in their western seats of power, so that they would change course and create the necessary conditions for favorable trading deals. At times, they were so effective in their pleas and threats that, on the back of their clamors, authorities in places like London, Paris, or Washington, DC, were left with no option but to take military action to support them. In 1839, Canton-based British merchants succeeded in fabricating a crisis that led to a full-blown invasion of Qing China when their opium exports to the mainland were suspended by the imperial authorities. In this opportunity, as in many others, "Navy personnel and ships were first responders to calls for the protection of British subjects."[171]

Diplomatic measures of a coercive nature, such as pressures and threats, were frequently used to obtain privileges, the restitution of capital or property, or punishment against sea raiders who had disturbed their self-given right to trade in foreign waters. Such pressures and threats often led to clear instances of intromission in the internal affairs of sovereign states and were regularly carried out under the menacing view of state-of-the-art gunships.

Armed suppression was at times seen as a necessary measure, indispensable to admonish those who engaged in maritime raiding or those who protected these activities. Bombarding cities and towns, for example, was a regular occurrence during these decades, from when the British shelled Ras Al-Khaimah in 1819 until the Americans and the French attacked Korean peoples along the banks of the Taedong River and on Kangwha Island, respectively, in 1866.[172] Collateral casualties, including women and children, constituted another important dimension of this story. On occasion, punitive expeditions resulted in bloodbaths, with men, women, and children massacred for no other reason than being members of groups that had been labeled as "pirates" who stood in the way of commerce. Most of the historical evidence of these massacres comes, precisely, from the agents of pirate imperial powers who were so enthralled by their self-given legal rights to protect trade that they often described them in detail, without expecting anything but praise. Agents that, in the words of Lauren Benton, even in the face of death and destruction "held tight to a pretense of Western innocence."[173]

In his masterful book *Necropolitics*, Achille Mbembe noted that "while control over international trade flows henceforth presumed mastery of the seas, the capacity to create unequal exchange relations became a decisive element of power" for European empires.[174] This statement reflects, in only a few words, the main argument of this chapter. To protect trade, Western imperial powers coerced, threatened, and murdered as they saw fit, and they justified these atrocities over non-white peoples on their refusal to open their ports to foreign trade, or on their failure to deal with maritime raiders who disturbed their commercial interests. It was a conscious approach, well-understood by agents of empire around the world. As Lord Palmerston put it in crystal clear terms in a letter to James Brooke in 1850, while tacitly approving his punitive expeditions against Southeast Asian amphibious communities, "It is certain that the extension of commerce depends upon the suppression of piracy."[175]

CHAPTER FOUR

Proto-Colonial Expansion and the Suppression of Maritime Raiding

On August 3, 1837, the US consul to the Straits Settlements, Joseph Balestier, wrote to Secretary of State John Forsyth describing the ways in which the Siamese had taken to the sea since their fleet had been defeated by the Vietnamese at the battle of Vàm Nao in 1833.[1] In this missive, Balestier referred to one of several new war vessels, "built and fitted out by the King of Siam," as a challenging "new naval power."[2] To him, the *Conqueror*, which had just arrived at Singapore "for the purpose of increasing her armament and other means of warfare," constituted a statement of intentions by a kingdom that had been involved in several colonial wars in the preceding years and was also under constant pressures from expanding Western pirate empires.[3] In addition to the *Conqueror*, Balestier correctly pointed out that other war vessels, including one of more than one thousand tons, were being fitted by King Rama III in what he perceived would become nothing short of a fresh naval menace in the region.

Balestier's observations were largely correct. After fighting colonial wars on at least three different fronts—Kedah, Patani, and

Indochina—between 1831 and 1833, the Siamese began complementing their already large fleet of war junks with newly acquired European vessels, some of which had been bought in Penang by Chao Phraya Nakhon from the British.[4] In fact, the *Conqueror* (1835) was added to their ranks around the same time they acquired or built the schooner *Ariel* (1835), the barques *Fairy* and *S. W. Scott* (1836), and the large tonnage ships *Victory* and *Caledonia* (1837).[5] Altogether, this rapidly assembled fleet, said to be "commanded and officered" by European seamen and carrying several hundred cannons, was soon put to use when the Malays, led by Tunku Mohamed Saad, took Kedah back from Siam for a second time in 1838.[6]

As soon as he heard about the fall of Kedah in mid-1838, Rama III sent his troops, once more, to wrestle the territory away from the rebels. In addition to a large army sent by land, the king was able to summon vessels capable of sharing a blockade of Kuala Kedah with their British allies. In the instructions sent to one of his generals, soon before he had sailed for Kedah, Rama III emphasized that he should take enough cannons "to keep off the pirates during the voyage," even though in his opinion these "pirates" were not likely to trouble him much during his journey.[7]

In addition to the blockade of Kedah, some of the new war vessels were later used by Siam to carry out enslaved Malays, who had been captured during the war against Kedah. On July 12, 1839, for example, Khun Sombatphakdi was reported to have taken 121 enslaved Malays in one of those vessels.[8] Likewise, according to General Luang Udosombat's communications, five more ships were used for the same purposes around the same time. If Udosombat's words are to be believed, by the end of July, 431 enslaved Malays had been seized and sent away to the Siamese districts of Phangnga and Phatalung on these vessels.[9]

As these episodes demonstrate, though it is less well documented, pirate imperialism was not exclusive to Western powers. The Siamese were one of a number of non-Western states—including the Russian, Ottoman, and Qing China empires—that, under the excuse of suppressing piracy, attempted to expand their national territories through colonial gains. Already in 1821, when they first took possession of Kedah, the Siamese had used piracy as a justification for their invasion and occupation, and they did so again in 1831, this time with the full complicity of the British. Not surprisingly, as their naval fire power grew stronger, labeling others, like Tunku Kudin in 1831 and Tunku Mohamed Saad in 1838 and 1839, as pirates turned into a frequent and convenient strategy.

Although the Siamese had been engaged in colonialist endeavors for centuries, there is little doubt that they were quicker than most to take advantage of the new technologies and approaches brought into the region by Western powers in the first decades of the nineteenth century. By being quick to modernize their army and navy, the Siamese were able to reinforce and legitimize their own conquests and territorial claims. Modernizing the fleet was a crucial step taken by Rama III to protect Siam from Western maritime powers, and also to preserve recent conquests. Even before new warships had been acquired, such conquests had typically been carried out through the use of extreme violence. During Tunku Mohamed Saad's trial for piracy in Penang in 1840, one of his attorneys, while digressing on what was to be considered an act of piracy and what was not, made a point of referring to the Siamese conquest of Kedah in 1821 as not only an exceedingly violent affair but also one that had been "piratical in every sense of the term."[10]

The Siamese invasion and occupation of Kedah from 1821 were not an exception.[11] In neighboring Patani, the Siamese also resorted to massacres and to the enslavement of local Malay populations in order to consolidate the colonial subjugation of this territory.[12] According to Francis R. Bradley, who did an in-depth examination of the surviving primary sources related to the invasion of Patani in 1832 the documents strongly suggests that "Patani's conquest was far more violent and systematically carried out than previously thought."[13]

Siam's continuous pirate imperialist undertakings, though idiosyncratic, were made possible not only by copying Western pirate imperialism but also by creating convenient alliances with Western states like Great Britain. Pacts between the Siamese and other nations are discussed at length in chapter 5. Suffice it to say here that the Siamese were successful when negotiating because at least until the 1850s they showed themselves to be smart operators and hard bargainers, who were not easily intimidated by their Western counterparts and who knew how to reach agreements that would allow them to continue their expansionist agenda.[14]

There is little doubt that colonialism was at the very epicenter of pirate imperialist actions during the period covered in this book. Under the guise of bringing about civilization, abolition, and commerce, pirate imperialist nations conquered, dispossessed, displaced, and repressed amphibious communities on a global scale. In his discussion of this new age of colonial expansionism, Michael Barnett coined the term "imperial humanitarianism" to refer to predatory behaviors justified by supposedly higher needs, which frequently required sacrifices by both the colonizer and the colonized.[15] Similar arguments were made by such historians as Felicity Jenz and Zoë Laidlaw; the latter going as far as to claim that during this period, even within the humanitarian movement, there was "much self-interest," a circumstance that often blurred the lines "between moral and political reform."[16]

Pirate imperialist states, particularly so Western ones, made use of their laws to nullify and take away what they wanted from maritime peoples, while simultaneously laying down Western universalist claims. The displacement, disarticulation, and dispossession of entire populations was possible only thanks to premises of civilizational superiority, which all too frequently were anchored by the Law of Nations and carried out through a combination of diplomatic and armed means. As Jennifer Pitts has convincingly argued, by riding the coattails of the Law of Nations, pirate imperialist states conquered and seized territories, imposed discriminatory trade regimes, and justified multiple abuses of power carried out by their agents.[17] In this process of territorial expansionism, then, suppressing real or imagined acts of "piracy," became "an integrated part of the intensified process of colonization."[18]

While imposing themselves over amphibious peoples and snatching control over their ancestral lands and waters, pirate imperialists used a variety of effective diplomatic and armed methods. For example, in Algiers and Morocco, the French and the Spanish cited offenses committed by "pirates" to justify their *causes de guerre*. In Hong Kong and Kowloon, the British also resorted to blaming maritime predatory activities for obliging them to occupy these territories, even though they did so against the wishes of the Chinese. On the island of Labuan, they took advantage of James Brooke's occupation of Sarawak and the previous chastising expeditions against the sultan of Brunei to acquire the island through an enforced treaty.

In the case of Kedah, through a combination of betrayals and alliances, the British took advantage of a historical conjuncture to expand their colonial possessions at the expense of this Malay kingdom. In a secret letter sent to Calcutta in late 1831, alongside the copy of an interview with the rajah of Ligore, Straits Settlements' governor Robert Ibbetson reported that his attempts to renegotiate the boundaries of the Province Wellesley with the Siamese had been successful.[19]

In 1831, Province Wellesley, located across the sea from the island of Penang, had an ambiguous border with Kedah, which the British set to rectify shortly after they supported the Siamese repression of the Malay revolt earlier that year. Through a series of negotiations, the British managed to expand their territories inland for an average of around five miles. To Ibbetson this was nothing short of a huge achievement, as these lands were "superior in every respect to the mangrove swamps" found nearer the coast and to which British settlements had so far been limited.[20] The new territories, he noted, were "uncommonly rich in Rice Ground" and had a large, and increasing, population as a result of waves of Malay war refugees who had run away from Kedah and Perlis.[21] In order to secure this land grab, the British reaffirmed their commitment to support the rajah of Ligore and Siam against any new Malay uprising. Before concluding his letter, Ibbetson also noted that this cooperation would likely be useful in any case, even if it were to "only operate in the suppression of Piracy."[22]

As pirate imperialist empires found out, the only way to stop maritime raiding in and around their new colonies was to subjugate or destroy nearby amphibious populations by any available means. When diplomacy failed, incursions were based on a torch and kill policy, a method widely accepted by fellow pirate imperialist states and generally seen as a necessary evil if colonialism and the "advantages" associated with it were to succeed. As Hannah Arendt put it, repressing and massacring these "natural" human beings who "lacked the specifically human character," as they saw it, was an acceptable transaction.[23] These attacks could be totally unprovoked, as was the case in October 1828 just outside Penang harbor when Captain Havers of the British brig *Cecilia* opened fire upon two prows he judged to be pirates by the way they sailed. This incident is similar to those of British Lieutenant Henry Lloyd when he spotted Greek sailors off Negroponte's northeast coast in 1854 (see chapter 3).[24]

Ultimately, and arguably to a larger extent than for the advancement of "civilization," abolition, or commerce, pirate imperialism resorted to the same coercive measures—namely, pressures, threats, and violence—to expand their empires into new physical spaces. Proto-colonialism and colonialism, however, were not simply terracentric endeavors; the securing of ocean, sea, and riverine trade routes was at their very core. Consequently, waterways were colonized by Western, and occasionally non-Western, empires. This colonization of aquatic spaces was at times apparent, even to those charged with colonizing them. A system of trading passes and licenses across Southeast Asia implemented by the British, Dutch, and Spanish from the mid-1830s onward served as a new hydrarchic way to mutually codify into a legal structure aquatic colonialist actions and behaviors. Relying on superior naval technologies, particularly after the introduction of steam vessels, Western pirate imperial states self-appointed themselves as the policemen of seas and rivers, thus legitimizing their rights over them and their peoples.

There is little doubt that colonizing enterprises, just as free trade endeavors did, served to arm amphibious peoples, who were frequently accused of being pirates. Pirate imperialist agents and merchants did their best to justify arms sales as a necessary evil, precisely under pretenses of curbing maritime raiding.[25] When the Marquis de Moges discussed the continuing arms trade out of Hong Kong and Singapore in the 1850s, he criticized Hong Kong's governor John Bowring for placing "quantity over quality" and for turning Hong Kong into "a rendezvous for all the pirates of the Canton river."[26]

At a loss as to why the British governor would throw caution to the wind in such a manner, he recalled how Bowring himself had once confessed to him that over the course of that year he had "sold to these pirates and owners of junks in the river no less than four thousand small cannons and swivels."[27] De Moges, who was writing for a French audience infused with imperial dreams, could not help but compare Bowring's free market approach to the trade of firearms with the reluctance of the French to carry out a similar commerce in Algeria.[28] Although the French, like the Spanish, seemed reluctant to engage in this trade, other Western imperial powers, like the Americans, traded firearms within their colonies and beyond.[29]

Colonizing others was crucial for the development of the metropoles. For the French, in the words of David Todd, "Imperial grandeur was crucial to the preservation of domestic stability."[30] For the British, the Spanish, the Dutch, and the Americans, among others, the prosperity of the colonies was not to be thwarted by any sort of resistance, even if that meant resorting to violent measures that denied the principles of "freedom, civilization and liberalism" that they regularly used to justify their actions.[31] As Achille Mbembe put it years ago, civil peace in the West has depended "in large part on inflicting violence far away, on lighting up centers of atrocities, and on the fiefdom wars and other massacres," all of which have accompanied "the establishment of strongholds and trading posts around the four corners of the planet."[32]

Mid-nineteenth-century colonialism was a business built first and foremost around mutual demands, requests, and pressures between pirate imperialist agents and their centers of power and among these agents themselves. Diplomatic and armed suppression measures were exerted by imperial agents upon the leaders of the peoples they were intent on dispossessing from their territories. Unsurprisingly, Western and non-Western empires frequently blamed the colonization of lands and aquatic spaces on the need to suppress piratical activities by the peoples who inhabited them.

For example, as the Riff people in northeastern Morocco carried out repeated attacks on foreign vessels that veered too close to their homelands, European nations, including France, Spain, and Great Britain, repeatedly debated the best ways of chastising them.

At times, newspapers in all three countries suggested creating temporary alliances to bring these incidents to an end once and for all.[33] And in fact, the Spanish imperialist invasion of Morocco in 1859 was, to an extent, a response to these repeated attacks, which had been happening for decades, "wounding" Spanish honor and "forcing" them to act.[34] Before the actual Spanish invasion took place, however, there were repeated calls for the French to advance on the Riff from their Algerian colony, expanding France's possessions in the region.[35] Various British officers posted to this part of the Mediterranean during these years reminded their superiors in the Foreign Office not to trust the French when it came to the Riff, and to act either alone or, if pressed, in concert with the Spanish rather than the French.[36]

In the mid-1850s, John Hay Drummond Hay's repeated calls for an invasion of the Riff became more elaborate and precise, a circumstance that speaks to how much thought he gave to such an expedition at the time. In a letter to the Earl of Clarendon, sent out of frustration in August 1854, he went as far as drawing an invasion plan that would, in his mind, achieve "the effectual punishment of the pirates."[37] Punishment aside, his suggestions implied nothing short of a pirate imperialist incursion into the Riff. He recommended burning villages and destroying or carrying away "cattle and other property of the pirates."[38]

Drummond Hay was hardly alone. A couple of years earlier, Captain Henry Wells Giffard exposed an ever more detailed plan of attack against the Riff to his superior officer, Admiral James Dundas. In this missive, Giffard recommended an all-out attack on the Riffians, using secrecy and stealth as the main tactics. In Giffard's opinion, such an expedition should attack in May, during the harvest time, and should consist of "2000 fighting men, including some artillery and a few sappers and miners," plus 400 men to carry away the wounded.[39] Giffard also recommended using the steamers and troops posted at Lisbon, Gibraltar, and Malta, and in what was to be a preemptive exercise to calm a possible backlash from public opinion, he advised drawing a proclamation in advance, "stating that the destruction" had been "made to punish the pirates."[40]

To a large extent, anti-slave trade operations themselves were undertaken under the premise that for several Atlantic states the slave trade was nothing but another manifestation of piracy. Therefore, linking pirate imperialist projects with piracy while pressuring the centers of power and public opinion was a common occurrence during this period. During the attack on Lagos in 1851 the British referred to this Atlantic port as a nest of piracy (see chapter 2).[41] In another notable case, the French Anti-Slave Trade Squadron combined the chasing of slavers in the 1840s with the prospecting of potential colonies, often degrading and debasing their inhabitants with multiple epithets, including that of pirates. In more than one occasion during those years, French navy captains were ordered to carry out scouting missions along the West African coast with the intention of turning "temporary barracks" into colonial establishments.[42]

When commander Auguste Baudin was commissioned with one such voyage, he advocated for the creation of more French colonial outposts in coastal towns such as Grand Bassam and Assinoé, both places where France had already built fortresses.[43] Baudin was quite impressed with Gabon, a place he considered as "an essential maritime port and a beautiful colony at the same time."[44] Baudin, Jérôme Félix de Monleón, and other commanders of the West African Squadron during this period justified the establishment of new colonies on the need to bring laws and civilization to men they considered rude, violent, and not inclined to work. Baudin in particular went so far as to suggest taking advantage of the slave systems existing in these places and conditioning the granting of freedom to those enslaved on years of labor within the new French colonies. In Baudin's mind, such "liberation" would be more effective than any "impotent repression by treaties and cruises" as it would have a moral basis.[45] Baudin was also careful to note, first, that Africans were "negroes" who should "be treated as such," and, second, that for such a slave-labor-based colony to survive and progress, the development of the French navy and navigation were crucial.[46]

In Southeast Asia during the same years, Dutch and Spanish colonialism grew slowly but assuredly throughout the so-called Eastern Archipelago. The Dutch expanded their territorial conquests through a combination of negotiation, persuasion, pressures, and violence. After the Treaty of Paris in 1824, they focused on consolidating their gains in Java (1825–30), Sumatra (1831–38), Bali (1846–50), and South and East Borneo (1820s–50s), under the direction of Dutch East Indian governors Godert van der Capellen, Leonard du Bus de Gisignies, Johannes van den Bosch, Jean Chrétien Baud, Dominique de Eerens, Pieter Merkus, and Jan Jacob Rochussen. Assigning residents and assistant residents from the early decades of the nineteenth century to such places as Pontianak, Sambas, and Landak allowed the Batavian government to exert all sorts of diplomatic pressures over indigenous populations—and over their own officers—under the guise of suppressing any activities that they thought of as piratical.

A case of this nature took place in December 1850, when the resident at Surabaya asked the local public prosecutor to put on trial a number of free men who had been deemed to be engaged in piracy. After carrying out an exhaustive investigation, however, the public prosecutor, J. de Wal, refused to do so, arguing that it had been "sufficiently demonstrated that these men [were] not pirates."[47] In an attempt to dissuade the resident to drop the matter, de Wal went as far as to insist that these men were "under the protection of the Government" and that there were "no terms" for him "to prosecute them."[48]

On occasion, the Dutch were able to benefit from failed expeditions to contested zones by other imperial states to further their colonial gains. For example, in 1844, when James Erskine Murray lost his life after sailing into the Mahakam River in Eastern Borneo in a butchered attempt to emulate James Brooke's exploits in Sarawak, Batavia promptly took advantage of the situation. The Dutch, who had signed treaties in 1817 giving them supposed rights over all the eastern part of Borneo, saw an opportunity and acted accordingly.[49]

As soon as the news of the expedition reached Batavia, the Dutch sent their navy to pressure the local sultan at Tenggarong to sign a treaty by which he acknowledged their sovereignty over his territory.[50] The negotiations, carried out under the guns of the war schooners *Zephijr* and *Egmond*, were quite swift and took place in a depopulated place, as by all accounts the local population had run into the rainforest at the sight of the war vessels.[51] Among the many concessions made by the sultan to the Dutch was a commitment to "never participate again in any act of piracy or to tolerate any equipment being provided for that purpose."[52] By the time the Dutch ships left, Batavia was in official possession of this section of Eastern Borneo, and the Dutch flag was flying next to the sultan's in their capital Kutei.[53]

The Spanish, too, gradually strengthened their hold on the Philippines during the middle decades of the nineteenth century. Throughout this period, the sultanates of both Maguindanao and Joló came under repeated pressures to submit to the Spanish one way or another.[54] Basilan, Davao, Balanguingui, Tongkil, and Joló, among many other regions, found themselves fending off Spanish advances and losing territories through shadowy negotiations that were imposed on them or through armed suppression expeditions.[55] Another example of the pressures exerted upon local polities by the Manila government took place a few years earlier, in 1836, when the Spanish forced a treaty, aptly called "Capitulations of Peace, protection and commerce," upon the sultan and dattos of Joló.[56] The document, signed by the captain of the frigate, José María Halcón, and by the sultan Jamamul Kiram I and twelve of his dattos, stipulated that from that date forward Joló would "avoid the piracies of the llanos and zamales in the Philippines."[57] As a backup, the Spanish forced the sultan to agree to a clause that would give the Spanish the right to pursue Joloan vessels suspected of engaging in piratical activities if they saw fit to do so. In fact, the Spanish forced on the sultan and his dattos a system of passes by which all Joloan vessels were required to carry licenses from the sultan, in order to be "free and safe."[58] Those ships seized by the Spanish navy without such licenses would "lose all their effects" as a direct result.[59]

As we have seen, an almost identical system of passes was established that same year by Bonham and Chads in Singapore, with the Dutch following suit soon after.[60] The British system of licenses or passes was established as a response to the complaints sent by Singapore-based merchants to Calcutta a year earlier, in 1835. Suggestions to control the paperwork of local traders had been made before. In fact, in April 1836, William Barrow had done so in a missive sent to the government of India, which also included recommendations as to the most efficient ways of implementing such a

The sultan of Joló. Edward Belcher, *Narrative of the Voyage of H.M.S Samarang, during the Years 1843–46* (London: Reeve, Benham, and Reeve, 1848), vol. 1.

system through the patrolling of the waters between Penang and Singapore.[61]

Proposals such as those put forward by Barrow were echoed by Bonham and Chads, and they were broadly accepted by British authorities throughout the Indian Ocean. Even in the rare occasions when the need for passes was questioned by someone like Straits Settlements' governor Kenneth Murchison, the counterproposals were limited to suggestions of not treating every vessel as a pirate "merely for the absence of a required pass."[62] Murchison was keen to stress that time was needed for the system to take hold, especially when it came to applying their rules to vessels "belonging to Chiefs under the Political influence of the Batavian Government."[63] It is quite plausible that Murchison was compelled to raise this criticism as he had learned about the raid carried out in late June by Captain Chads and HMS *Andromache* on three Dutch-controlled villages in Galang Island.[64]

These fears were not unfounded, and clashes between British, Dutch, and Spanish warships and local traders from all three spheres of influence were frequent. At times these clashes escalated to the point of turning into diplomatic crises, some of which are discussed in chapter 5. Licenses or passes allowing non-European ships to carry guns were not always welcome by Western pirate imperialist agents. This was especially the case when such measures were taken without consulting them or, as in the case of China, were issued during the First Opium War as a way of defending against British attacks. In January 1845, John Francis Davis, British governor of Hong Kong, lamented the large number of "Chinese junks and boats" that retained the licenses to "carry arms which were granted to them during the war with England."[65] In Davis's opinion, former combatants were using these licenses for "piratical purposes," and he suggested that it would become necessary to bring this issue up with the Chinese government. In the meantime, he advised Thomas Cochrane that it would be "ultimately necessary to seize and destroy all vessels whose armament and other circumstances prove their criminal pursuits."[66] It is hard to miss how ironic this situation was for Davis, Cochrane, and the British in general, as the only reason these legal licenses existed was precisely the British invasion of China six years earlier.

To be sure, after the Treaty of Nanjing had secured a British victory against Qing China in 1842, navy commanders like Cochrane and Chads had continued to pressure the governments at Hong Kong and London for the implementation of stricter measures against Chinese "pirates," who were a nuisance for their new island colony. In July 1843, Chads wrote to his superior, Vice Admiral William Parker, calling his attention to a supposed "force of hundreds of junks" that had been assembling "at Shippo."[67] After receiving this missive, Parker duly forwarded it to Hong Kong governor Henry Pottinger, who immediately questioned "the credence of the rumours" reported by Chads and dismissed his claims as "almost superfluous."[68] Pottinger's rebuke of Chads's hawkish assertions was so robust that Vice Admiral Parker felt compelled to jump to his defense, arguing that even if exaggerated, Chads's only intention had been not "to neglect this information."[69]

All in all, whether pressuring their own officers, foreign Western agents, or the peoples whose lands they had their sights on, pirate imperialist agents did everything in their power to exaggerate threats and to engineer situations that allowed them to make demands and to lay the ground for more severe approaches. When diplomatic pressures did not yield the expected results, threats of a different kind took center stage in their land appropriation schemes.

In December 1849, José Alemany forwarded a missive from the governor of Zamboanga, Cayetano Suárez de Figueroa, to the captain general of the Philippines, Narciso Clavería. In it, he discussed how a group of refugees who had survived the attack against Balanguingui earlier that year had settled in the island of Tongkil.[70] Alemany also communicated how the governor had threatened the chief of Tongkil, Planglima Bombali, with a severe "punishment and a lesson" should he choose to continue sheltering these men, women, and children. To Governor Suárez de Figueroa, such a deference was tied to the fact that the Panglima had sworn obedience to the queen of Spain and had "renounced forever to piracy."[71] Something similar happened in 1826 when the governor of Bombay, Mountstuart Elphinstone, sent a menacing letter to Rahmah ibn Jabir al-Jahami, strongly suggesting that he stop plundering boats within the British colonial waters in the Persian Gulf.[72] In this note, Elphinstone first insisted that it was his duty to suppress "indiscriminate acts of plunder," and then threatened al-Jahami again with drawing down on him "the enmity of all nations."[73]

As they did when protecting their commercial privileges, piratical imperialist officers seldom hesitated to parade their gunboats before their foes in order to consolidate territorial gains. On occasion, gunboats could take on a protagonist role in the commercial treaties signed by the British with nations they had subdued in one way or another. One example is the supplementary treaty to the Treaty of Nanjing, signed at Bogue by the British and the Chinese in October 1843. The document, which had an intrinsic trading regulatory character, included an article on gunboat guarantees, which gave lie to the notion that the British were indeed exercising any sort of "free" trade with China. Article 10 stipulated that each port opened to British trade would harbor a British cruiser, purportedly charged with enforcing "good order and discipline amongst the crews of merchant shipping."[74] In reality, of course, the main reason for this permanent presence was to dissuade the Chinese from attempting any form of regulation beyond those imposed by force by the British at the end of the First Opium War.

Perhaps there is no better example of how pirate imperialism operated during this period than that of James Brooke's colonial endeavors in Western Borneo from the early 1840s forward. Brooke snatched a large territory in Sarawak from the sultan of Brunei. In spite of his repeated protestations of innocence in following years, Brooke went on record, at least once, stating that he had taken Sarawak from Muda Hashim "under the guns of the 'Royalist,' " his well-armed yacht.[75] Such a land grab was indirectly sanctioned by the British government on more than one occasion, notably in 1844, when Captain Keppel supported Brooke's piratical attack on the Dayak people of the Skrang and Saribas Rivers, who had dared refusing to accept his rule.

It came as a surprise to no one that Brooke's actions were comprehensively questioned by many of his contemporaries, especially in Singapore and London. Joseph Hume, MP, who invested significant amounts of time in investigating Brooke's shady conduct in Borneo throughout the 1840s, concluded in 1852 that he had taken Sarawak in defiance of both "the Law of England and the Law of Nations." To Hume, Brooke had managed to hold on "to the territory over which he rule[d] as much on a piratical tenure, as if he were a Malay or Illanun rover."[76]

That Hume accused Brooke of behaving like a pirate did not surprise anyone. Over the years Brooke had engaged in spreading rumors about the supposed involvement of the Dayak, whose lands he had just taken by force, with piracy. Finding a propitious excuse in the very rumors he had disseminated, Brooke conducted at least two major expeditions against these amphibious populations, massacring, kidnapping, and displacing them in the process. His claims of Dayak involvement in so-called piratical activities, however, were almost universally questioned and refuted by British merchants operating in the region at the time. One merchant commented that he had "never heard of Dyak pirates till the expedition of the 'Nemesis.' "[77] Two other traders, who admitted to having heard about the Dayak headhunting habits in the late 1830s, also were keen to point out that they had never heard of them being involved in any sort of piracy.[78] Another merchant based at Singapore, who confirmed to have visited Brunei and Sarawak many times between 1833 and 1843, agreed.[79]

Others were even more specific as to when exactly they had first heard rumors of Dayak involvement in piracy. One of them, named Guthrie, confessed to have "never heard of Dyak pirates until 1842," and another, a Mr. Napier, resident in Singapore, gave a similar date, 1843, as the first time he had ever heard the Dayak being referred to as pirates.[80] Another person, named Crane, who had been a merchant also based in Singapore since 1824, was eager to stress that he had never "heard of Dyak pirates till 1840 or 1841."[81] Keeping in mind that Brooke's initial land grab occurred in 1841, it is nearly impossible not to see a direct chronological correlation between his taking over of Sarawak, supported by British gunships, and the sudden appearance of reports of Dayak piracy in the region.

Brooke's gunships and those of the East India Company were also instrumental in the cession by force of the island of Labuan by the sultan of Brunei to the British, eventually leading to the creation of a new colony, strategically placed in the maritime routes that connected India with China and with conveniently abundant coal reserves. Although Brooke had been singing the island's praises for years, noting that it could become a key coaling station for the steam vessels in the region, it was not until the British sent Captain Charles Drinkwater Bethune in 1844 to examine the island that the idea of a new colony took shape.[82] The Treaty of Labuan, by which Brunei ceded ownership of the island to the British, was signed within sight of a number of British gunships, which arrived in Brunei to make sure that the sultan would oblige.[83]

This treaty, just like the idea of snatching Labuan from the sultan, had been in the works since Captain Bethune arrived in Southeast Asian waters two years earlier. In fact, in August 1845, three British steamers, the *Vixen*, the *Nemesis*, and the *Pluto*, carried Bethune and Brooke to Brunei, where they tried to get the sultan to sign another treaty, by which he would commit to stopping all involvement in piratical activities while guaranteeing the

British more extensive trading rights in the region. In these negotiations, once again, suppressing piracy, expropriating lands by force from other people, and diminishing any influence that Brooke's antagonists could have upon Sultan Omar Ali Saifuddin II were all intrinsically linked. Later that summer, when the sultan refused the treaty, the three gunships attacked and destroyed the quarters of Pangeran Usop, the most senior member among those at the Brunei court opposing the treaty and any sort of pressures coming from Brooke. This attack, meant to serve as a warning to other high-ranking Brunei chiefs, ended in the unnecessary killing of many of Usop's people. After destroying Usop's houses and forcing all survivors to run or swim for their lives, British "officers had some trouble to make the men cease fireing [*sic*]."[84] Edward H. Cree, once again reporting a case of British overkill of "savages," noted that such behavior seemed to be "always the case."[85]

Ultimately, as they were not able to achieve their objectives, the steamers retreated to Labuan to reprovision themselves with coal before continuing to Marudu Bay, where they undertook an all-out attack on another local chief, Syarif Osman, who had also opposed Brooke's attempts to control the sultan of Brunei. This attack, too, was the result of Brooke's intentional image distortion of someone he perceived as a foe and who had too much influence over the sultan. As with the assault against Usop's quarters, this attack was meant as a warning to the local chiefs still opposing Brooke's expansionist agenda in West Borneo.

As Bianca M. Gerlich has argued in more than one place, once Brooke decided Syarif Osman was a pirate, the British accepted his judgment without much questioning and committed to destroying Osman's headquarters at Marudu.[86] In fact, Captain Bethune admitted as much, when he wrote that it was precisely because of Osman's obstructions to "the development of Mr Brooke's judicious policy" that it had become "necessary to attack him in his stronghold."[87] Bethune also noted that the main reason behind this expedition had been "the experience of Mr Brooke," who had found it impossible "to establish influence at Bruné" until "the power of the Sheriffs in the North and on the North-West had been altogether annihilated."[88] Even after Syarif Osman's influence had been eliminated, Brooke and Cochrane continued their violent

Destruction of Pangeran Usop's piratical stockades by HMS *Vixen*, by Edward H. Cree. © National Maritime Museum, Greenwich, London.

assaults across the region, in order to consolidate their supremacy. A year later, when the sultan again refused to accept Brooke's demands, Admiral Cochrane bombarded his palace, driving "him and his people into the wilds" and subsequently sending "strong military parties to hunt him in the forests."[89]

The armed action against Syarif Osman constitutes a representative case of how when pressures and threats to amphibious populations failed to deliver the expected results, they were soon turned into violent aggressions that would facilitate proto-colonialist and colonialist agendas. By late 1849, Brooke had subdued Marudu, cemented his influence on the sultan of Brunei, given Labuan to the British crown as a gift, massacred the Dayaks on various occasions—often with the support of the Royal Navy—and taken possession of Sarawak as a ruler.[90]

In the middle decades of the nineteenth century, rapacious pirate imperialist agents never struggled to fabricate new opportunities to

Cutting the boom at Malludu (Marudu). Drinkwater Bethune, *Views in the Eastern Archipelago, Borneo, Sarawak, Labuan, &c, &c, &c. From Drawings Made on the Spot by Capt. Drinkwater Bethune, R.N.C.B., Commander L. G. Heath, R.N. and Others* (London: The Descriptive Press by J. A. St. John, 1847).

extricate amphibious populations from their own lands and waters through the use of violence. Accusations of piracy were commonly levied whenever all pirate imperialist powers set their eyes on a new realm. This predatory behavior was clearly observable during the Second Opium War, when the British decided to take the Kowloon Peninsula from China, under the pretense that only they could stop the "pirates" residing there from continuing their depredations in the region.

The war itself had been nothing short of a personal project for the British governor of Hong Kong, John Bowring.[91] Although the hostilities had begun over a disagreement between Bowring and the Chinese vice-consul, Ye ming-chen, Bowring was quick to take advantage and claim access to Canton by force, a circumstance that unleashed a protracted military conflict.[92] By 1860, however, Bowring was gone, after a series of scandals and a failed assassination attempt that resulted in the death of his wife. Almost as soon as his replacement, Hercules Robinson, arrived in Hong Kong, he picked up where Bowring had left off, devising a plan to occupy and ultimately take permanent possession of the Kowloon Peninsula. British accusations against Kowloon "pirates" had been piling up for many years, and expeditions sent from Hong Kong, right across Victoria Harbor, had been frequent.[93] The Portuguese, too, had carried out punitive expeditions against Kowloon from Macau in previous years. In 1855, for example, a Portuguese fleet had attacked and destroyed various villages on the peninsula, chasing and firing upon their inhabitants, who had escaped to the hills upon seeing the Portuguese force arrive.[94]

There is little doubt that the plan to snatch Kowloon from the Chinese had been in the works for some time. In 1860, the colonial secretary, William Thomas Mercer, who had served in various roles in the colony since 1844, produced a "Memorandum on the Kowloong Peninsula Question," which informed the actions subsequently taken by Governor Hercules Robinson and General James Hope Grant, eventually leading to the expropriation and annexation of Kowloon to Hong Kong.[95] In this document, Mercer justified the need to wrestle the peninsula away from Qing China to reduce piracy in the waters between Hong Kong Island and the peninsula. In fact, Mercer's colonialist ploy became transparent when he commented that achieving this feat would legally turn these waters into a British "mare nostrum," where they would be able to exercise British law accordingly.

Shamelessly, he then went on to offer a number of reasons why such an annexation would be welcome by Qing China. To Mercer, it was clear that the Chinese had "no authority" over this land and that they drew "no revenue" from it.[96] He also commented that the "ground" was "worthless to them," and that by occupying and colonizing it, the British would be doing the Chinese a favor by protecting them from potential future conflicts "with other powers or with lawless foreign banditti."[97]

In an attempt to allay fears that this rapacious annexation would lead to Chinese claims for indemnification, Mercer insisted that he had demonstrated how the land was "worthless to them."[98] He thought that "it would be sufficient to tender the smallest sum" to turn their nominal occupation into a legal colony. Not only that, but taking Kowloon from the Chinese would "entail no expense" on the British, as he anticipated that sales of land on the "new site,"—the same land that he had insisted was worthless to the Chinese—would "increase the Colonial Revenue" of their now larger colony.[99]

Mercer's "Memorandum" was music to Robinson's and Hope's ears. The latter, provided with a copy of the lease of the peninsula, began planning an expedition in mid-March 1860 to take over Kowloon by force.[100] Robinson fully endorsed this move, praising Hope for his "intention to encamp troops" in Kowloon "to maintain order among the thieves and pirates" who were said to have established their headquarters there.[101] Robinson was also enthusiastic about the possibility presented to them that this encampment could "pave the way towards obtaining from the Chinese Government eventually a cession of the opposite promontory."[102] Echoing Mercer's argument and clearly stating his colonialist intentions, Robinson contended that although the peninsula was "valueless" to the Chinese, it was "absolutely essential for the security and accommodation of the growing community of Hong Kong."[103]

Mercer's claims, later echoed by Robinson, Hope, and others, were rather superfluous and indeed made up. Under the supposed "need" of securing the future of their Hong Kong colony, they devised a plan to extricate the Kowloon Peninsula from Qing China and presented this seizure by force and violence as an act of good will, done chiefly for the benefit of the Chinese. As with Brooke's actions in securing Labuan a few years before, gunships and Royal Navy personnel played a central role in what was another example of pirate imperialism by the British against an amphibious community that stood in their way.

The British, however, were just one of a number of pirate imperialist powers practicing this sort of seizure and violent expropriation of territories belonging to amphibious populations during the period. In order to keep their northern African colonies, the Spanish frequently resorted to violent attacks on the seafaring peoples of the Riff, whom they never hesitated to accuse of being pirates. In 1856, Spanish soldiers posted to the Peñón de Vélez de la Gomera shot at and captured several boats belonging to the people of the Riff.[104] In a diary he left about his cruise along this coast, the British consul in Tangier, Drummond Hay, recorded what he learned about the attack when the first reports had reached Tangier. Drummond Hay was received by both the Spanish governor of the fort, José Agustín Calvo, and by local Riff chiefs. The latter explained to him that they had been "shot at first by the Spanish garrison."[105] After Drummond Hay directed a series of threats at them, they told him that the Spanish were regarded as enemies "for having settled in the land of the mussulman," and that they would have never bothered them should they "keep within the walls of their fortress and not seek provisions from the Moorish land."[106] In other words, the local chiefs all but confirmed that the main reason behind the ongoing conflict was the Spanish occupation and the colonial reach of their garrisons in the region.

Shooting at Riff peoples both on land and at sea from these Spanish outposts was a common occurrence during the period. Only a year later, for example, Drummond Hay again commented that the Spaniards did not "hesitate in dealing with the Reefians in as summary a manner as that in which the latter treat them whenever they have an opportunity for doing so."[107] In the years leading up to the Spanish invasion of Morocco, numerous vessels belonging to Riff communities had been sunk by successive Spanish governors of Melilla, and soon after the start of this invasion in 1859, Spanish newspapers boasted to their readers about the African blood that had "run in torrents" as their troops marched on.[108]

The Spanish colonial expansion in the Philippines in the middle decades of the century was also conducted through the use of excessive violence. The expedition to Zamboanga in 1852, for example, was nothing short of a textbook piratical venture. During this attack, the Spanish burned down villages, destroyed crops, and stole all sorts of property in the name of repressing amphibious communities they had singlehandedly designated as pirates.[109] A similar story of extreme violence characterized the expedition against Joló a year earlier, when the town was reduced to ashes and its population sustained a substantial loss of human lives.[110]

In another case of this kind, in 1857, the Spanish found a way to acquire the Puerto de Santa Maria in Mindanao, by using piracy as an excuse and employing dishonest stratagems and unnecessary violence.[111] They forced a treaty on the local prince at Siocon, who relied on the Spanish to defeat his enemies. The Spanish took advantage of his struggles against other amphibious communities, which he had portrayed as pirates, to take possession of the town and region by questionable means.[112] Even on dubious occasions, as it happened in 1841 when some minor excesses committed by pirates along the coast of Albay were reported, Spanish gunships were dispatched to punish the alleged pirates with excessive force.[113]

South of Joló, in Sulawesi, the Dutch also made use of disproportioned violence to bring the Kingdom of Boné, at times accused of sponsoring and harboring pirates, under their colonial rule. During the second Dutch-Boné war, fought between 1859 and 1860, Dutch forces killed and displaced several hundreds of Boné residents, set towns and villages on fire, and destroyed everything they found in their way.[114] Violence against supposed pirates was an intrinsic part of Dutch pirate imperialism and its territorial appropriations throughout this period. Barely a few months after their attack on Boné, the Dutch carried out two punitive expeditions against a supposed group of pirates that had sought refuge in the island of Sailoos, not far from Boné. The first expedition against this group, undertaken by the Dutch war vessel *Reinier Claeszen* under the command of Lieutenant Willinck, departed from Bima in early December 1860. This initial attack on the inhabitants of Sailoos resulted in the destruction of several prahus and of the "robbers' village."[115] Seeing that many of their targets were successful in retreating to the interior of the island, Lieutenant Willinck decided to return to Bima for reinforcements. A few days later, on December 27, the *Reinier Claeszen*, now accompanied by the *Gedeh* under the command of Captain A. F. Siedenburg, sailed for Sailoos again. This time the rooting out of the alleged pirates was complete.

By February 3, 1861, all the Dutch enemies had been captured, killed, or had run away, and the Dutch East Indies government rejoiced on the destruction of "the core of the pirate power, that had been making the Celebes waters unsafe for several years."[116] According to a letter sent by Siedenburg to the governor of the Celebes Islands on February 6, the "robbers" had suffered at least 15 casualties during the second attack, and if we are to believe Lieutenant Willinck's initial reports, likely many more during the first one.[117]

In an analogous fashion, a few years earlier the Dutch did something similar throughout Southern Borneo when, at the request of the sultan of Sambas, they carried out a brutal war against the sultan's enemies in what is known as the Kongsi Wars (1850–54). "Villages were burned down, inhabitants were shot," and an escalation of the armed conflict led to thousands of casualties, "particularly among the non-combatant population."[118]

Like the Spanish and the British in neighboring regions, the Dutch demonized amphibious communities in order to be able to justify numerous atrocities. They, perhaps better than their imperial rivals, knew that colonizing the seas around their Southeast Asian possessions was just as important as wresting lands away from their rightful owners. Cornets de Groot had made this point transparently clear when he referred to these waters as "Our Indian Sea" in 1837.[119] Time and again, Dutch gunboats navigated these waters killing and displacing local populations, in what J. A. de Moor has described as the "long decade of expansion" that took place between 1846 and 1862.[120]

This sort of indiscriminate colonial violence turned on occasion into inhumane actions against alleged or real pirates and their communities. The Dutch-Boné war of 1862 provides a categorical example of how far Dutch pirate imperialist scions were willing to go to expand their territorial gains in Southeast Asia. The initial assault occurred shortly after the Boné rulers had challenged Dutch supremacy in the region by ordering that all their ships entering Boné waters fly the Dutch flag upside down.[121] As happened in cases like this, the Dutch government in Batavia perceived the order as an insult that needed to be urgently answered to preserve Dutch "honor and superiority in these provinces."[122] The violence employed by the Dutch in their subsequent attack on Boné was excessive in extreme and resulted in what can only be referred to as a massacre.

A poem left by a Boné survivor, Daéng ri Aja, provides a rare primary source describing in detail this ferocious pirate imperialist incursion. In this poem, the sound of firing Dutch cannons is described as a "rolling thunder," and Boné's ordinary inhabitants appear as "shivered in fear" while the assailants advanced on them. The poem describes the burning of Taponngé and the multitude of "corpses [that] lay scattered" after the battles were over.[123] This exceptional elegy then recounts how the Dutch, now "delighted" with "the conquest of the cherished villages" and "the burning of the lands," finally left on the same ships they came on.[124]

On July 1849 James Brooke, supported by Royal Navy gunboats, undertook a punitive expedition against the peoples living on the banks of some of the rivers of Sarawak. This time, more "than a thousand innocent persons" were killed, as a result of what some of Brooke's contemporaries considered to be an "alleged but unproven charge of piracy."[125] Brooke's actions, according to numerous firsthand witnesses, among whom was J. W. Miller, the surgeon of the East India Company steamer *Nemesis*, had been nothing short of a "cold-blooded slaughter."[126] In a letter sent to London from Melbourne, where he was on sick leave, Miller noted that Brooke's men had "wantonly beheaded" four innocent men they had found in the river, that a Dayak woman had seen her husband and son decapitated in front of her, and then their heads "had been roasted before her" in the canoe where Brooke had placed her, after allowing for her to be enslaved by "a Balloo Dyak."[127] Before concluding this missive, Miller described various other cases just as bloodied as these and pointed out to Joseph Hume that he "had sufficient proof of his [Brooke's] cold-blooded slaughter in the Kaluka river."[128] Miller confirmed that his "boar's crew and officers in the expeditions" were all "most anxious to have his [Brooke's] doings made known to the Government."[129]

To be sure, Miller was not the only one to denounce Brooke's massacres to the British government. Some newspapers with a significant weight in public opinion, such as the Singapore-published *Straits Times* and the *Illustrated London News*, printed detailed accounts of the events of July 1849. In an article appearing in the *Illustrated London News*, by B. Urban Vigors, another firsthand witness of the events, Commander Farquhar was accused of being responsible for the massacre of Dayaks, together with Brooke.[130]

Seeing himself under increasing scrutiny, Brooke resorted to all kinds of subterfuges to dismiss the testimonies of an increasing number of witnesses, who accused him of unspeakable crimes. He first did everything in his power to convince Lord Palmerston that extreme violence had been necessary against the Dayaks, yet again, on the grounds that they were pirates. As early as 1850, before his crimes had become well known across the British Empire and beyond, Brooke attempted to justify his actions by pointing out that "no act of inhumanity [had been] committed" and that those he had attacked "were known to be pirates."[131] In the same letter, however, he betrayed his earlier claims of innocence when he pointed out that the armed operation had been "consonant with the interests of humanity, with the interests of commerce, and with the maintenance of our national position in the Archipelago."[132] In other words, Brooke was eager to present his extreme actions as absolutely necessary for the strengthening of Britain's colonial interests in Southeast Asia. Not surprisingly, in his brief reply to Brooke, Palmerston stated that his actions in 1849, were "perfectly satisfactory" to the British government.[133]

At the time Brooke's massacres in Borneo were coming under scrutiny, the Spanish were carrying out some truly atrocious crimes in the Philippines. In addition to the previously discussed bloodbaths in places like Balanguingui in 1848 and Joló in 1851, the Spanish's superior firepower was on display, with ghastly consequences for local amphibious communities accused of piracy, on other occasions and for years to come.

Soon after the attack and destruction of Joló, which resulted in hundreds of deaths for the defeated and a treaty of peace with the sultan, Spanish vessels continued to scour the Sulu Sea, which by this date they considered part of their colonial jurisdiction, in search of "small pirate hordes."[134] Across this sea, on its western limits, they carried out a new massacre only a few days after subduing Joló. This time, a Spanish fleet under the command of Lieutenant Claudio Montero came across four local vessels at the northern extreme of the island of Palawan. Without much ado, they deemed the men to be pirates, based on the fact that they carried weapons with them. Once they decided that the vessels were manned by pirates, the order of attack did not take long to come forward.[135]

The action began with a Spanish demand of surrender, which was duly ignored by the four local vessels. Instead, the men on board prepared for a battle, knowing well their chances of victory were slim. Once the assault began, the Spanish gunboats opened fire, keeping up an exchange that lasted for at least ten minutes. In an unexpected twist, the powder magazine on one of the Spanish ships was hit, resulting in a "deadly explosion" and on the sinking of the vessel.[136] Even though most of its crew managed to survive—the Spanish lost a total of eleven men in the entire exchange—the response to the explosion was ruthless. Antonio Giménez, in a letter to the governor of the Philippines, Antonio de Urbiztondo, mentioned how this event had "irritated" his men, spurring them to board the enemy vessels, shooting numerous enemies point blank as they made their way.[137]

Describing his personal experience while boarding one of the vessels, Giménez commented that he had encountered its deck covered with dead bodies and blood. Aware that fighters were still hiding inside the vessel, Giménez then gave the order to set it on fire, drawing seventeen of these men out into the open, where they were arrested. After looking unsuccessfully for any survivors from their own blown-up ship, Giménez and his men sailed to a nearby beach, where they summarily executed all seventeen men at dawn the next day.[138]

Reporting on these events a few weeks later and in an attempt to justify the excessive violence, Urbiztondo referred to the "moors' resistance" as "ferocious and merciless."[139] To the Spanish governor, his men had acted with honor and courage, exterminating "properly savage" men, who in a "bloody trance" had fought until the end with "ferocity."[140] Somehow, although the Spanish had likely killed in battle or summarily executed more than one hundred men in less than a day, showing no mercy and acting more viciously after being "irritated" by the blowing up of one of their vessels, Urbiztondo managed to paint a distorted picture for Madrid, in which all the barbarous and inhumane actions had been supposedly committed by the people who had been slaughtered. For good measure, and without any shred of proof to back up his assertions, Urbiztondo claimed that these four vessels "without a doubt" were part of the fugitive naval forces belonging to Joló that had escaped the destruction of the sultanate's capital earlier that year.[141]

For good measure, only a few days later, Urbiztondo found himself writing again to Madrid, to explain yet another instance of excessive violence carried out by one of his men, Lieutenant Luis Gayoso, against three local vessels that had been spotted by his gunboat in "the most occulted part of the coast," near Iloilo.[142] Without vacillation, after concluding that they were almost certainly pirates, Gayoso gave orders to attack, giving them a "stern chastisement," which resulted in numerous fatalities, which in his eyes and in those of Urbiztondo, were also necessary.[143]

Over the next decade, as the Spanish attempted to consolidate their colonial claims on the Sulu Sea and the Philippines, their use of unwarranted violence became a common occurrence, although it was not until 1861 that a new massacre was recorded. This time, Governor José Lemery e Ibarrola, just as Urbiztondo had done ten years earlier, felt compelled to write to Madrid to justify the need for carrying out the sort of punishment that he considered to be necessary to bring to an end "piratical expeditions" within the colonial boundaries.[144] To be precise, Lemery was referring to the actions undertaken by Lieutenant José Malcampo against a number of vessels that he had encountered along the coasts of Iloilo a few weeks earlier and that he had swiftly deemed to be engaged in piracy.

The account of this new massacre was described by officer Eusebio Salcedo in a letter sent to Lemery in mid-June. In it, Salcedo explained to the governor that the account was really Malcampo's, who was the commander of the Iloilo naval division, and who had communicated it to him directly.[145] According to Salcedo, after spotting a fleet of "pirates," Malcampo and his vessels had come under fire, prompting a severe response.[146] Once they began to return fire, Malcampo and his men did so with everything they had. They used their "cannons and all sort of portable weapons, with such a success, that it could be considered to be horrific."[147] Salcedo described in detail how the superior firepower created havoc among their enemies, the "shrapnel sweeping them away" and the "expansive force of the gunpowder . . . launching them away from their ships."[148] After every shot, Salcedo casually commented to Lemery, "Masses of men were sent flying into the air, falling into the water, dismembered, far from their vessels."[149] This gruesome description concluded with a reference to the numerous "corpses floating in the water around their vessels," and with an approximate calculation of the number of deaths caused by the attack, which, in his opinion, were no less than two hundred.[150]

To be sure, further reports of disproportionate brutality by Malcampo and his men continued in the weeks to come. New actions against maritime communities living under his jurisdiction soon followed. Only a few days after the events described by Salcedo, Malcampo found "four pirate ships" not far from the site of his previous attack.[151] Without hesitation, he ordered a new attack, rapidly overrunning the four vessels with his ships' superior firepower and killing at least "ten pirates."[152] Those who managed to escape were given chase by Malcampo's men. Malcampo threatened "skinning them alive," justifying his threats by the fact that they would only understand this kind of "inhumane customs."[153] Against all the odds, about nineteen or twenty of the men managed to elude capture; they were reported to have landed on the island of Negros, north of Mindanao, a few weeks later, in the last days of August.[154] Ultimately, in addition to those that had been killed, fourteen "moros" were seized and sent to face trial before the navy court.[155]

Two well-known massacres of extensive proportions in nearby Chinese waters, justified by the need to suppress "piracy," were carried out in 1849 by British ships under the command of John Charles Dalrymple-Hay during and after the battle of Tysami, between September 28 and October 1, and then between October 20 and 22, at the battle of the Tonkin River. Due to their nature, these events were described by multiple witnesses and discussed widely by politicians and the press, both in Hong Kong and Britain. According to Scott Beresford, who in 1851 published a book filled with primary sources about these massacres, the reason behind these extreme actions was the constant threats presented by the fleets of Chui-a-poo and Shap-ng-tsai to the Hong Kong colony.[156]

The first of these two actions was undertaken by Dalrymple-Hay, who, commanding HMS *Columbine* and accompanied by the steamer *Canton*, sailed in pursuit of Chui-a-poo's fleet, which had been spotted days earlier in the neighborhood of Mirs Bay. On September 29, the British ships found a fleet of fourteen heavily armed junks near Tysami and proceeded to attack from two flanks. By the end of the day, most of the Chinese vessels had been destroyed, sunk, or severely damaged, and a large number of men had been blown into pieces by the guns of the *Columbine* and *Canton*. Those who escaped regrouped in nearby Bias Bay, where they were later found by the two British vessels, now also accompanied by HMS *Fury*.[157]

Edward H. Cree, who was on board the *Fury*, recalled the events of October 1, when Chui-a-poo's fleet was finally destroyed. He described in detail how some of the "junks were blown up by the shell from the Fury" while many others were "set on fire."[158] He reported that twenty-seven junks had been destroyed, calculating that "400 of the pirates" had perished. Almost two years later, the *Illustrated London News* speculated that at least 1,400 had been killed in the actions of September 29 and October 1.[159] Chui-a-poo himself managed to escape, but he was seized and turned over to the British by his own followers in February 1850. He was then immediately put on trial in Hong Kong, found guilty, and sentenced to transportation. While waiting to be deported, he took his own life a month later, in March.[160]

In an attempt to bring maritime raiding activities near their Hong Kong colony to an end, Dalrymple-Hay gathered the *Phlegethon*, *Columbine*, and *Fury* at Hong Kong a week after destroying Chui-a-poo's fleet and sailed for the coast of China in search of Shap-ng-tsai. After touching down at Hoi-How in Hainan Island, these three vessels were joined by a small number of Chinese war junks, under the command of acting major general Wang-hai-quang, which also participated in the naval battle that would take place only days later at the Gulf of Tonkin.[161] The encounter itself began on October 20 and ended two days later.

In his report to Admiral Francis Collier, written right after the battle had ended, Dalrymple-Hay mentioned that they had totally "destroyed by fire" a grand total of "58 piratical vessels mounting about 1200 guns, and with crews of 3000 men."[162] In another letter, also written in the aftermath of the confrontation and sent to the Chinese governor of Hainan, he was explicit about having "annihilated" Shap-ng-tsai's fleet, with the support of General Wang.[163] Dalrymple-Hay then proceeded to boast about having slain "about 1700 of their crews," while rejoicing that those few who had managed to escape had perished "for want and the weapons of the Cochin Chinese" in the vicinity of the Tonkin River.[164] Dalrymple-Hay's narrative of the destruction of Shap-ng-tsai's vessels and of the fate of their crews was backed up by Cree's written description and his watercolors depicting the action and its aftermath. Some of them show the Chinese vessels being blown up, and others depict the local people of the Tonkin River spearing those who had swum ashore after surviving the British-Qing China joint attack.[165]

The combined death toll—between 2,100 and 3,100—of the actions of September and October against the fleets of Chui-a-poo and Shap-ng-tsai was extremely high, even for the pirate imperialist standards of the period. Nevertheless, it would not be far-fetched to argue that other extremely violent actions, often worthy of being considered as massacres, were undertaken by British officers during this period. One such case took place only two weeks before Dalrymple-Hay attacked Chui-a-poo's fleet. On this occasion HMS *Amazon*, while on its way to Macau under the command of Lieutenant William Mould on September 16, 1849, attacked a number of supposed pirate junks, resulting in the killing of "59 pirates."[166]

A few months later, on March 4, 1850, Captain William Lockyer was ordered to sail toward Mirs Bay, with the intention of destroying a fleet of "16 Chinese Piratical Junks" that had been spotted in the vicinity.[167] Accompanied by two Chinese men who were expected to help him identify the "piratical vessels," he set out that same day on the steamer *Medea*. Within twenty-four hours, Lockyer reported that he had found thirteen junks at Mirs Bay, twelve of which hurried toward the shore while the one remained "an anchor, without offering the slightest resistance."[168] Even though in his own words the crews of the junks did not fight back, Lockyer confessed that when many men "jumped overboard, endeavouring to make for the shore," 150 among them "were destroyed" without any mercy by the *Medea*'s "shell and musketry."[169]

In a similar case of overkill, Commander William Arthur, of HMS *Nimrod*, was called into action in December 1860, when he received intelligence about "a pirate attack on a European vessel" that had taken place on the coast of China, near Hong Kong.[170] Upon arriving at a place that he called Tanne Bay, Arthur's men were forced to disembark in pursuit of the supposed pirates, engaging in a battle that raged for more than thirty hours. Although in his report Commander Arthur was not able to provide his superiors with an approximate number of Chinese killed by his troops, he assumed the number was quite high. From "the number of bodies" found after the combat Arthur deduced that "the loss of the pirates must have been great."[171]

Although the majority of the massacres recorded by pirate imperialist agents against supposed pirates during the middle decades of the nineteenth century took place in China and Southeast Asia, cases were reported elsewhere.[172] Notable among them were the actions undertaken by various US pirate imperialist agents in Liberia as retribution for some questionable acts of piracy carried out by local peoples against the US merchant ships *Mary Carver*, *Atalanta*, and *Edward Burley* between 1842 and 1843.[173]

The evidence collected by those who implicated the Africans for these acts of violence suggested that they were likely responding to American abuses and murders, but the official version of events, which circulated among politicians and the general public in the United States, indicated otherwise. The *Mary Carver*, the *Atalanta*, and the *Edward Burley* had all been attacked in 1842 and 1843 while trading with local peoples in the Bereby region of West Africa, not far from the colony of Liberia, an area upon which Liberian colonists had had their eyes set for some time.

Perhaps the most notorious, and certainly the one with the most significant consequences, among these attacks was the one on the *Mary Carver*, on April 24, 1842. That day, after the *Mary Carver*'s captain, Eben Farwell, had forced Little Bereby trader Crack-O to give him a canoe as compensation for a delay in loading the goods he had purchased, a violent attack on the American crew ensued, where all of them were killed by a group of local men and women. Once the news reached Monrovia, it was immediately forwarded to Washington. Abel P. Upshur, the secretary of the navy, dispatched Commodore Matthew C. Perry, the same officer who would years later force the shogunate to open Japanese ports to foreign trade, to chastise the attackers. Amy Van Natter has suggested that this attack served colonization agendas in the area, providing "Upshur, [President John] Tyler, and other Americans" with a "new justification for the Africa Squadron."[174] To support their strategy, they did not hesitate to present their new African foes as "savages and pirates."[175]

Upon arriving in Liberia a few months later, Commodore Perry proceeded to assess the situation and organized a retaliatory expedition against the Bereby people. He soon came to realize that the peace and trading relations between colonists at Liberia and the people living near the colony were far from friendly. There is little doubt that neighboring peoples had been repeatedly abused by American colonists. Almost a year after carrying out his attack on the Bereby people, with its attendant massacre and burning of several towns along the coast, Perry was forced to admit that although the colony's neighbors had been violent, quite often their behavior had not been without reason. In a letter to his superiors in Washington, sent in September 1843, he explained, "In most cases the natives [had] been as much sinned against as sinning."[176] Perry added later that "if accompanied by a recital of all the facts which had led" them to commit violent actions against American vessels, "some apology might be allowed to the natives."[177]

On March 31, 1843, the *Liberia Herald*, published in Monrovia, concurred with Perry. Addressing this uneven and problematic relationship between the locals and the colony, the newspaper stated that the Africans living in the vicinity of the American colony had been "feeling abused and cheated by white men," which had led to some of them growing "increasingly indignant and violent."[178] The same article also stated, "Some white men pretended to trade, only to lure Africans into vulnerable positions and rob them of their goods."[179]

Irrespective of his understanding of the situation, upon arriving in West Africa, Perry proceeded to consolidate the US colonialist position along this coast, strengthening the land and trading supremacy claims of the Liberian colonists. In the words of Eugene S. van Sickle, "Perry pleased Liberian administrators by honing the tactics of 'Powder and Ball Diplomacy' that would make [him] famous in Japan in 1853."[180] By early December, Perry, joined by a number of navy officers and by some colonists, including Liberian governor Joseph Jenkins Roberts, arranged a palaver with Crack-O to discuss the events of April 24. In this meeting, Crack-O denied having started the quarrel and blamed the *Mary Carver*'s captain, Eben Farwell, for the violence that ensued.

According to the report, a rare instance of recording of evidence provided by an African man considered to have committed piracy, Crack-O remonstrated to Perry that the nearby town of Old Crack-O had sent two boys with goods for Farwell, who had subsequently refused to accept them. Instead, he explained, Farwell "became infuriated, and finally murdered the boys."[181] These needless murders were the reason why the late king of Old Crack-O "declared Farwell guilty and sentenced him to death."[182]

Unwilling to consider Crack-O's account of the events, Perry was said to have approached him with the intention of advising him to stop lying. Perhaps feeling threatened, Crack-O attempted to run away, but he did not go far; he was shot on the spot by a marine and then speared for good measure by others. What followed was nothing short of carnage. Following Perry's orders, his men began shooting at will and setting villages on fire all across the area. Some US marines took the slaughtering of natives almost as a sport. Charles Heywood, who left a personal account of his actions, confessed later that he had become "possessed of a very strong inclination to shoot somebody."[183] Because night had fallen and visibility was limited, Heywood found himself frustrated at not finding any targets. However, he soon saw "two natives in the water," which appeared to him as "the most beautiful chance" to shoot an African or two.[184] Just as he and Horatio Bridge, the USS *Saratoga*'s purser, were about to shoot these men "with intent to kill," they "learned that they were Kroomen, from the Macedonian," who had jumped into the water precisely to avoid being shot by the American sailors with whom they had been sharing a vessel until a few hours earlier.[185] Another witness, Jabez C. Rich, observed in disbelief the bloodbath and destruction unfolding before his eyes. Recalling these moments, he questioned the moral right of the US marines to "inflict this course of punishment" on the Africans of Bereby.[186] Horatio Bridge, the purser who had gone on a shooting rampage alongside Heywood, also left a spine-tingling, self-congratulatory account of the way in which he and his mates had acted that night:

> Man is perhaps never happier than when his native destructiveness can be freely exercised, and with the benevolent complacency of performing a good action, instead of the remorse of perpetrating a bad one. It unites the charms of sin and virtue. Thus, in all probability, few of us had ever

> spent a day of higher enjoyment than this, when we roamed about, with a musket in one hand and a torch in the other, devastating what had hitherto been the homes of a people. . . . But when man takes upon himself the office of an avenger by the sword, he is not to be perplexed with such little scrupulosities, as whether an individual or a family be less guilty than the rest.[187]

The massacre of the Bereby people served to consolidate the Liberian colony, just as the US government, Commodore Perry, and Governor Roberts had expected it would. In August 1843, Perry wrote to Upshur supporting Roberts's requests for having an "imposing [naval] force before the towns and along the neighboring coast," with the intention of "impressing upon the natives greater awe of the American flag."[188] A few months later, in January 1844, he doubled down in a letter to Upshur's successor, David Henshaw, stating that "the retributive chastisement" they had inflicted on "those tribes that had acted in bad faith towards the Americans" was the best remedy to prevent what he referred to as a "recurrence of their piracies."[189]

There is little doubt that Perry had conflicted thoughts about the situation developing in front of his eyes, though. In another missive sent to Upshur in September 1843, he contradicted himself when describing the extent to which these "piracies" had occurred and the reasons behind them. This time, Perry stressed that the "government at home [had] heard but one side of the story" with respect to the conflict between colonists and traders on one side, and the Bereby people on the other.[190] He made it a point to make Upshur aware that it was "not known that masters of trading vessels often maltreat the natives," and yet it was "in proof that town and fishing villages have been fired into, and lives destroyed."[191] Perry's brand of pirate imperialism, which he would deploy later in Japan, ultimately reasserted ideas about "savage and pirate" Africans, ideas that then were used to legitimize extreme violence and massacres of the people who happened to live near the only American colony in West Africa.

In their efforts to expand territorial gains across the world, pirate imperialist agents did not hesitate to accuse amphibious communities of piracy in order to justify their advances. In many cases, these accusations were followed by punitive expeditions, which had violent piratical actions at their core. The questioning of pirate imperialist stratagems, both in the metropoles and in and around new or potential colonies, was a vital part of this process. Such questioning led, in some exceptional occasions, to public debates about the merits of exercising violence while expanding empires, and to the unreliable ways pirate imperialist agents had used to decide who was to be considered as a pirate and who was not. But, not surprisingly, the supporters of pirate imperialism fought back. In a piece published in *The Times* of London on December 22, 1849, the author felt compelled to address the "audacious assertions" and "malicious calumnies" presented against "bloodthirsty officers" who had declared peoples in various parts of Asia as pirates, only "to gratify their own butcherly propensities" and to "give a pretext for naval armaments."[192]

Men like James Brooke, José Malcampo, John Bowring, and Matthew C. Perry, among many others, did not vacillate in labeling any amphibious population that stood in the way of their respective colonial interests as pirates. As we have seen before, bestowing upon them other convenient appellatives, such as "uncivilized," "savages," and "heathen," also served to justify their ultimate aims of wrestling their lands from them by force, if necessary. Transforming predatory nests into civilized colonies, often by shell and fire, was a discursive line that fit perfectly into their "imperial humanitarian" duties.

In other cases, colonial officers benefited from a lack of distinction "between piracy, robbing and warfare," thus allowing them to carry out various strategies to expand their imperial conquests.[193] The Dutch, as Anita van Dissel and others have posed, did so while incorporating new territories into their East Indian colonies, especially so as Governor van den Bosch introduced a new cultivation system in Java from 1830, de facto commandeering part of every farmer's crop for government export purposes.[194]

The colonial ploys and subterfuges carried out all around the world by pirate imperialist agents were not just terracentric endeavors aimed at stealing and appropriating other peoples' lands. To them, the colonization of waterways, including seas and rivers, was as central to their pirate imperial schemes as the appropriation of lands was. At times they succeeded in colonizing entire seas and adjacent lands, establishing exclusively controlled zones, which they transformed into textbook examples of private or shared seas. The British, for example, turned the Persian Gulf into a de facto mare nostrum after 1819, as did the Spanish with most of the Sulu Sea, and the Dutch with the Celebes, Banda, and Java seas throughout the 1840s, 1850s, and 1860s.

The principles of civilizational superiority often wielded while planning to colonize or while colonizing other peoples were validated by the Law of Nations and implemented by pirate imperialist agents, who used both diplomacy and their navies and military to take possession of lands and waterways. The rapacious actions of these imperialist agents were vindicated by supposedly higher needs associated with progress and civilization. Ultimately, new colonized spaces became the lifeblood of these pirate empires, contributing to the development of political stability and metropolitan wealth, and reinforcing ideas of superiority of the white man over peoples they had been "forced" to repress and colonize, for their own good. Many years later, while discussing such pirate imperialist behaviors, Henry Labouchère captured the essence behind the sort of pirate imperialist violence associated with colonialism, perhaps better than anyone else, when he wrote:

> Seize on his ports and pastures,
> The fields his people tread;
> Go make from them your living,
> And mark them with his dead.[195]

CHAPTER FIVE

Inter-imperial Cooperation and Conflict around the Suppression of Maritime Raiding

IN THE LATE AFTERNOON OF AUGUST 22, 1849, the governor of Macau, João Maria Ferreira de Amaral, went for his customary horseback ride across the streets of the Portuguese colony, accompanied by his aide-de-camp, Lieutenant Jerónimo Pereira Leite. Around 6:30 p.m., as night fell and they approached the gate that separated the colony from the Chinese territory, they were ambushed by a group of men armed with short swords. Within a few minutes, Amaral was killed, and his head and remaining hand—he had already lost an arm during the Brazilian war of independence in 1823—were cut off and taken across the border into China. Lieutenant Leite, who managed to escape with a wounded leg, immediately rushed to get reinforcements. By the time the Portuguese soldiers made it to the scene of the crime, however, the mutilated body of Amaral lay on the street, and his Chinese assassins were nowhere to be found.

Reporting the event to the Portuguese government a few days later, the members of the Council of Government of Macau pointed out that the governor had been warned many times that his life was in danger.[1] For months Amaral had been antagonizing his Chinese neighbors through a series of ill-advised measures. These included the closing of the Chinese custom house in Macau, the razing of an ancient Chinese burial ground, and severe punishment dispensed to those captured and deemed to be engaged in piratical actions.[2] In a letter sent a week after Amaral's murder to George Bonham, at the time British governor of Hong Kong, Canton's governor, Xu kuang-chin, noted that Amaral had been known to have a "violent temper," and that he had aggrieved Macau's Chinese residents for a long time.[3] In April, he had imprisoned various Chinese merchants during a religious procession. This decision, according to Xu, had created panic among the Chinese in Macau, who had begun to move to Huangpu "to avoid unexpected trouble."[4]

Just two months before his death, in June 1849, Amaral had irritated his British neighbors in Hong Kong when he ordered the arrest and imprisonment of a British subject who had failed to take his hat off during another Catholic procession in the city. As a result of this measure, Captain Henry Keppel of the Royal Navy, who had supported James Brooke's first bloodthirsty expedition against the Dayak populations of Sarawak and participated in the suppression of maritime raiding in the South China Sea, decided to teach a swift and unambiguous lesson to his Portuguese neighbor. Imbued with a sense of grievance, he took his ship HMS *Meander* to Macau and invaded the city, taking advantage of the brief absence of Amaral, who at the time was visiting an American vessel. Keppel's pirate imperialist attack, which eventually resulted in an apology to Portugal by the British government of John Russell, led to the freeing of the British subject in question but also to the murder of a Portuguese soldier.[5]

Despite Amaral's reputation for no-nonsense confrontation, since his arrival in Macau he had managed to collaborate effectively with his Chinese and British counterparts in various endeavors. This was evident in their joint efforts to combat "piracy" in the South China Sea, particularly in the vicinity of Macau and Hong Kong. For instance, in February and April 1847, after receiving requests from the authorities in Canton to pursue a group of pirates who had attacked some Chinese vessels, he sent Macau's lorchas out to sea to find and punish these men.[6] Collaboration with the British in Hong Kong around the suppression of maritime raiding had been frequent even before Amaral's appointment to Macau's governorship in 1846, and it continued unabated during his tenure. In fact, virtually from the moment the island was ceded to Britain in 1841, collaborative anti-piratical expeditions that would persist for decades after Amaral's death were carried out.[7]

Amaral's assassination had significant reverberations in the days, weeks, and months to come. Soon after his death, the Council of Government of Macau organized an armed expedition to chastise the Chinese and avenge their late governor. For this mission they requested support from the British, and Captain Edward Troubridge immediately sailed for Macau and disembarked a British force to hold the city. Simultaneously, the Portuguese marched toward the border, where the Chinese had concentrated at the Pak Shan Lan fort, known as Passaleão to the Portuguese. After conferring with various foreign diplomats who were on site, including the French, Spanish, and US consuls to China—Alexandre de Forth-Rouen, Sinibaldo de Más, and John W. Davis—a military action in which the Portuguese prevailed, now remembered as the Battle of Passaleão, ensued.

Over the next few days, not only did the British offer all their support to the Portuguese but American vessels hurried to their assistance and a detachment belonging to the French corvette *La Bayonnaise* disembarked in Macau.[8] And yet, in spite of the obvious signs of Western hydrarchic cooperation against the Chinese, only a few months later one of Lisbon's main newspapers went to lengths to warn their readership that "the English, the Americans, the French, the Dutch and the Spanish, all want[ed] to buy Macau from the Portuguese."[9] Tensions and competition, it seemed, could be temporarily set aside when dealing with a common foe, but they were resurrected as soon as the crisis was over.

Events that unfolded in response to Amaral's murder, referred to as "a most barbarous act of atrocity" by US businessman and Macau resident Robert de Silver in a letter to the US secretary of state, John M. Clayton,[10] highlight how, in spite of ongoing distrust and instances of open conflict, pirate empires were able to cooperate and sustain each other in the face of threats posed by other empires or by amphibious communities they deemed to be piratical. That the British would disembark troops in Macau twice in less than three months, the first time to attack the Portuguese garrison and the second one to support it, reveals how fast and adaptable policies and actions could be. In the case of Macau and Hong Kong, a continuing joint struggle against maritime raiding seems to have aided with the speed and flexibility shown by the British in June and August 1849.

The Portuguese, aware that they had support among other Western powers represented in the region, were quick to blame the Chinese government for Amaral's assassination. By October 1849 they had complained profusely about the delays in returning Amaral's head and hand.[11] In reality, Governor Xu kuang-chin and the inspector general of Canton, Ye ming-chen, seem to have done everything in their power to please their Portuguese counterparts in Macau, often using Hong Kong's Governor Bonham as their intermediary. By mid-October, they had seized and executed the band's leader, Shen zhi-liang.[12] Not long after, they were also able to account for the rest of the killers. Notably, three among them were said to have "joined the pirate" fleets of Chui-a-poo and Shap-ng-tsai shortly after they escaped from Macau.[13] Two of them died during the naval battles that took place in late September and early October between these fleets and the British and the Chinese.[14] Amaral's head and hand, however, remained in Chinese hands until they were finally delivered to Macau in January 1850. Their return was dependent on the release of three Chinese border guards who had been made prisoners right after Amaral's death. Soon after these guards were freed by the Portuguese in late December 1849, the Chinese reciprocated, returning Amaral's body parts, as previously agreed.[15]

In spite of the many differences and disputes existing between pirate imperial powers in the middle decades of the nineteenth century, the suppression of maritime raiding and of the autonomy of amphibious communities was the common theme that brought them, more often than not, together. These suppression activities concealed further agendas, which included the acquisition of commercial advantages, the consolidation of colonies, and the displacement or extermination of amphibious communities allegedly standing in the way of Western "civilization" and the abolition of slavery and slave-trading activities.

Even when hydrarchic confrontations and alliances happened around trade and colonialism, it is fair to say that civilization and abolitionism were also used and abused. Collaboration and struggle were fluid positions that could be rapidly altered, depending on the range of benefits at play for the pirate empires involved. Whenever needed, non-Western pirate imperialist states were included in alliances, to the point of securing unexpected concessions from their Western counterparts. On other occasions, they were challenged or even betrayed, as new alliances were formed and old treaties deemed redundant.

Western pirate imperialist agents labored under the impression that they were harbingers of progress—and they did everything in their power to convince others of this claim. Army and navy officers, agents, and ideologues alike found ways of drumming up their own echelons of civilization in an effort to portray themselves as more enlightened and sophisticated, and thus worthier of conquering and colonizing other peoples. Throughout the nineteenth century, the French thought themselves superior to others, and so did the Americans, the Dutch, the Spanish, the Portuguese, and certainly the British.

To "civilize" declining amphibious populations, whom they all too readily accused of being pirates, they at times formed alliances and backed each other unconditionally. In other cases, as Stefan Eklöf Amirell has pointed out in his discussion of how the British developed a colonialist policy in Southeast Asia, they had no qualms in blaming other Europeans for the backward fate of those they had set out to conquer and colonize. While contrasting Dutch oppression of the Malays with the new principles of the British, Thomas Stamford Raffles proposed bringing civilization and progress to them by focusing first and foremost on the suppression of "piracy and slave-raiding."[16]

In fact, Raffles's praise of British imperialism in Asia was hardly unique. Years after Raffles made his claims of British superiority,

Sherard Osborn accused both the Dutch and the Spanish of "ball-cartridge and grape-shot" policies of "tyrannical despotism," which had failed to lead "the naturally mercantile Malay to legitimate sources of emolument and occupation."[17] The French, too, developed their own arguments to highlight their uniqueness and superiority over competing empires. In a letter to Emperor Napoleon III in 1854, Jean-Baptiste Philibert Vaillant, marshal of France, was keen to emphasize that French civilization towered above all others, portraying it as the legitime heir of classical cultures, including the Roman Empire. Writing of French influence in Algeria since its conquest and colonization in 1830, Vaillant argued that "in almost all parts of Algeria French civilization does nothing but resume, in a way, at long intervals of long centuries, the interrupted work of Roman civilization."[18]

To Western pirate imperialist agents, bringing "progress" to "savage" peoples was considered to be such a worthy venture that they could put differences aside to achieve their goal. They did so in numerous occasions during the middle decades of the nineteenth century, always emphasizing that their actions, even the use of excessive violence, were justified by the positive results their joint civilizing missions would bring to those they considered as savages and heathen.

The Spanish support of the French invasion of Da Nang in the late 1850s is one such example. In a letter written in September 1858, Colonel Bernardo Ruiz de Lanzarote, commander of the Spanish forces in the Cochin China, observed that the time for "the Spanish and French armies to fight together in favor of the cause of religion, humanity and civilization" had finally arrived.[19] For good measure, in the same missive Ruiz de Lanzarote found a way of making China responsible for their need to invade their southern neighbors. To him, the policy of the "Celeste Empire" was to "fight western civilization to death." As a result, he noted, the Cochin China had been following their neighbor's lead, thus justifying the use of force by the Franco-Spanish invading forces, which bombarded and occupied Da Nang that year.[20]

This hydrarchic alliance was praised not only in Madrid but also in Paris, where newspapers and other printed publications thanked their Spanish counterparts for their support in attacking

Da Nang. *L'observateur du Dimanche*, for instance, in its issue of December 1858, acknowledged Spain's support to their troops, which were attempting to become "masters of the city where Tu Duc reside[d], and from where he dictate[d] his bloodthirsty decrees."[21] While repeatedly denigrating their enemies, the anonymous author of this article also paid tribute to the "Christian spirit" that animated the two allied armies, which reminded them of "the time of the Crusades."[22]

On occasion, however, the sheer violence of these joint actions was called out by some of those very agents of pirate imperialism. A case in question is that of the French attempt to colonize the island of Basilan in 1845. This effort, which was supported by British HMS *Semarang*, resulted in the unnecessary destruction of property and the displacement and murder of scores of locals who had been accused of piracy. One of the French members of the expedition, Melchior-Honoré Yvan, who witnessed the entire affair, commented years later on how the supposedly "civilized and Christian soldiers" had sacked and burnt whole villages while crying out, "Malheur aux vaincus."[23] Here, as it happened many other times during this period, the implementation of a regime of armed peace "opened the door to atrocity."[24]

On this particular occasion, the British decided to support the French attack on Basilan, as it aligned well with their own attempts to conclude a treaty with the sultan of Joló. Such a treaty, they hoped, would allow them to snatch parts of the southern Philippines from the Spanish sphere of influence. Tensions around this supposed "nest of pirates" had been in crescendo since Brooke had grabbed by force the region of Sarawak from the sultan of Brunei in the early part of the 1840s. By the middle years of the decade, the Spanish found themselves on the defensive, fending off French, Dutch, and British efforts challenging their claims over the southern Philippines and northern Borneo. In spite of some temporary alliances that interrupted these clashes, the Spanish continued to complain about British interference at least until the late 1850s. In 1859, José García y Ruiz, while diminishing the peoples of the Philippines as "mistrustful, suspicious and treacherous" also found time to squarely lay the blame of their access to fire guns on imports from British Borneo.[25]

The steamer *Phlegethon* and the boats of the squadron of Rear Admiral Sir Thomas Cochrane repelling an attack from the forts at Borneo proper, July 8, 1846. Drinkwater Bethune, *Views in the Eastern Archipelago, Borneo, Sarawak, Labuan, &c, &c, &c. From Drawings Made on the Spot by Capt. Drinkwater Bethune, R.N.C.B., Commander L. G. Heath, R.N. and Others* (London: The Descriptive Press by J. A. St. John, 1847).

Even as these tensions developed in the years following the First Opium War, the Spanish, the Portuguese, and the British found ways to collaborate when it came to putting down amphibious communities along the coast of China. Nicolás Cañete y Moral, Spanish consul to Macau in the late 1850s, was keen to encourage cooperation with other Western nations in the face of the violent resistance offered by the Chinese, which "affected much the character and interests of the civilized nations" present in the region.[26] In a letter to the governor of the Philippines, Cañete y Moral stressed that all the treaties signed in previous years with the Chinese, which had cost "money and blood to the Europeans," could easily become null and void. He then explained that these treaties had been signed only because the Chinese had found themselves compelled “under the muzzles of enemy cannons.”[27]

The Chinese were often perceived as falling short of European civilizational standards. As a result, they faced repeated challenges from hydrarchic alliances of Western nations accusing them of being incapable of controlling lawless maritime raiders on their seas. The author of an editorial published in *The Times* in September 1849 stated that the Chinese government was both “weak and disaffected,” that it was questionable whether Qing China’s leaders were able to “suppress piracy,” and that even if they could, they certainly had “no intention to do so.”[28] Similar arguments were put forward by W. S. Bridges in 1856, in a letter sent by the secretary of state for the colonies, Henry Labouchère. In this missive, Bridges denounced the lack of cooperation of the Chinese, going as far as stating in unambiguous terms that in his opinion the Chinese government was “barbarian in the fullest and strongest sense of the word.”[29]

Curiously, when Chinese officials used the term “barbarian” to refer to the British, the latter did not hesitate to remonstrate against what they considered to be a deeply offensive expression. In 1841, Edward H. Cree complained that the Chinese authorities in Ningbo had “sent an insolent message” to the British, “directed to the English barbarians, the most inferior natives.”[30] The letter was sent back without a reply. Later that decade, in 1849, George Bonham communicated to Lord Palmerston how he had obtained a promise from Wu, the imperial commissioner in Canton, that the word “Barbarian” would not be used again “in documents enclosed to officers of the British government.”[31] Bonham justified such a duplicitous request on the need to “remove the hostile feeling of the [Chinese] people against foreigners,” those same foreigners who had invaded and slaughtered them only a few years earlier and who would invade and slaughter them again a few years later.[32]

In spite of these constant lamentations and complaints by Western pirate empires that interacted with China after 1842, there is evidence that Chinese authorities frequently collaborated with them and attempted to meet their requests. The support offered to the British gunships that attacked and defeated the fleets of Chui-a-poo and Shap-ng-tsai in late 1849, the satisfactions offered to the

Portuguese government in Macau following the assassination of Governor Amaral, and even the occasional invitations extended to Western powers to attack "pirates" on their national territory attest to this fact.

A relevant case of this kind took place in May 1865, when the Portuguese lorcha *Maria do Carmo*, with a Chinese and European crew belonging to Macau, was captured by HMS *Bustard* off the coast of China for having engaged in maritime raiding activities.[33] After the vessel was taken to Amoy, the local Chinese authorities were quick to direct the Chinese to Hong Kong to testify before a British court there, before being returned to Amoy to face charges of "piracy and murder on the high seas."[34] William Henry Pedder, British consul at Amoy, saw this concession as a good precedent for future cases where extradition would be needed. In his letter, he stressed that great care be taken "for the matter to be so managed as that the mandarins may have no reason to regret the course they are taking."[35] To Pedder as well as to his colleague James F. Wardlaw, Portuguese consul in Amoy, behavior of this kind conformed to Western rules of civilization and laws, and as such it should be valued and encouraged.

Collaboration among Western pirate empires around the suppression of maritime raiding had a core element of learning, imitation, and competition. Efforts deemed successful in "civilizing," alongside repressing or colonizing, were widely shared and imitated. The Dutch in Southeast Asia, for instance, often discussed how the British had brought progress to their Asian possessions, by becoming "pioneers of development and civilization."[36] They saw the work of the Dutch navy not simply as that of consolidating their territorial gains in the region but also as a "beautiful, honorable and civilizing task."[37] In northern Africa, soon after Prince Adalbert's doomed expedition against the Riff, calls to join forces to avenge this affront on Western imperialism were made in various parts of Europe. French writer H. de T. D'Arlach went as far as to suggest that "civilized nations [should] come together to obtain a brilliant revenge," while warning that such a combined force would engage in a "battle between civilization and barbarism" where victory was "not in doubt."[38]

Pirate imperialist alliances and conflicts around the need to "civilize" amphibious communities accused of sea raiding and violence were often coupled with abolitionist narratives. Here, too, a combination of real-life occurrences and deliberate lies allowed for further excuses to coordinate real or make-believe anti-slave trade and anti-slavery actions that resulted in the suppression, displacement, and colonization of entire amphibious populations. For good measure, such excuses were also used to break hydrarchic alliances and occasionally led to mutual accusations between pirate empires of engaging in those same activities they sought to end.

When it came to implementing abolition, it was apparent that pirate empires still engaged in the trafficking of human beings, particularly in the Atlantic Ocean, would not willingly collaborate to bring an end to a commerce and institution that were still lucrative. Despite receiving backlash from public opinion and some of their fellow pirate imperialist agents, the margins of profit were too significant to commit to a swift and radical change of policies and practices. When they made changes, it was because they were forced to do so. Even when slave traders violently resisted arrest, going as far as murdering some among their captors, they were still protected by their own governments (see chapter 2). However, in some cases when they incorporated maritime raiding into their repertoire, they found themselves hunted and punished by coalitions that included abolitionist and slave-trading Atlantic states.

Especially within the Atlantic realm, examples of inter-imperial cooperation in suppressing both slave trade and piracy abound. The arrangement and acceptance of witnesses' testimonies in foreign courts and some exceptional cases of extradition illustrate the extent to which pirate imperialist states were willing to support each other while dealing with pirate/slave traders, and yet, on occasion, when these men were protected by their states such partnerships were left in tatters.

Anti-slave trade patrols were a constant presence in West and West Central African waters for most of the first seven decades of the nineteenth century. Where the British led, the French, the Americans, the Portuguese, and others eventually followed, at times even challenging British supremacy in this vast geographical area.[39] While multiple cases of Franco-British anti-slave trade collaboration were recorded from the 1830s onward, there is one—that of slave dealer Manuel Garra in December 1849—that especially highlights the depths of such commitment to each other. At some point earlier that year Garra had seized the British schooner *Grant* and taken it to his base in Balantes Bay—somewhere in the river Gêba—near the Bissagos Islands. Upon discovering the hideout of Garra and the place where he was keeping the *Grant*, Commodore Arthur Fanshawe ordered the recovery of the schooner and the chastising of those who had seized it and murdered its captain and part of its crew.[40] As a result, the French ship of war *Rubis*, alongside HMS *Teazer*, and the boats of HMS *Centaur*, mounted a concerted attack on the pirates/slave traders, which resulted in the destruction of their settlement and the recovery of the lost vessel.[41]

Other instances of inter-imperial collaboration to suppress piracy/slave trade are those of the *Defensor de Pedro* in the late 1820s and the *Panda* in the mid-1830s (see chapter 2). In the latter case, the support offered by the Royal Navy to the American government did not stop with the capture of the *Panda* pirates in West Africa and their transportation to England. In an early case of international extradition, the British surrendered all prisoners to the American government and even allowed the main officer involved in their capture, Captain Henry Dundas Trotter, to travel to Boston to testify before the court that had convened there to try the men.

Collaboration among pirate imperialist states around the case of the *Defensor de Pedro* was even more widespread. Upon the arrests of Benito de Soto in Gibraltar and many of his crew in Cádiz, British and Spanish authorities worked jointly to put together a case against this group of pirate/slave traders. Exchanges of witnesses were quite complicated at the time, mostly as a direct result of the yellow fever epidemic that had been affecting Gibraltar since mid-1828. As garrison Lieutenant Colonel Daniel Falla pointed out in early 1829 in a letter to Colonel Stephen Chapman, Soto had entered Gibraltar in May 1828, a short time before the epidemic swept through the town. From that moment onward, he subsequently noted, it had been nearly impossible to move between the British enclave and the Spanish territory.[42]

In spite of these obstacles, communication between the Spanish and British authorities in Gibraltar was constant. In addition to Governor George Don's repeated missives, the British consul in Cádiz, John Brackenbury, kept both his own government and the

Spanish apprised of any developments in the case for months. This was particularly evident during the trials that eventually resulted in multiple executions on both sides of the border. For example, Brackenbury was tasked with communicating the execution of Benito de Soto to Spain's secretary of state, Manuel González Salmón, on January 25, 1830.[43] Moreover, he was also charged with explaining to the Spanish government, over a year before, that the authorities of Gibraltar would be unable to extradite Soto as a consequence of the "state of public health in Gibraltar."[44]

Inter-imperial cooperation in this case also involved representatives of the Brazilian Empire. According to González Salmón, it had been the Brazilian consul in Naples who had given to his Spanish counterpart there the background information necessary to understand the extent of the *Defensor de Pedro*'s piratical activities.[45] Without this information, the Spanish may have never learned that the vessel had left Rio de Janeiro for the Gold Coast in a slave-trading expedition. It was thanks to this letter that they also learned that the crew of the ship had taken arms when their captain, Pedro Maris de Souza Sarmento, had landed with some sailors with the intention of procuring a human cargo from the local traders at Woe.[46]

Cooperation around the suppression of slave-trading activities associated with maritime raiding in the Atlantic was not, however, without dissent. Numerous cases of confrontation between pirate imperialist agents, both at sea and on land, attest to such disagreements. Some cases discussed above, including those of the *Veloz Pasagera*, *Gaio*, and *Galgo*, among others, reveal how pirate imperialist states were quick to protect their own nationals, even when faced with unquestionable charges of piracy.

Beyond the Atlantic, abolitionism was also used as a pretext to suppress amphibious populations who stood in the way of pirate imperialism. In places like Southeast Asia and the South China Sea a consensus began to emerge as the century progressed, suggesting that especially Western actors in these regions were fully committed to bringing any sort of slave-trading or enslaving activities to a closure. However, historical evidence seems to suggest that whenever endorsing and practicing abolitionism was not convenient, ways to ignore the slave trading could be found.

This was especially the case on those occasions when this trade was carried out by an ally, rather than a competitor or an enemy. In spite of written remonstrations by a number of pirate imperialist agents, the suppression of slavery and human trafficking was a priority only when there was something to gain from it. Stamford Raffles, for example, wrote in 1823 about the need to relieve the inhabitants of the new lands colonized by the British from "oppression and exaction."[47] In this letter, written barely a couple of years before the British signed the Burney Treaty, which created an alliance with the Siamese that condemned thousands of Malays into slavery in Siam, Raffles praised England for "advocating the cause of the captive or the slave."[48]

There is little doubt that the British, in particular, were able to look the other way on occasions when one of their allies was accused of "committing unheard atrocities."[49] That the Siamese carried thousands of enslaved Malays from Kedah and Perlis to Bangkok and other Siamese cities was a well-documented fact at the time, even by British officers like Henry Burney or William Balhetchet.[50] Slave trade and enslaving activities were regularly reported by Burney and by other British agents for most of the 1825–41 period, and it was extensively condemned by the British public in Penang. In 1840, Belhetchet went as far as describing the traffic of enslaved Malays from Kedah who had been taken to Bangkok in five junks and given to "the King, princes and his ministers." More poignantly, he stressed that these men, women, and children, "about a thousand in all," had tried to escape this fate, only to be "driven back by the English ship of war," thus explicitly accusing his countrymen of complicity in the slave hunting and trading operation.[51]

Throughout the period, the British repeatedly accused Kedah's Malays of being pirates bent on destroying their alliance with Siam, and they did everything in their power to stop them from retaking their own country. When Tunku Kudin expelled the Siamese from Kedah in April 1831, Straits Settlements governor Ibbetson gave strict instructions to the commanders of the vessels *Zephyr* and *Emerald* to cooperate with the Siamese in order to retake Kedah. Kudin and his men should be considered as "pirates" and treated "as such" should they be captured.[52]

Ibbetson, as Governor Bonham would do years later, considered cooperation with Siam to be a priority, and he was willing to look the other way should it help to "efface the unfavourable impression" that the British had apparently given by allowing the Malay to retake Kedah and enslave its people.[53] But where Ibbetson was concerned, Bonham was defiant. Ten years later, as Tunku Mohamed Saad was put on trial under his watch at Penang, Bonham ignored twenty years of reports of Siamese enslavement and trafficking of Malays into Bangkok; instead he attempted to present the Malays as pirates who deserved to suffer the most severe punishment. To Bonham, it was the Malays who had "ravaged" their own country, and the Siamese who had suffered from their "rapine and bloodshed."[54]

As we have seen, the Spanish and the Dutch willingly worked together, linking slave trade with maritime raiding whenever it was convenient, in order to suppress amphibious communities across Southeast Asia. In 1851, for example, the Dutch East Indies governor Jan Jacob Rochussen communicated to General Urbiztondo how Dutch vessels had freed "61 natives of various parts of the archipelago of the Sunda islands who had been made slaves by pirates."[55] In the same letter, Rochussen was keen to express his gratitude to the Spanish government in Manila for spoiling "the attacks of the pirates who hide in its domains."[56]

Nonetheless, the agents representing each of these pirate imperialist states often blamed each other for failing to join forces to suppress slave trade and piracy. In recounting his time in Southeast Asia years earlier, Sherard Osborn suggested that the Dutch pepper plantations in Sumatra had been the "great mart for the disposal of the slaves" in the region.[57] In the same paragraph he went further and accused Dutch planters on the coast of Borneo of participating in a large enslaving operation.[58]

In the mid-1840s, Portuguese authorities in East Timor all but implied a similar connection between Dutch sailors and planters and the continuation of slave raids, piracy, and slavery in the neighboring Dutch possessions. On October 3, 1845, Julião Jozé da Silva Vieira, governor of East Timor, issued orders to "examine and stop, if possible, the traffic of slaves, or better said the piracy, being practiced along that coast by Makassan ships flying the Dutch flag."[59]

In the same letter, the Portuguese governor explained how the behavior of the Dutch in the area was in reality very different from what "European gazettes" would divulge, and that they would frequently "violate Portuguese territory" and would get involved in both slave trade and piracy.[60] In another letter, written in early 1846, Vieira again suggested that the Dutch had set their eyes on the Moluccas and Makassar, where they were establishing large coffee plantations, for which they were "buying or stealing the inhabitants of Timor and Solor, promising them their freedom after ten years [of work]."[61]

For agents of pirate imperialism, slavery and the slave trade were often tolerated or even endorsed when such actions helped forge alliances that advanced their commercial or colonial interests. Equally, and for the same reasons, these alliances could be called into question whenever it was convenient to do so. Commercial interests were often at the center of these hydrarchic alliances and disagreements between pirate imperialist states. Threats to trading routes, for example, were used as justification for joint attacks on amphibious peoples accused, with reason or not, of being pirates, more so than the vague excuses of needing to civilize them or to abolish enslavement and human trafficking.

As pirate imperialist states expanded around the world in search for new markets, they took with them their commercial practices based on Western laws, regardless of whether they had been drafted to support free trade or protectionist approaches. These expansionist and commercial practices were continuously performed by pirate imperialist agents from different states, who saw the need for backing each other as crucial for the success of their trading interests. Imposing Western models of commerce, based on Western laws, was the rule throughout the period. Those who resisted, like China, Japan, and even Siam, were eventually persuaded through a combination of diplomatic and armed approaches, that at times resulted in full-blown wars, for example, the two Opium Wars with Qing China between 1839 and 1860.

By the end of the First Opium War, a fragile alliance had been imposed by the British upon the Chinese. Against the will of the latter, Hong Kong was snatched from Qing China and five ports were opened to foreign trade, a circumstance that was quickly taken advantage of by other Western states interested in furthering their trading goals. Americans, French, Spanish, and Portuguese flocked to Chinese ports to carry out trade under the new regime. Even states with a lower profile in the region, such as Belgium, jumped at the opportunity and sent their ships to trade under the protection of British gunboats.[62]

The Americans in particular had been concerned about the effect that the tense relationship between Britain and China from the late 1830s onward could have on their business in the region. Already in May 1839, shortly before the war had begun, the US consul in Canton, Peter Wanten Snow, had warned his government that things were reaching a crisis level and that traders, especially British ones, had been leaving Canton "as fast as possible."[63] Over a month earlier, his fellow US consul in Singapore, Joseph Balestier, had informed Washington of the deterioration of relations between China and all foreign traders, referring to inauspicious accounts "as to the permanence of trade with Europeans, among whom Americans are included," in China.[64]

An even clearer indication of the US prospects of imposing their own commercial rules in the region, while still maintaining collaboration links with other pirate imperialist states, can be seen in Commodore Perry's "opening" of Japan to foreign trade in the mid-1850s. Not only was he inspired to some extent by Britain's exploits in China, but while discussing the need to open Cochin China to foreign ships, Perry recalled previous British, French, and American failures to do so.[65] While on his way back to the United States in 1854, Perry went as far as suggesting that the secretary of the navy use "small steamers of light draught" to "command respect and as a consequence, secure the friendship of these singular people."[66] Equally, around the same time, US trader Townsend Harris, following British negotiations with Siam in the mid-1850s, had supported the use of gunships to open Siamese ports to foreign trade and had concluded that for the United States to achieve a similar result "the proper way to negotiate with the Siamese" should be sending "two or three men-of-war" in order to force them to comply.[67]

Fractious interactions between Western and non-Western empires were in fact very common during the period. After the Treaty of Nanjing in 1842, relations between China and Britain around the suppression of piracy were repeatedly strained by mutual accusations of indolence and transgression. At the same time, both empires collaborated to make trading routes, especially in the seas around Hong Kong, safer for all trading vessels. Whereas the British often displayed their naval superiority, the Chinese made the best out of a difficult situation, and as C. Nathan Kwan has recently argued, Qing China officials frequently succeeded in coopting "the Royal Navy into their own administration."[68]

In 1843, only a few months after the Treaty of Nanjing had been signed, the governor of Hong Kong, Henry Pottinger, informed Vice Admiral William Parker that he had received news from the mainland confirming that the Chinese authorities there were "about to take active measures for the total suppression of piracy." In spite of what Pottinger considered to be a positive development, he lamented that when he had offered to cooperate in these efforts, the Chinese had "civilly declined."[69] As the months went by and the raids at sea continued, British officers in the region grew suspicious of their Chinese counterparts' real intentions and at times carried out indiscriminate attacks against Chinese vessels that they deemed to be pirates.

One such case took place in 1844 when Captain Bruce opened fire upon some Chinese boats without having authorization to do so, provoking a diplomatic incident that had to be dealt with by the British governor in Hong Kong, John Francis Davis. As would happen on many other occasions, Captain Bruce's superior officer, Thomas Cochrane, was quick to jump to his defense, noticing that officers like Bruce were "placed in a very peculiar position," having to deal with two civil powers within the same area, and often falling into a situation in which they could be accused of not having "manifested sufficient zeal on the one hand, and indiscretion on the other."[70]

The exchanges between Governor Davis and the Chinese governor of Kwangtung and Kwangsi, High Imperial Commissioner Keying, are illustrative of the existing tensions between the two empires around the issue of suppressing maritime raiding in the South China Sea. In early December 1844, for example, Davis wrote to Keying pointing out that his government had failed to inflict any punishment on "pirates attacking the English and their vessels."[71] Not content with remonstrating for the supposed lack of action by the Chinese, Davis resorted to unambiguous threats, when, using self-defense as a right, he warned Keying that unless things improved, he would send British ships to "the haunts of these lawless robbers" with the aim of rooting them out "with the greatest severity."[72]

Keying received Davis's threatening letter a few days later, and he soon replied, highlighting the many obstacles he faced in suppressing maritime raiding and placing the blame squarely on the "traitorous villains of the Triad Society."[73] In his letter, Keying also pointed out that the British were not without fault, indicating that many of these men had gone to Hong Kong "to hide themselves there," where they remained outside his jurisdiction. Before concluding, he subtly implied again that the British were responsible for the escalation of this crisis and recommended that "these perfidious villains" should "in one body be arrested" without delay by the British authorities in Hong Kong.[74]

Keying's suggestions fell on deaf ears. A few days later, Davis was still using the "self-defense" argument in a letter to Cochrane, in which he wondered to what extent the needs to protect British subjects were "to prevail over the respect which is undoubtedly due in the first instance to the independent rights of China."[75] To Davis, Chinese concerns about the ways in which these men had been using Hong Kong as a hideout were dismissible. Instead, he almost provided a template for Cochrane to carry out armed actions against Chinese vessels. Davis recalled how the Chinese had refused British cooperation when Pottinger had offered it, using this refusal as another reason to overrule the supposedly reciprocal rights and obligations agreed upon between the two states.[76] Cochrane's response was predictably in tune with Davis's complaints. He started by pointing out that this was not a new concern, that he had told Pottinger years before that so long as the "Chinese government permits their boats to carry arms," it would be impossible to find "any adequate means of suppressing their acts of aggression."[77]

In the years that followed the destruction of the fleets of Chui-a-poo and Shap-ng-tsai these tensions continued, eventually intensifying before the start of the Second Opium War in 1856. For instance, in 1852, as maritime raiding in Chinese waters had significantly diminished, British officers and traders continued to criticize the Chinese for failing to accept British support to suppress piracy in the region, and for buying the loyalty of Shap-ng-tsai's leaders after the destruction of their fleet three years earlier.[78] A year later, in 1853, as the Taiping Rebellion diverted the imperial authorities' attention and resources toward a more pressing matter, British acting governor in Hong Kong, William Jervois, expressed his fears that this new conflict would make Chinese efforts futile, leading to a "tenfold increase to the piratical fleets already overrunning these waters."[79] After the end of the Second Opium War, however, cooperation between British and Chinese authorities around the suppression of maritime raiding seemingly improved. In 1861, William Thomas Mercer credited the Treaty of Tientsin for providing the "measures for the suppression of piracy" that were to be taken "in concert by the British and Chinese governments."[80]

At virtually any given time during this period, pirate imperialist states supported each other, while never failing to take advantage of any opportunity that, to the expense of other pirate imperial states, would allow them further their own commercial aims. The Dutch, for example, often supported British or Spanish expeditions against amphibious populations that had troubled their commercial interests. Very often they went out of their way to make sure that their actions were known to the British and Spanish governments in Penang, Singapore, and Manila.

One illustrative case is that of the British merchant cutter *Paul Jones*, which was allegedly attacked by pirates in 1846 while on its way from China to the Swan River in Australia. Soon after the attack was brought to his attention by the captain of another British vessel, the Dutch governor of Ambon Island, Johannes Baptista Cleerens, took the necessary steps to assist the *Paul Jones*'s crew and to locate and punish its attackers, although with little success.[81] For their part, both British and Spanish pirate imperialist agents were also keen to study Dutch anti-piracy expeditions within their territories and waters, in the hope of learning from them. Arguably, even James Brooke's activities in Borneo may have been inspired to some extent by campaigns carried out by the Dutch navy, especially by the one conducted by Dirk Hendrik Kolff from 1829 against amphibious populations in the Makassar Straits and across the Celebes, Moluccas, Timor, Banda, Flores, and Java Seas. In a discussion in the House of Commons in London in 1846, following the translation into English of Cornets de Groot's *Notices Historiques*, it was stressed that every year the Dutch would follow these "pirates" into "their haunts, to make an example of them, to burn their ships, to carry off their arms, and to spread terror and confusion" among them.[82]

Dutch relations with their neighbors in this region, when it came to protecting trade rights, were far from ideal. Frequent incursions from British and Spanish vessels, which often targeted peoples considered to be under the protection of the Netherlands, occurred. For example, in 1856, a number of Dutch subjects were shipwrecked at Mindanao and promptly taken captive by the locals to Siocon. Upon requests from Charles Ferdinand Pahud, his Dutch counterpart in Batavia, Governor Norzagaray did everything in his power to free these men, ordering a punitive expedition the next year. As a result, the men were released, and, conveniently, the expedition gave the Spanish an excuse to seize for good the port of Santa Maria in Mindanao.[83]

A few years later, in 1862, the Spanish steamer *Elcano* attacked and sunk a vessel hoisting the Dutch flag, which, as on many other occasions, was deemed to be a pirate because of the way it sailed.[84] Unlike many other attacks on supposed pirate ships belonging to local amphibious communities, this incident escalated into a diplomatic crisis when the ship's crew members, all Dutch subjects, were arrested and imprisoned. As a result, the Spanish were compelled to release and compensate the ship's master and crew and to issue a series of profuse apologies to their Dutch counterparts.[85]

Conflicts with the British were, if anything, even more frequent. Sumatra often played a central role in these differences. In 1827, John Prince, a British merchant residing in Batavia, informed a colleague in Singapore about a vessel that the Dutch had sent to the coast of this island to "induce the natives to discontinue the purchase of salt" from the British.[86] In the same letter, Prince pointed out that there were no "exertions or pains" that Dutch merchants were not ready to take in order to destroy Singapore. Logically, upon being briefed about this Dutch move, Governor

Robert Fullerton proceeded to launch a charm offensive along the coast, letting the locals know that trade between Siak and the Straits Settlements had continued to increase "to the mutual advantage of these countries."[87] Regardless, disputes about trading rights along the Sumatran coast continued in the years to come, as the Viscount of Pontón communicated to the Spanish minister for the colonies in 1866. Quoting a letter from their consul in Singapore, the viscount noticed "a certain aggression of the Dutch against the Western coast of Sumatra, which, as expected, provoked the ire of the English on this residence."[88]

So-called anti-piratical expeditions to protect trade in the region were particularly prone to lead to further conflict among these two representatives of pirate imperialism. The offensive launched from Singapore by Bonham and Chads in 1836 highlights how stakes could rise significantly in a very short period of time. To Bonham in particular, Dutch control of trade in places like Riau and Lingga constituted an obstacle to the newly launched British all-out attack on the amphibious communities of the regions, which he and Chads considered to be infected by pirates. Before setting out on their expedition in June 1836, Bonham wrote a note accusing the rajah of Riau of sheltering and supporting pirates and suggesting that their first move should be to persuade the Dutch to cooperate with their new plan.[89]

A few days later, when the Dutch declined his request of cooperation against the rajah of Riau, Chads deemed the reasons for this refusal insufficient "to defer the punishment called for by the aggression on the British flag, in which Mr. Bonham fully concurred."[90] Chads then sailed for Galang Island, destroyed three villages and all the vessels he found there, subsequently congratulating himself for having "broken up" such a "horde of pirates."[91] Although this attack led to multiple remonstrations from Batavia, neither Chads nor Bonham were ever admonished by Calcutta or London. In fact, later that year Chads wrote a minute lamenting that Galang Island had again become a "piratical depôt" allowed by the Dutch "to the sole injury of property going to British ports."[92] He then concluded that they were necessarily pressed to "gain an intimate knowledge of all the probable resorts of the Pirates . . . in spite of all jealously or impediments" presented by the Dutch.

Chads, as Bonham had done earlier that year, suggested ignoring the Anglo-Dutch Treaty of 1824, which had defined pirate imperial spheres of influence in the region. This treaty was regularly at the center of Anglo-Dutch disputes around trade and the suppression of maritime raiding during the period. When in 1848 numerous complaints of Dutch interference against British vessels trading in the Celebes and Makassar reached the governor of the Straits Settlements, he quickly pointed out that such actions were taken in "contravention of the commercial treaty dated 17th March 1824."[93] Governor William John Butterworth, however, was forced to admit that there had been "considerable difficulty in obtaining information of a conclusive nature, proving an infraction of the Treaty," a circumstance that kept his hands tied for the time being.[94]

In the Mediterranean Sea, too, trade and maritime raiding were inextricably linked, and at the center of pirate imperial cooperation and competition. From Gibraltar and the Riff Coast in the Western Mediterranean to the Greek and Ottoman territories in the east, pirate empires jostled for commercial supremacy, and they often joined forces to impose their trading practices upon the various amphibious peoples who inhabited this sea. The united front presented by the Spanish and British against slave traders accused of having carried out piratical attacks, such as Benito de Soto and the crew of the *Defensor de Pedro*, are a case in point. More often than not, they also came together to put down Greek, Ottoman, or northern African amphibious communities that they accused, with proof or not, of being involved in acts of piracy.

As was happening elsewhere in the world during those years, in the Mediterranean real or alleged punitive activities were used as a way to gain and expand trading rights and spheres of influence—or even to support smuggling activities. For example, in 1838, after pledging British support to Count Joseph-Constantin von Ludolf of the Kingdom of Naples to combat "Albanian pirates" in the Adriatic Sea, Lord Palmerston reneged on his promise.[95] Instead of delivering support, Palmerston suspended British aid until von Ludolf gave assurances that his kingdom had "abandoned its intention of violating the Treaty of 1816 between Great Britain and Naples," which guaranteed the former priority in acquiring the sulfur produced by the kingdom.[96] A few years later, in October 1847, Jean François Théodore Béchameil complained to the French minister of the navy about the extensive smuggling activities carried out by British vessels out of Gibraltar, which supplied their enemy, Emir Abd el-Kader, with shipments of sulfur, landing shipments "between Melilla and the Algerian part" of the coast.[97]

Pirate imperialist rivalries over territories and their waterways were also a central part of the story of suppression of amphibious populations in the middle decades of the nineteenth century. From Southeast Asia and China to the Mediterranean and the Atlantic, imperial powers haggled for potential colonies and, on occasion, collaborated to subjugate those who refused to accept their rule. There is little doubt that agents of pirate imperialism watched each other's exploits, at times with envy, and did their very best to further the colonial possessions of their metropoles.

In 1857, in a book dedicated to the Spanish conflict with the amphibious peoples of the southern Philippines, Emilio Bernaldez emphasized how France, the Netherlands, and Britain, "animated by the natural desire of expanding their commerce, and stimulated by jealously when looking at the conquests of the other two," had continuously tried to wrestle some of the southern islands of the archipelago from Spain.[98] Bernaldez's fears were well founded. In the mid-1840s, Spanish authorities in Manila had seen James Brooke's success in Borneo and Labuan, and his subsequent attempt to take possession of Joló through diplomatic means, as a continuous threat.

To some extent, as Bernaldez admitted, the Spanish attack on Joló in June 1849 was not so much the result of repeated acts of piracy on Spanish ships but a response to the manifest designs of the British upon that sultanate.[99] The Spanish were certainly aware of the sort of subterfuges the British had employed in taking Hong Kong from China and Labuan from the sultan of Brunei. In a letter to Madrid, written in mid-1849, Governor Narciso Clavería went so far as to state that the British were resorting to disinformation in their press, "just as they had done when the violent occupation of Labuan," to justify their attempts on Joló.[100] In a similar case years earlier, Francisco María de Marcaída, a Spanish lawyer based in Manila, stressed in a letter to the Philippines postmaster general that the British had originally promised the Chinese imperial commissioner that they would use Hong Kong Island only to anchor their vessels and not establish a colony. Yet they went back on their word and settled there through the use of deception and force.[101]

The French, too, had been intent on gaining on their fellow pirate empires in this region. In 1845, years before they finally secured a foothold in Vietnam, they had tried to extricate Basilan from the Spanish sphere of influence. In a letter written in November 1843, François Guizot, minister of foreign affairs, made it clear that it was not "convenient to France to be absent from . . . this part of the globe, where other nations have already settlements."[102] This need for appropriate territories to colonize was behind the drive to settle in Basilan. In the same letter, Guizot mentioned the importance of having the French flag "fly on the China seas" and for the French to find a place to colonize, as the British had done in Hong Kong.[103]

Years before Brooke sailed for Joló, British authorities in Calcutta and the Straits Settlements had discussed a possible expedition to wrest that territory from the Spanish sphere of influence, justifying the move with the need to stop piracy across the Sulu Sea. In July 1838, Henry Prinsep, responding to a letter written by Bonham, communicated that the governor of India was "prepared to approve of any measures" he would take, together with Commander Chads, "for punishing the Soloo Chiefs."[104] What began before Brooke's attempts continued long after they had occurred. As late as 1862, Charles Wood felt it was worth asking the governor of India, the Earl of Elgin, to get "a copy of the treaty conferring sovereignty" of "Sooloo archipelago" to Spain, as it was not clear to the British to what extent Spain had indisputable rights to these islands.[105]

According to Amirell, Brooke's actions in 1849 had been nothing but a response to fears of an impending Dutch colonial expansion in northern Borneo and Sulu.[106] In fact, years before such fears had been expressed by Colonel Torrens in a letter to Prinsep in Calcutta, when he warned the British government to avoid getting caught in any sort of "prelude to territorial occupation or political aggrandizement by the Dutch," and to require that "the stipulations of the existing treaty" should be "insisted upon" in any bilateral talks.[107]

Unsurprisingly, the Dutch expansion along the northeastern coast of Borneo was provoked by another British adventurer, James Erskine Murray. Inspired by none other than Brooke himself, Murray sailed to Tenggarong, hoping to seize a piece of land from the sultan of Kotei through a combination of deception and force.[108] Soon after Murray lost his life, ending his expedition, the attention of Jean Chrétien Baud, the Dutch East Indian governor at the time, was immediately drawn to this region, which, according to Graham Irwin, had been totally neglected by the Dutch since 1834.[109] Thus in spite of the agitation in the British press for the Royal Navy to punish those who had murdered Murray, the quick manner in which the Dutch took control of the sultanate of Kotei impeded them from doing so.[110]

Anglo-Dutch tensions in the region around declared rights to particular territories were long-standing, and predated the 1824 Anglo-Dutch Treaty. However, these tensions reached new levels after Bonham and Captain Chads undertook their anti-piracy offensive in mid-1836. As we have seen, Bonham and Chads did not hesitate to chastise amphibious populations inhabiting areas that had been recognized as Dutch by the 1824 treaty. In a letter to Bonham written during one of his expeditions in the Malacca Straits, Chads insisted that they should gather intelligence and punish pirates "in spite of all jealously or impediments of the Dutch."[111]

In Bonham, Chads had an equally belligerent partner in a seat of power. From his position of governor of the Straits Settlements, Bonham repeatedly questioned the rights and commitment of their Dutch neighbors with regard to suppressing maritime raiding. Bonham also repeatedly justified all sorts of incursions into Dutch spheres of influence and was keen to "induce the Dutch to co-operate" in pirate imperialist endeavors.[112] Even so, and in spite of their aggressive approach against amphibious communities and competing pirate empires in the region, Bonham and Chads did not seriously attempt to occupy and claim any new territories for the British crown. It was not until 1846 that the British, relying on the advice of Brooke, took the island of Labuan from the sultan of Brunei through a combination of diplomacy and gunships.

Ceremony of hoisting the British flag on the island of Labuan, northwest coast of Borneo, by Captain Rodney Mundy. HMS *Iris*, December 24, 1846. Drinkwater Bethune, *Views in the Eastern Archipelago, Borneo, Sarawak, Labuan, &c, &c, &c. From Drawings Made on the Spot by Capt. Drinkwater Bethune, R.N.C.B., Commander L. G. Heath, R.N. and Others* (London: The Descriptive Press by J. A. St. John, 1847).

The occupation and colonization of Labuan was a critical moment in the pirate imperialist story in this part of the world, as it consolidated the position of the British in Southeast Asia as arguably the main maritime power, especially following their victory in the First Opium War. Labuan was strategically placed between Singapore and Hong Kong, and it had large reserves of coal that could now be readily accessed by a rapidly increasing number of British steamers. This advantage was not lost on the US consul in Singapore, Joseph Balestier, who reported to Washington, soon after the British had claimed the island, that its commanding position "in the China sea and its proximity to the city of Brunei" had given the new colony a "great importance as a military and commercial station."[113]

In spite of all their disputes and mistrust, Western pirate imperialist powers rarely hesitated to help each other in suppressing amphibious populations that threatened the consolidation of their new colonies. For instance, regardless of their qualms and misgivings against the British, Dutch, French, and others, the Spanish more often than not lent their hands to "piracy" suppression endeavors that benefited the strengthening colonial grip of their competitors in places like Hong Kong, Vietnam, and Borneo.

A representative case was recorded in August 1856, when a British merchant ship out of Hong Kong was taken at sea, east of the island, by maritime raiders. Needing to take immediate action to pursue the attackers but not having any gunships to his disposition at that very moment, Hong Kong's governor, John Bowring, requested help from Commander Eugenio de Agüera, whose steamer, *Reyna de Castilla*, happened to be anchored in Hong Kong harbor at the time.[114] Upon receiving Bowring's request, the Spanish commander immediately agreed to help and readied his vessel to leave at once. Just as the *Reyna de Castilla* was about to depart, HMS *Coromandel* arrived in the colony, and after some delays and consultations, the two ship commanders agreed to go out together on a pirate-hunting expedition along the coast of China.[115]

The extensive correspondence between Spanish and Dutch authorities in Southeast Asia from the mid-1820s until the late 1860s attests to a close collaboration and support, which frequently mixed attacks against amphibious peoples with the occupation and colonization of their ancestral homes. In 1851, for example, Governor Urbiztondo assured his counterpart in Batavia, Governor Rochussen, that the Spanish would "not neglect any means to spoil the attack of pirates," who were resisting Dutch advances in Borneo and then seeking refuge in Spanish-controlled territories.[116] In 1855, Dutch governor Duymaer van Twist reciprocated, when he assured the Spanish of "his desire to cooperate with the Spanish Government in the extermination of piracy on the seas of India."[117]

Not surprisingly, soon afterward the Spanish secretary of state, Juan de Zavala, wrote to his fellow secretaries of war and the navy encouraging a sort of colonialism à la carte approach, by which the Spanish and the Dutch would mutually recognize each other's rights over Joló and Borneo, respectively.[118] To Zavala, it seemed, partnering with the Dutch carried a lesser risk than doing so with the British, who had continued to threaten Spanish supremacy over the southern part of the Philippines. Barely a few months later, Leopoldo O'Donnell, acting secretary of state in the absence of Zavala, was even clearer in a letter to the Baron Gravestins, diplomatic envoy of the Low Countries in Madrid. In this letter, O'Donnell pressed the need to "concur of common accord to extirpate the piracy" that infected Southeast Asian seas and "made insecure the coasts of our colonies in those remote regions."[119] Mixing the suppression of "piracy" with their colonial intentions, O'Donnell then explained that in order to "obtain" and "overtake" those islands and "to reduce their inhabitants to a way of living" they found more acceptable, the Spanish government was ready to "sign an agreement with the government of the Netherlands."[120]

Another example of Spanish cooperation with a fellow Western pirate empire took place in the mid- and late 1850s, when old quarrels around the French attempts on Basilan were forgiven and the Spanish lent their support to the French invasion of Vietnam. Although in the early stages of this conflict, the Spanish were not certain that the French had colonial ambitions, it soon became apparent that this was indeed the case. In November 1858, these intentions were so transparent that the Spanish governor in the Philippines wrote to Madrid describing how the French had begun fortifying Da Nang, with a view of establishing a colony similar to the ones the British had founded in Hong Kong and Singapore, thus fulfilling the wishes expressed by Guizot a decade earlier.[121] This letter constituted a radical turnaround from the narrative espoused in the initial correspondence between the Spanish expeditionary forces to Vietnam and Manila a few weeks before, which insisted that French intentions were all about "civilizing" the Annamites and about opening their country to foreign trade.[122]

Collaboration between Western and non-Western empires was generally less forthcoming, and any alliances formed to suppress maritime raiding were much more fragile. In the mid-1840s, after snatching Hong Kong from Qing China and forcing their opium trade on the Chinese, the British began a half-hearted charm offensive to appear as willing partners to the same people they had bombarded and occupied only a short time before.

Only a few months after the British victory and the signing of the Treaty of Nanjing, which he had negotiated, Henry Pottinger, at the time administrator of Hong Kong, wrote to Vice Admiral William Parker to bring him up to speed on recent developments in the vicinity of the colony. As we have seen before, Pottinger's approach was "civilly declined"; his Chinese counterparts communicated to him that they were "about to take measures for the total suppression of piracy" and did not need any foreign help.[123]

Over the coming months and years, amiable approaches continued. On repeated occasions British officers in the region claimed to have made offers to cooperate with their Chinese counterparts, only to be turned down more often than not. In virtually every one of these Chinese refusals, the British saw an aggravated offense against their efforts to suppress amphibious communities along the coast of China. Pottinger's successor in the government of Hong Kong, John Francis Davis, wrote to Lord Stanley a year later, in 1844, warning that "the Chinese police can never be trusted" in the colony under his command.[124] A few weeks later, when the Chinese decided to execute a man called Chintae, who was supposed to be a notorious pirate at the time, Davis saw the action as "a breach of good faith."[125] In his opinion, the imperial commissioner, Keying, had failed to surrender Chintae to the British, placing his country in breach of the treaties signed two years before. This circumstance, he pointed out, would make him "more cautious" when deciding whether to deliver future prisoners to "the authorities on the mainland."[126]

The correspondence between British officers during this period leaves little doubt that any decision taken by their Chinese counterparts regarding the problem of piracy, without consulting them, was viewed as an infringement of their supposedly cordial relationship and mutual trust. Based on these judgments, whenever maritime raiding activities in the region increased, they were quick to blame the Chinese for the lack of interest they had shown to punish these outlaws. In December 1844, Davis again complained about his counterparts, and he threatened Keying with taking measures to "root [Chinese pirates] out with great severity" irrespective of whether or not they were allowed to do so by the Chinese authorities.[127]

Years later, after the Chinese had voluntarily joined and participated in the naval operations against the fleets of Chui-a-poo and Shap-ng-tsai in the autumn of 1849, the British redoubled their complaints. In a letter sent to Lord Palmerston that October, Governor Bonham commented that he was certain that "the Chinese Government [was] altogether unable to cope with the Pirates."[128] In Bonham's opinion, the Chinese were more likely to bribe these maritime raiders into submission, cutting deals, offering them gifts, and then using them to attack their "former confederates."[129]

A similar dynamic of reproachment and mistrust took place among the people of the Riff, in northern Morocco, and the European powers who came to the region intent on suppressing the amphibious populations and taking away their lands. After their occupation of Algiers in 1830, the French did not hide their desire to expand their colonial territories toward the west. Perhaps due to their success in Algiers, the French considered themselves as the only European power capable of subduing the people of the Riff, arguing that Spain and Britain had little chance of organizing a successful colonial expedition toward what they considered to be a combined force of between eighty and one hundred thousand well-armed men with a superior knowledge of the terrain.[130]

The French were aware that the Spanish garrisons along the coast were little more than outposts and had very limited communication with the people of the Riff. Despite efforts to cultivate friendlier relations with those whose lands they had seized, the Spanish—like the British—often failed to establish any genuine rapport. Any success they achieved was largely due to threats and military force. In 1856, the British consul, Drummond Hay, tried to intercede, with little success, to stop the constant attacks between the Spanish at Melilla and Peñón de Vélez de la Gomera, and Saed Mohammed Katif and the Basha of the Riff.[131]

Drummond Hay was well aware of French colonial intentions, and he often raised them with the sultan of Morocco and with his superiors in London. That same year, 1856, he communicated to the Earl of Clarendon that should the sultan ignore advice regarding the need to suppress maritime raiding along the Riff Coast, he would likely provoke a French invasion and "occupation of his territory."[132] Drummond Hay was very clear about what he considered to be a French colonial threat when he stated that he doubted that the French would ever return any occupied territory in the region, and that, instead, they were likely to continue their campaigns "for the aggrandizement connected with their Algerine colony."[133]

Drummond Hay's fears were probably well-founded; only a few weeks earlier he had been forced to send a British cruiser toward the Riff, dreading that the French had "entered" or were about "to enter the Reef with an army."[134] In addition to sending a gunship, Drummond Hay considered sending an army to prevent French troops from moving west toward Morocco.[135] All in all, France's colonial ambitions in this part of the world hindered any sort of collaboration between them and the local populations and in fact resulted in long-term military conflicts. In the meantime, their main competitors, the Spanish and the British, bided their time by allying with the sultan of Morocco and local chiefs, while keeping diplomatic channels open with the French.

The anonymous author of an article focusing on European affairs in East Asia, published in 1860 in the French magazine *Revue des deux Mondes*, praised the support France had received from Spain during its recent Cochin China campaign. After discussing how the French had for years been observing with jealously the advances of other European colonial powers in the region, and noticing the relevance of this unusual Franco-Spanish coalition, the author proceeded to probe the real intentions of the expedition. In a line that brought into question the raison d'être of the attack on the Cochin China, he commented that the "desire to avenge the murder of a bishop," the main excuse given by the French for launching the attack, did not seem to him "a sufficient motive" to carry out such a large and complex military venture.[136] In a few lines, the author succeeded in implying both that the alliance had been a success mostly thanks to the Spanish support and that it had clearly been instigated by concealed motivations.

Inter-imperial relations were rarely unidirectional or stable, often fluctuating according to metropolitan policies, trading ambitions, or colonial enterprises. On occasion, empires could come together to face what they considered to be a common foe, and other times they would not hesitate to take advantage of each other. As David Todd stated while examining mid-nineteenth-century Anglo-French imperial relations, on occasions when these two empires collaborated, such collaboration was "neither perfectly balanced nor stable," mostly due to Britain's "naval and economic superiority."[137] The Anglo-French relationship was not unique, and the reasons behind the lack of balance referred to by Todd were frequently found in other inter-imperial relationships.

In spite of their frequent disagreements, pirate imperial powers occasionally found ways to collaborate, especially when it came to subduing and conquering others. That they found common ground in the suppression of the amphibious peoples they decided to label as "pirates" should not come as a surprise to anyone. Suppression efforts helped pirate empires fulfill an array of further ambitions: acquiring trading advantages and privileges; expanding and strengthening their colonial possessions; dislodging and annihilating "savage" seafaring communities that stood in the way of commerce, "civilization," and the abolition of slavery and slave trading.

On some occasions, fighting amphibious peoples also brought together Western and non-Western empires. Non-Western imperialist states, such as Siam, took advantage of conflicts fueled by their European counterparts, at times outplaying them in the process to secure their own goals. They did so while showing a deep awareness and distrust of their Western counterparts. As Chao Phraya Prayurawongse, governor of Southern Siam at the time, warned Siamese officers in recently reconquered Kedah in 1839, "The English had had for a long time a desire to wait for an opportunity . . . to make Mueang Sai (Alor Setar) their own."[138] He then ordered the swift appointment of a governor of Kedah, as any delays would have given the British an opportunity to claim the territory as theirs.[139]

Disagreements between empires were frequent and deep rooted in their trading and colonial ambitions. Western and non-Western empires often confronted each other, sometimes over minor concerns and other times while seeking hyperbolic restitution or reparation claims for what they considered to be affronts to their flags and honor. These disagreements were frequently fueled by local merchant and colonial elites, eager to expand their spheres of influence and profits and using and altering "European doctrines of international law in conflicts over sovereignty and self-determination" to do so.[140]

Ultimately, the symbiotic relationships between Western and non-Western pirate empires were defined by complex dynamics based on self-interests and ambitions. Pirate empires fought each other, fed off each other, and inspired each other, from the actions of the Portuguese in Macau to the ways that joint abolition efforts along the African coast turned into independent prospecting proto-colonial expeditions, which served as a preamble to the scramble for Africa decades later.

Conclusions

> The conquest of the earth, which mostly means the taking it away from those who have a different complexion or slightly flatter noses than ourselves, is not a pretty thing when you look into it too much.
>
> —JOSEPH CONRAD, *The Heart of Darkness*, 1899

ON THE MORNING OF NOVEMBER 15, 1861, a Spanish naval force commanded by Frigate Captain Casto Méndez Núñez began a truly unconventional attack on an amphibious community at the cotta (fort) of Pagalungan, in Mindanao's Rio Grande, within the sultanate of Tumbao (Kabuntalan). According to Antonio Vázquez de Aldana and Valentín González Serrano, who chronicled the event fifteen years later, Méndez Núñez had no option but to attack the fort after its inhabitants had fired at his vessels' crews when they had tried to interact with them. To these two chroniclers, the real reason behind the assault, however, had been the need to quell the "savage instincts of rapine against the Christian people" of the river.[1]

Infused with the conceit typical of pirate imperialist agents during that era, Méndez Núñez positioned his vessels in front of the Pagalungan fort. Within the small fortress, hundreds of men had entrenched themselves, anticipating an armed assault. Méndez Núñez ordered a dual attack, by both land and water. Giving lie to the notion that the Spanish were the more civilized party in this dispute, he turned down a negotiating party sent by his adversaries. He extinguished any chance of a possible peaceful solution to the crisis by telling them that they were not there "to make treaties, but to castigate their provocation."[2]

Seeing that resisting would be their only option, the delegation returned to the fort and prepared for battle. The Spanish force, numbering several ships and a large contingent of men, proceeded to attack the fort by land. In an unexpected twist, their advance was hindered by an overlooked ditch; this glaring blunder resulted in significant casualties among their ranks. Remarkably, among the officers who commanded this attack were two who would go on to play crucial roles in the pirate imperialist history of Spain in years to come. José Malcampo, a lieutenant at the time, would eventually be appointed captain general of the Philippines. In that position, he would lead a bloody invasion against Joló years later, in 1876. Pascual Cervera, his second-in-command, would go on to become admiral of the Spanish navy and would command the Spanish fleet famously destroyed by the US Navy just outside the harbor of Santiago de Cuba at the end of the Spanish-American War in 1898.

Two days after the first assault was repelled, on the seventeenth, Méndez Núñez chose a form of attack never seen before. Taking advantage of the fact that his steamship, the *Constancia*, was a state-of-the-art, iron-plated vessel, he decided to lunge the ship forward at full steam, charging the fort with its bow, a move that allowed his sailors to jump from the ship directly into the yard of the fortress. This truly peculiar development was praised by the Spanish press for years to come, and it was immortalized in a watercolor by Rafael Monleón, which captures the precise moment at which the prow of the *Constancia* crashed through the fort's walls.

In their narrative, Vázquez de Aldana and González Serrano noted how unique this attack had been. They emphasized that previously boarding actions had always been "from ship to ship," and that with this assault the Spanish navy had given the term "boarding" a new meaning.[3] The crashing of the *Constancia* into a "pirate" fort by Méndez Núñez and his men is, perhaps, the most

Attack on the cotta of Pagalungan on November 17, 1861, by the Spanish forces under the command of D. Casto Méndez Núñez, by Rafael Monleón. Museo Naval de Madrid.

apt metaphor for the sort of pirate imperialism discussed in the pages of this book. This sort of pirate imperialism, supported by a new armed peace regime, had become by then common practice in virtually every corner of the world. Its consequences, too, are reflective of the outcomes of pirate imperial actions worldwide during these years.

Not only had the Spanish decided to attack following what would barely register as a provocation, blaming the local amphibious community for the carnage that followed, but they did so after their would-be victims sought to negotiate a peaceful outcome to the crisis. Once the Spanish decided to launch their offensive, they were implacable. According to Méndez Núñez's calculations, at least two hundred "moros" had been killed and many others had been wounded.[4] The bodies of the dead defenders were everywhere; they were eventually thrown into the river, to "serve as witnesses to the river inhabitants of what a few Spaniards had done to the proud defenders of the impregnable cotta of Pagalungan."[5] Their "savage howls" silenced by their deaths were, to Vázquez de Aldana and González Serrano, a clear sign of the "triumph of the cross."[6] Nevertheless, to the ancestral inhabitants of the river and their families, the events of the cotta of Pagalungan, like many before, were nothing but a needless massacre, an unwarranted loss of life carried out in the name of the Christian god for commercial and colonial purposes.

This story of overpowering brutality repeated itself, throughout the world, time and again during the nineteenth century. Comparable acts of pirate imperialism were documented in Atlantic Africa, across the Mediterranean Sea and the Persian Gulf, along the Indian Ocean, in the South China Sea, and in numerous other regions. During the mid-years of the nineteenth century, when Western pirate imperialist powers were in full swing, scarcely any amphibious community escaped their devastating impact. Such actions were part of a global regime of armed peace. In the words of Lauren Benton, "In the long nineteenth century, armed intervention was defined as a European right," and based on this assumption, virtually every type of behavior, especially when carried out far away from the metropolitan centers, was viable, and more often than not accepted and even cheered.[7]

The full-on charging of the Pagalungan fort by a state-of-the-art, iron-plated steamer also reveals the extent to which technological advancements played a key role in the pirate imperialist victories of this period. This attack constitutes an archetypical instance of what historian Priya Satia has called "mechanized killing" and "mechanized warfare."[8] By the mid-nineteenth century newly introduced, more advanced weapons came accompanied by superior vessels, making possible more decisive and lethal actions against amphibious populations. Although pirate imperialist powers continued to expand through a combination of diplomatic and armed means, technological advances allowed them to carry out many of their diplomatic negotiations under the long-range, more accurate guns mounted on their state-of-the-art steamers.

Both the diplomatic and the armed types of suppression of maritime raiding were claimed to be absolutely essential for the spread of "civilization"; for the abolition of slavery and the slave trade (although not for other forms of indentured labor); for the opening of foreign ports to Western products, whenever possible at preferential prices; and, finally, for the consolidation of colonial territorial gains. These claims, however, were constantly undermined by the behavior exhibited by pirate imperial leaders, agents, and army and navy officers in different parts of the world, which occasionally included conflicts among themselves. Efforts to suppress "piracy" in the nineteenth century, when scrutinized, can be revealed for what they truly were, namely, proxies for formal and informal imperialist ventures.

The imperative to civilize and Christianize amphibious populations served as a pivotal component within the narratives propagated by pirate imperialism. This rationale was employed to validate both diplomatic and military strategies. Intertwined with the aims of expansion and the imposition of Western laws on non-Western societies, notions of civilization were both utilized and manipulated by every Western pirate empire of that era. By categorizing amphibious communities into civilized or uncivilized groups, Western pirate imperialist agents created a system of exclusion, which, in the words of Priyamvada Gopal, worked "to effect colonial divisions," and, more important, justified the "appropriation of their land and labour."[9] Such a system also served to justify extreme acts of violence, including massacres, and at least tentatively, it provided an ideological footing to those who argued for replacement theories.

Likewise, mid-nineteenth-century pirate imperialism adeptly capitalized on the growing and impassioned demands for the abolition of the slave trade and slavery. Behind this façade agents could further their aims of extending trade routes, strengthening commercial privileges, and expanding colonial dominion. Cloaking themselves in this noble cause, the proponents of pirate imperialism imposed treaties and dispossessed amphibious communities. In certain instances, this coercion forced many communities to resort to maritime raiding as a means of survival.

Abolition, therefore, served as a convenient tool, but its application was tailored to individual circumstances. Whereas numerous pirate imperialist nations wholeheartedly engaged in efforts to curtail human trafficking conducted by their adversaries in certain regions, such as the South China Sea or Southeast Asia, they simultaneously provided either implicit or explicit support for the slave trade and enslavement practices in their colonies across the Atlantic world. More important, their willingness—or lack thereof—to prosecute "pirates" involved in slave trading took on an even more distinctive character, invariably influenced by such factors as the skin color, nationality, and cultural background of those who were apprehended while engaged in the trafficking and enslavement of fellow human beings. Ultimately, as many authors have indicated over the years, there was much hypocrisy associated with abolitionist efforts across the world.[10] When it came to prosecuting slave traders caught red-handed in acts of piracy, pirate imperial laws were fully applied or not, depending on whether those accused were Western white Christians, or not.

The deployment of civilization and abolition tropes, while serving their purposes, ultimately amounted to justifications for ideas and actions that would have otherwise faced condemnation. In contrast, the needs to consolidate commercial routes and expand markets for pirate imperialist products, were very real and consequential reasons behind efforts to intimidate, suppress, displace, and massacre amphibious populations. As Nathan Perl-Rosenthal put it recently, the suppression of maritime raiding allowed the "British and others" to further expand their "internationalist claims over maritime law."[11] In doing so, they succeeded in seeking and establishing new corridors of commerce, altering trading dynamics wherever they arrived and regularly encroaching on local amphibious populations and forcing many of them to turn to maritime raiding in order to survive. The Spanish assault on the fort of Pagalungan is but one among many cases where pirate imperialist agents felt the need to chastise those who opposed their presence, under the guise of avenging bogus affronts against their flags, honor, ships, or men.

Whether done in the spirit of protectionism or free trade, these actions epitomized a sanctimonious belief in the superiority of Western cultures and laws, with its right to impose "superior" forms of trade upon other peoples, even upon those who, like the Siamese or the Japanese, initially refused to accept them. Pirate empires systematically extended their spheres of influence across the globe, employing a blend of diplomatic negotiations and military force. When make-believe acts of friendship failed to work, they resorted to threats and violence to achieve their aims. The commercial rewards they promised to amphibious populations did not entail parity of access or profit but, as these communities soon found out, were instead devised for the benefit of pirate imperialist powers.

The ultimate consummation of pirate imperialism was the dispossession, by deception or force, of amphibious populations' lands and waters. As with the need to advance trade opportunities, dispossessing amphibious communities of their ancestral lands and waters was frequently presented to the public as a necessary step—as the only way of bringing these amphibious peoples into the fold of the family of civilized and lawful nations. To imperial nations, exceptional circumstances justified extraordinary actions, even when these actions were exceedingly brutal and, at times, tantamount to genocide. And so, through a combination of deception and violence, those peoples designated as "pirates" by Western expansionist states, regardless of whether they were involved in maritime raiding or not, soon found themselves at the end of all sorts of diplomatic subterfuges and cannonades.

Pirate imperial agents were so immersed in their diplomatic schemes and colonial conquests that they documented them in great detail, expecting accolades from their contemporaries. The men involved in this work rarely foresaw how perceptions of different peoples would evolve over time. On multiple occasions attacks were directed against amphibious communities accused—with reason or not—of participating in maritime raids, with the resulting conquest and colonization of their lands and waters, or at the very least in attempts of doing so. From the stratagems employed by James Brooke throughout Borneo to the calculated expropriation of Kowloon at the end of the Second Opium War, the British demonstrated exceptional proficiency in expanding their colonial territories during this era. But they were by no means the sole actors in this endeavor. Western and non-Western empires alike frequently and unapologetically engaged in pirate imperial activities, often resorting to brute force without hesitation to accomplish their objectives.

As their empires and commercial benefits expanded throughout the world in the middle decades of the nineteenth century, they fought each other for privileges and territories that had belonged to distant amphibious communities for generations. Even after entering into treaties and agreements, which almost invariably favored them at the expense of these same communities, they persisted in exploiting each other's weaknesses to stake claims on lands, waterways, and spheres of influence. Occasionally, however, they also found ways to set aside their differences and forge formidable alliances against the peoples they had singled out as their targets.

Not surprisingly, these amphibious communities, often dubbed as "pirates" in most of the primary sources we have inherited, did not go quietly. In this book I have focused on the actions of pirate imperialist states and agents and did not delve into the other side of the story—the courageous and recurrent acts of resistance carried out by the men, women, and children in defense of their ancestral lands and waters. But the global history of the suppression of maritime raiding and amphibious communities has a corresponding counterpart: the resistance to pirate imperialism. This little-studied aspect of the story requires comprehensive exploration, not in the fragmented accounts recounted thus far but as an integral component of global history.

Although the majority of existing primary sources on this topic were generated by these very same pirate imperialist states, there are compelling reasons to suggest that there is ample material to construct a history of the resistance to their hydrarchic advances. Numerous cases discussed in the chapters of this book offer insights into the specific choices made by those who faced attacks from British, Spanish, Siamese, or Ottoman forces during that era.[12] Further study is needed.

Diplomatic and armed strategies, justified by a Western legal corpus and often involving deception and disproportionate violence, constituted the primary features of pirate imperialism and its interactions with amphibious communities worldwide during the mid-nineteenth century. Wielding the power of Western traditions and the principles of the Law of Nations, pirate empires and their agents arbitrarily determined who would be classified as a pirate and who would not. The repercussions of these decisions were significant and frequently fatal. The excessive violence linked to the expansionist projects of pirate imperialism was evident even to those who represented it in various forms. It is no wonder that at the end of the century one of the most notorious champions of the British Empire, author Rudyard Kipling, referred to these actions as "the savage wars of peace," while adding his voice to those that attempted to present these violent armed actions as a necessary evil.[13]

In the afterword of a recently published book focusing on the issues of maritime raiding and its suppression worldwide, Lauren A. Benton highlighted the need of "repositioning sea raiders as full participants in regional politics."[14] Doing so, she contended, would enable scholars to put forward "alternative narratives of piracy in international law."[15] In this book, I have tried to follow Benton's advice, not by examining those who were labeled as "pirates" but by focusing instead on those who labeled and suppressed them. I have done so in the hope of exposing, as Richard Drayton has requested from historians of imperialism, the exploitation and inequalities embedded in global imperial interactions of the period.[16] This approach serves to illuminate the active involvement of native populations in regional politics while prompting questions and categorizing the methods through which pirate imperial powers identified and repressed them throughout the era. The result, I hope, is precisely an alternative global history of these suppression efforts, their true motivations and intentions, and the severe consequences they had upon the amphibious communities that had the bad fortune of becoming their targets.

Notes

Introduction

1. Bonham to T[homas] H[erbert] Maddock. Prince of Wales Island, February 27, 1841. National Archives of Singapore, Singapore (hereafter NAS): R. 6 Governor's Letters to Bengal. Jan. 1840–Feb. 1841.
2. Minute by the Honorable A. Amos Esq. [1841]. British Library, London (hereafter BL): IOR/F/4/1920.
3. Minute by the Honorable A. Amos Esq. [1841]; See also Bonham to Maddock. Prince of Wales Island, January 26, 1841. BL: IOR/F/4/1920.
4. Minute by the Right Honorable the Governor General [Lord Auckland]. March 13, 1841. BL: IOR/F/4/1920. For an insight into the extensive negotiations that led to the signing of this treaty, see *The Burney Papers* (Bangkok: Vajiranana National Library, 1910), vol. 1.
5. Bonham to Maddock. Prince of Wales Island, January 26, 1841. NAS: R. 6. Governor's Letters to Bengal. January 1840–February 1841.
6. Orlando Fals Borda, *Historia doble de la costa* (Bogotá: Carlos Valencia Editores, 1979), vol. 1, 19A–22B. For a more recent evaluation of the concept of "amphibious cultures," see Valeria Mantilla Morales, "Amphibious Landings: Free People of Color, Food Supply, and Contested Land Tenure on the Magdalena River Network," *Atlantic Studies* 21, no. 1 (2024): 70–89.
7. Lauren Benton, *They Called It Peace: Worlds of Imperial Violence* (Princeton: Princeton University Press, 2024), 19.
8. Peter Earle, *The Pirate Wars* (London: Methuen, 2003), 111. See also Stefan Eklöf Amirell, *Pirates of Empire: Colonisation and Maritime Violence in Southeast Asia* (Cambridge: Cambridge University Press, 2019), 27–31.
9. Richard Drayton has argued for the need to recognize and discuss in more depth the power imbalances, often tainted by violence, associated with the ways in which Western empires exerted domination over various

parts of the world. See, for example, Richard Drayton, "Where Does the World Historian Write From? Objectivity, Moral Conscience and the Past and Present of Imperialism," *Journal of Contemporary History* 46, no. 3 (2008): 671–85.

10. Richard Drayton, "Imperial History and the Human Future," *History Workshop Journal* 74, no. 1 (2012): 156–172.
11. See, for example, Henry Arderne Ormerod, *Piracy in the Ancient World* (New York: Dorset Press, 1987); Philip de Souza, *Piracy in the Graeco-Roman World* (Cambridge: Cambridge University Press, 2002); and Richard J. Evans and Martine De Marre, eds., *Piracy, Pillage, and Plunder in Antiquity: Appropriation and the Ancient World* (London: Routledge, 2020), among others.
12. Some recent works on maritime raiding in the Middle Ages are: Dirk Meier, *Seefahrer, Händler und Piraten im Mittelalter* (Ostfildern: Thorbecke Jan Verlag, 2004); Jill Eddison, *Medieval Pirates: Pirates, Raiders and Privateers, 1204–1453* (Stroud: The History Press, 2013); and Peter D. Shapinsky, *Lords of the Sea: Pirates, Violence, and Commerce in Late Medieval Japan* (Ann Arbor: University of Michigan Press, 2014).
13. The system worked for most of the time, although bad weather often caused serious issues to its ships. At least once, the fleet was successfully attacked and seized, just outside the harbor of Matanzas, by Dutch privateer Piet Hein. See Ronald Prud'homme van Reine, *Admiraal Zilvervloot: Biografie van Piet Hein* (Amsterdam: De Arbeiderspers, 2003). For the sixteenth-century attacks to Havana and the rest of Cuba, see Carlos Alberto Hernández Oliva, *Corsarios y piratas en La Habana: Siglo XVI* (Seville: Ed. Renacimiento, 2020).
14. Salvatore Bono, *Corsari nel Mediterraneo* (Perugia: Oscar Storia Mondadori, 1993).
15. Angelo Mercati, *Saggi di storia e letteratura* (Rome: Storia e letteratura, 1982), vol. 2.
16. James K. Chin, "Merchants, Smugglers, and Pirates: Multinational Clandestine Trade on the South China Coast, 1520–50." In Robert J. Antony, ed., *Elusive Pirates, Pervasive Smugglers Violence and Clandestine Trade in the Greater China Seas* (Hong Kong: Hong Kong University Press, 2010), 43–57.
17. Among the most insightful studies of Golden Age piracy are: Marcus Rediker, *Villains of All Nations: Atlantic Pirates in the Golden Age* (Boston: Beacon Press, 2004) and David Head, ed., *The Golden Age of Piracy: The Rise, Fall, and Enduring Popularity of Pirates* (Athens: University of Georgia Press, 2018).
18. For early examples of this romanticizing of pirates, see Douglas R. Burgess Jr., "Piracy in the Public Sphere: The Henry Every Trials and the Battle for Meaning in Seventeenth-Century Print Culture," *Journal of British Studies* 48, no. 4 (2009): 887–913.

19. Peter Linebaugh and Marcus Rediker, *The Many-Headed Hydra: Sailors, Slaves, Commoners, and the Hidden History of the Revolutionary Atlantic* (London: Verso, 2000).
20. For recent studies of piracy and privateering in the Atlantic World before the nineteenth century, see Mark G. Hanna, *Pirate Nests and the Rise of the British Empire, 1570–1740* (Chapel Hill: University of North Carolina Press, 2015), and Ernesto Bassi, *An Aqueous Territory: Sailor Geographies and New Granada's Transimperial Greater Caribbean World* (Chapel Hill: University of North Carolina Press, 2017).
21. Charles James Fitzmorris to Robert Monroe Harrison. St. Barts, May 22, 1822. Arquivo Nacional de Torre da Tombo, Lisbon (hereafter ANTT): Ministerio dos Negocios Estrangeiros. Cx. 113.
22. Fitzmorris to Monroe Harrison. St. Barts, May 22, 1822. ANTT: Ministerio dos Negocios Estrangeiros. Cx. 113.
23. [Apollinaire] Boutineff to Le Reiss Effendi (or Head Clerk). Constantinople, December 17, 1829. Başbakanlık Osmanlı Arşivi, Istanbul (hereafter BOA): HR.TO 1532/1.
24. Robert J. Antony, "Scourges on the People: Perceptions of Robbery, Snatching, and Theft," *Late Imperial China* 16, no. 2 (1995): 99.
25. Antony, "Scourges on the People," 99–100.
26. Dian H. Murray, *Pirates of the South China Coast, 1790–1810* (Stanford: Stanford University Press, 1987).
27. Nicholas Tarling, *Piracy and Politics in the Malay World: A Study of British Imperialism in Nineteenth-Century South-East Asia* (Melbourne: F. W. Cheshire, 1963); and *Imperial Britain in South-East Asia* (Kuala Lumpur: Oxford University Press, 1975); James F. Warren, *The Sulu Zone, 1768–1898: The Dynamics of External Trade, Slavery, and Ethnicity in the Transformation of a Southeast Asian Maritime State* (Singapore: NUS Press, 1981); Alfred P. Rubin, *The Law of Piracy* (Newport, RI: Naval War College Press, 1988); J. L. Anderson, "Piracy and World History: An Economic Perspective on Maritime Predation," *Journal of World History* 6, no. 2 (1995): 175–199; Joseph N. F. M. à Campo, "Discourse without Discussion: Representations of Piracy in Colonial Indonesia, 1816–1825," *Journal of Southeast Asian Studies* 34, no. 2 (2003): 199–214; Amirell, *Pirates of Empire;* Sandy J. C. Liu, "Violence and Piratical/Surreptitious Activities Associated with the Chinese Communities in the Melaka-Singapore Region, 1780–1840," in In Y. H. Teddy Sim, ed., *Piracy and Surreptitious Activities in the Malay Archipelago and Adjacent Seas, 1600–1840* (Singapore: Springer, 2014), 51–76; and Simon Layton, "Discourses of Piracy in an Age of Revolutions," *Itinerario* 35, no. 2 (2011): 81–97.
28. Sugata Bose, *A Hundred Horizons: The Indian Ocean in the Age of Global Empire* (Cambridge, MA: Harvard University Press, 2006), 44.
29. James F. Warren, "The Structure of Slavery in the Sulu Zone in the Late Eighteenth and Nineteenth Centuries," *Slavery & Abolition* 24, no. 2 (2003): 111–112.

30. Kristie Flannery, *Piracy and the Making of the Spanish Pacific World* (Philadelphia: University of Pennsylvania Press, 2024).
31. Patricia Risso, "Cross-Cultural Perceptions of Piracy: Maritime Violence in the Western Indian Ocean and Persian Gulf Region during a Long Eighteenth Century," *Journal of World History* 12, no. 2 (2001): 315.
32. Layton, "Discourses of Piracy," 84.
33. Manuel Barcia, "Cause and Consequence: Slave Trade, Piracy, and the Law in the Cases of the Spanish Schooners *Panda* and *Amistad*," *Journal of Early American History* (forthcoming).
34. Leonidas Mylonakis, *Piracy in the Eastern Mediterranean: Maritime Marauders in the Greek and Ottoman Aegean* (London: I. B. Tauris, 2021), 18–19.
35. Risso, "Cross-Cultural Perceptions."
36. *Treaty between His Britannick Majesty and the King of the Netherlands Respecting Territory and Commerce in the East Indies.* Signed at London, March 17, 1824 (London: R. G. Clarke, 1824).
37. Jennifer Pitts, *Boundaries of the International: Law and Empire* (Cambridge, MA: Harvard University Press, 2018), 6, 19.
38. Emerich de Vattel, *Le droit des gens ou principes de la loi naturelle appliqués à la conduite et aux affaires des nations et des souverains* (London: n.p, 1758), 2 vols.
39. De Vattel, *Le droit des gens*, 2.
40. Benton, "Legal Spaces of Empire: Piracy and the Origins of Ocean Regionalism," *Comparative Studies in Society and History* 47, no. 2 (2007): 724.
41. Benton, *They Called It Peace*, 19.
42. Benton, *They Called It Peace*, 17–18.
43. Pitts, *Boundaries*, 6.
44. Benton, "Legal Spaces," 724. See also Judith E. Tucker, "Piracy of the Eighteenth-Century Mediterranean: Navigating Laws and Legal Practices," in Judith E. Tucker, ed., *The Making of the Modern Mediterranean: Views from the South* (Berkeley: University of California Press, 2019), 123–148.
45. Benton, "Toward a New Legal History of Piracy: Maritime Legalities and the Myth of Universal Jurisdiction," *International Journal of Maritime History* 23, no. 1 (2011): 225–226.
46. Gerrit W. Gong, *The Standard of "Civilization" in International Society* (Oxford: Clarendon Press, 1984), 24.
47. Gong, *Standard of "Civilization."*
48. See C. H. Alexandrowicz, David Armitage, and Jennifer Pitts, eds., *The Law of Nations in Global History* (Oxford: Oxford University Press, 2017).
49. John Crawfurd, *A Descriptive Dictionary of the Indian Islands and Adjacent Countries* (London: Bradbury & Evans, 1856), 353. In recent years, Crawfurd's conclusions have been challenged in Jennifer L. Gaynor, *Intertidal History in Island Southeast Asia: Submerged Genealogy and the Legacy of Coastal Capture* (Ithaca: Cornell University Press, 2016).

50. Amedeo Policante, *The Pirate Myth: Genealogies of an Imperial Concept* (London: Routledge, 2015), 127.
51. Layton, "Discourses of Piracy," 88.
52. See, for example, the way in which Chappell has discussed such protocols between states. Jonathan Chappell, "Maritime Raiding, International Law and the Suppression of Piracy on the South China Coast, 1842–1869," *International History Review* 40, no. 3 (2018): 473.
53. Layton, "Discourses of Piracy," 86.
54. Amirell, *Pirates of Empire*, 7.
55. à Campo, "Discourse without Discussion," 202. For the original report, see Rapport van de Ch. Van Angelbeek omtrent Zijne Zending naar naar Riouw, 1825. Nederland National Archief, The Hague (hereafter NNA): Ministerie van Kolonien, 498.
56. Butterworth to F[rederick] J[ames] Halliday. Singapore, April 12, 1850. NAS: R. 15. Governor's Letters to Bengal. Jan. 1847–April 1851.
57. Kim A. Wagner. *Thuggee: Banditry and the British in Early Nineteenth-Century India* (London: Palgrave Macmillan, 2007), 200.
58. Henry Wise to the Earl of Malmelsbury. Lloyds, London, April 26, 1852. Oxford University Weston Library, Oxford (hereafter OUWL): Papers of the Brookes of Sarawak. MSS Pac. s. 66.
59. See, for example, Yi-faai Laai, "The Part Played by the Pirates of Kwangtung and Kwangsi Provinces in the Taiping Insurrection" (PhD diss., University of California at Berkeley, 1950), 74–77.
60. This problem is far from over. Some recent titles have continued to use the terms "piracy" and "pirate" in the same uncritical way. See, for example, Graham A. Thomas, *Pirate Killers: The Royal Navy and the African Pirates* (Barnsley: Pen & Sword, 2011) and Julio Albi de la Cuesta, *Moros; España contra los piratas musulmanes de Filipinas, 1574–1896* (Madrid: Desperta Ferros, 2022).
61. Charles Belgrave, *The Pirate Coast* (London: G. Bell and Sons, 1966); Bose, *Hundred Horizons*, 44; and Layton, "Discourses of Piracy," 84; and "The 'Moghul's Admiral': Angrian 'Piracy' and the Rise of British Bombay," *Journal of Early Modern History* 17, no. 1 (2013): 75–93.
62. See, for example, the otherwise excellent works by Iain Ward, *Sui Geng: The Hong Kong Marine Police, 1841–1950* (Hong Kong: Hong Kong University Press, 1991); Patricia Lim, *Forgotten Souls: A Social History of the Hong Kong Cemetery* (Hong Kong: Hong Kong University Press, 2011); and Robert J. Antony, "Violence and Predation on the Sino-Vietnamese Maritime Frontier, 1450–1850," *Asia Major* 27, part 2 (2014): 87–114.
63. Anderson, "Piracy and World History."
64. J. L. Anderson, "Piracy in the Eastern Seas, 1750–1850: Some Economic Implications," in D. Starkey, E. S. van Eyck van Heslinga, and J. A. de Moor, eds., *Pirates and Privateers: New Perspectives on the War on Trade in the Eighteenth and Nineteenth Centuries* (Exeter: University of Exeter Press, 1997), 190.

65. Anderson, "Piracy and World History," 181.
66. Anderson, "Piracy and World History," 181.
67. Among these exceptions are Amanda M. Evans, "Institutionalized Piracy and the Development of the Jamaica Sloop, 1630–1743" (PhD diss., Florida State University, 2005); Emrys Chew, *Arming the Periphery: The Arms Trade in the India Ocean during the Age of Global Empire* (London: Palgrave Macmillan, 2012); and R. J. Blackmore, "The Politics of Piracy in the British Atlantic, c. 1640–1649," *International Journal of Maritime History* 25, no. 2 (2013): 159–172.
68. Warren, *Sulu Zone;* Lauren Benton, *A Search for Sovereignty: Law and Geography in European Empires, 1400–1900* (Cambridge: Cambridge University Press, 2009); Patricia A. Risso, *Merchants and Faith: Muslim Commerce and Culture in the Indian Ocean* (London: Taylor & Francis, 2018); Amirell, *Pirates of Empire;* and David Wilson, *Suppressing Piracy in the Early Eighteenth Century: Pirates, Merchants and British Imperial Authority in the Atlantic and Indian Oceans* (Woodbridge: Boydell Press, 2021).
69. Pitts, *Boundaries*, 9.
70. Pitts, *Boundaries*, 21; Julia Gaffield, "The Racialization of International Law after the Haitian Revolution: The Holy See and National Sovereignty," *American Historical Review* 125, no. 3 (2020): 841–868; and James Forde, *The Early Haitian State and the Question of Political Legitimacy: American and British Representations of Haiti, 1804–1824* (London: Palgrave MacMillan, 2020).
71. Marqués de Olivart, *Colección de los tratados, convenios y documentos internacionales celebrados por nuestros gobiernos con los estados extranjeros desde el reinado de Doña Isabel II hasta nuestros días* (Madrid: El Progreso Editorial, 1890), vol. 1.
72. Anita M. C. van Dissel, "Grensoverschrijdend optreden. Zeerof en zeerofbestrijding in Nederlands-Indië," *Leidschrift* 26, no. 3 (2011): 165.
73. J. P. P. Cornets de Groot, *Notices Historiques sur les Pirateries, commises dans l'Archipel Indien-Oriental, et sur les mesures prises pour les réprimer par le gouvernement Néerlandais, dans les trente dernières années* (La Haye: Belinfante Fréres, 1847), 55.
74. See "Foreign Anti-Slave Trade Bill" (Hansard, May 1815), and "An Act to Protect the Commerce of the United States and Punish the Crime of Piracy." March 3, 1819, specifically the amendments made in 1820. See also Randy J. Sparks, "Blind Justice: The United States's Failure to Curb the Illegal Slave Trade," *Law and History Review* 35, no. 1 (2017): 53–79.
75. *Treaty of Amity and Commerce between His Majesty and the Emperor of Brazil. Signed at Rio de Janeiro, August 17, 1827* (London: R. G. Clarke, 1828).
76. *Convention between Her Majesty and the King of the French for the Suppression of the Traffic in Slaves. Signed at London, May 29, 1845* (London: T. R. Harrison, 1845).

77. Treaty between Her Majesty and the Oriental Republick of the Uruguay for the Abolition of the Traffick in Slaves. Signed at Montevideo, July 13, 1839 (London: T. R. Harrison, 1842); General Treaty between Her Majesty and the Republick of Texas, for the Suppression of the African Slave Trade. Signed at London, November 16, 1840 (London: T. R. Harrison, 1842); Treaty between Her Majesty and the Queen of Portugal for the Suppression of the Traffick in Slaves. Signed in Lisbon, July 3, 1842 (London: T. R. Harrison, 1842); and Treaty of Friendship and Commerce between Her Majesty and the Sultan of Borneo. Signed in the English and Malay Languages, May 27, 1847 (London: T. R. Harrison, 1849).
78. Risso, "Cross-Cultural Perceptions," 315.
79. Hideaki Suzuki, *Slave Trade Profiteers in the Western Indian Ocean: Suppression and Resistance in the Nineteenth Century* (London: Palgrave Macmillan, 2017), 43.
80. Fahad Ahmad Bishara, *A Sea of Debt: Law and Economic Life in the Western Indian Ocean, 1780–1950* (Cambridge: Cambridge University Press, 2017), 32.
81. Carl E. Franklin, *British Rockets of the Napoleonic and Colonial Wars, 1805–1901* (Stroud: Spellmount, 2005).
82. Priya Satia, *Empire of Guns: The Violent Making of the Industrial Revolution* (New York: Penguin Press, 2018), esp. chapter 9.
83. For an extended discussion of the Paixhan cannons, see Henry Thomas Adams, "L'évolution du canon obusier Paixhans et sa place dans la marine française de la première moitié du XIX siècle" (PhD diss., Paris-Sorbonne University, 1994).
84. Satia, *Empire of Guns*, chapter 6.
85. James P. Baxter III, *The Introduction of the Ironclad Warship* (Cambridge, MA: Harvard University Press, 1933).
86. See W. H. Hall and W. D. Bernard, *The Nemesis in China, Comprising A History of the Late War in that Country; with an Account of the Colony of Hong-Kong* (London: Henry Colburn, 1847); and Adrian G. Marshall, *Nemesis: The First Iron Warship and Her World* (Stroud: The History Press, 2016).
87. Lawrence Sondhaus, *Naval Warfare, 1815–1914* (London: Routledge, 2001), 74–76.
88. Policante, *Pirate Myth*, 139. For a discussion on the use of extraterritorial violence in Europe before 1800, see the introductions and essays in Janice E. Thomson, *Mercenaries, Pirates, and Sovereigns: State-Building and Extraterritorial Violence in Early Modern Europe* (Princeton: Princeton University Press, 1994).
89. Policante, *Pirate Myth*.
90. See, Risso, "Cross-Cultural Perceptions," 293.
91. Van Dissel, "Grensoverschrijdend," 162.
92. Policante, *Pirate Myth*, 130.

93. Tarling, *Imperial Britain;* Sultan Muhammad Al-Qasimi, *The Myth of Arab Piracy in the Gulf* (Abingdon: Routledge, 1988); Charles E. Davies, *The Blood-Red Arab Flag: An Investigation into Qasimi Piracy, 1797–1820* (Exeter: University of Exeter Press, 1997); Robert J. Antony, ed., *Elusive Pirates;* Amirell, *Pirates of Empire;* Layton, "Discourses of Piracy."
94. See, for example, the slave trade voyages undertaken by the *Príncipe de Guiné* in 1826 (voyage id: 2965); the *Voladora* (776) and the *Midas* (777) in 1829; the *Segunda Socorro* in 1833 (2435); the *Formidable* (2469) in 1834; the *Eagle* (2615) and the *Clara* (2682) in 1839; the *Venus* (3458) in 1844; the *Veiga* (4082) and the *Harriet* (3812) in 1850; among many others. All identifying numbers correspond to those given to each of these voyages in the Transatlantic Slave Trade Database: https://www.slavevoyages.org.
95. Arthur Farquhar to Rear Admiral Francis Collier. HMS *Albatross*, Sarawak, August 25, 1849. House of Commons Parliamentary Papers (hereafter HCPP): Correspondence respecting Piracy on the Coast of Borneo, 1852.
96. Konemenos to Ali Pacha. Samos, September 25, 1851. BOA: HR.TO 416/5.
97. Marcus Rediker, *Outlaws of the Atlantic: Sailors, Pirates, and Motley Crews in the Age of Sail* (Boston: Beacon Press, 2014), 2–3; See also Rediker, "Hydrarchy and Terracentrism," in Alex Farquharson and Martin Clark, eds., *Aquatopia: The Imaginary of the Ocean Deep* (Nottingham: Nottingham Contemporary, 2014), 106–117; Rila Mukerjee, "Escape from Terracentrism: Writing a Water History," *Indian Historical Review* 41, no. 1 (2014): 87–101; Peter D. Shapinsky, *Lords of the Sea: Pirates, Violence, and Commerce in Late Medieval Japan* (Ann Arbor: University of Michigan Press, 2014); David Armitage, Alison Bashford, and Sujit Sivasundaram, eds., *Oceanic Histories* (Cambridge: Cambridge University Press, 2018); and Liam Campling and Alejandro Colás, *Capitalism and the Sea* (London: Verso, 2021).
98. Rediker, "Hydrarchy and Terracentrism."
99. Sherard Osborn, *My Journal in Malayan Waters; or the Blockade of Quedah* (London: Routledge, Warne and Routledge, 1860), 22, 156.
100. The *Hyacinth* was one of the vessels sent from Penang to establish a blockade of Kedah in 1838, shortly after the Malays retook the capital, Alor Setar, from the occupying Siamese forces. Osborn, *My Journal in Malayan Waters*, 22.
101. Ibbetson to George Swinton. Singapore, April 25, 1832. NAS: R. 1. Governor's Letters to Bengal. May 1831–August 1832.
102. José de Espronceda, "Canción del pirata," in *Obras* (Valparaíso: Imprenta del Mercurio, 1844), 103–106; for the *Long, Low Black Schooner*, see Rediker, *Outlaws of the Atlantic*, 154, 215.
103. Badger to A. K. Forbes. Aden, June 5, 1861. National Archives of India, New Delhi (hereafter NAI): Foreign. Political-A. Nos. 248/250.

Chapter One. Civilization and the Suppression of Maritime Raiding

1. Fernando de Norzagaray to the Secretary of State and Overseas Colonies. Manila, August 3, 1858. Archivo Histórico Nacional, Madrid (hereafter AHN): Ultramar, 5172/15.
2. James C. Warren, "In Search of Julano Taupan: His Life and His Times," *Journal of Indian Ocean World Studies* 4 (2020): 17–19.
3. Warren, "In Search of Julano Taupan."
4. Governor Narciso Clavería to the Secretary of State. Manila, February 28, 1848. National Archives of the Philippines, Manila (hereafter NAP): Cartas, 1847–1848.
5. Norzagaray to the President of the Council of Ministers. Manila, December 22, 1858. AHN: Ultramar, 5172/15.
6. Norzagaray to the President of the Council of Ministers. Manila, December 22, 1858. AHN: Ultramar, 5172/15.
7. Norzagaray to the President of the Council of Ministers. Manila, December 22, 1858. AHN: Ultramar, 5172/15. See also Warren, "In Search of Julano Taupan," 22–23.
8. Warren, "In Search of Julano Taupan."
9. Warren, "In Search of Julano Taupan."
10. Warren, "In Search of Julano Taupan," 23–24.
11. Eric Tagliacozzo, "Kettle in a Slow Boil: Batavia's Threat Perceptions in the Indies' Outer Islands, 1870–1910," *Journal of Southeast Asian Studies* 31, no. 1 (2000): 71.
12. James Kent, *Commentaries on American Law* (New York: O. Halstead, 1826), vol. 1, 171. In the decades following the publication of this lecture, Kent was frequently cited by authors defending "anti-piratical" activities carried out by piratical empires. See, for example, Scott Beresford, *An Account of the Destruction of the Fleets of the Celebrated Pirate Chieftains Chui-Apoo and Shap-Ng-Tsai, on the Coast of China, in September and October, 1849* (London: Saville and Edwards, 1851), 31.
13. Kent, *Commentaries on American Law*, vol. 1, 171–172.
14. Herbert Spencer, *Social Statics; or, the Conditions Essential to Human Happiness Specified and the First of Them Developed* (New York: Appleton, 1872), 464. See also Brett Bowden, *The Empire of Civilization: The Evolution of an Imperial Idea* (Chicago: University of Chicago Press, 2009), 133.
15. Bowden, *The Empire of Civilization*, 146–149; See also, Ellen P. Sullivan, "Liberalism and Imperialism: J. S. Mill's Defense of the British Empire," *Journal of the History of Ideas* 44, no. 4 (1983): 559–617.
16. John Crawfurd, *Journal of an Embassy from the Governor-General of India to the Courts of Siam and Cochin China; Exhibiting a View of the Actual State of Those Kingdoms* (London, H. Colburn and R. Bentley, 1830), 373.
17. Crawfurd, *Journal of an Embassy*, 373–374.
18. Bowden, *Empire of Civilization*, 147–148.

19. John Stuart Mill, "Civilization," *London and Westminster Review* (April 1836); *Dissertations and Discussions: Political, Philosophical and Historical* (London: John W. Parker and Son, 1859), 2 vols.; and James Mill, *The History of British India* (London: Baldwin, Cradock and Joy, 1817), 3 vols.
20. See, among others, Manuel Sales y Ferré, *Civilización Europea: Consideraciones acerca de su presente, su pasado y su porvenir* (Seville: José Ma. Ariza, 1887); *Historia e memorias da Academia Real das Sciencias de Lisboa* (Lisbon: Academia das Sciencias, 1825), esp. 126–127; and 156–157; F. W. Hostmann, *Over de beschaving van negers in Amerika, door kolonisatie met Europeanen, of beschouwingen omtrent de maatschappelijke vereeniging der negers in Afrika, den staat, waarin zij door den zoogenaamden slavenhandel komen, en later door abolitie en emancipatie overgaan Negers, niet door abolitie en emancipatie, maar alleen door kolonisatie te beschaven* (Amsterdam: J. C. A. Sulpke, 1850).
21. Matthew Burrows, " 'Mission civilisatrice': French Cultural Policy in the Middle East, 1860–1914," *Historical Journal* 29, no. 1 (1986): 109–135. See also David Todd, *A Velvet Empire: French Informal Imperialism in the Nineteenth Century* (Princeton: Princeton University Press, 2021), 48–51.
22. Jennifer Pitts, *A Turn to Empire: The Rise of Liberalism in Britain and France* (Princeton: Princeton University Press, 2009), 4.
23. Benton, *They Called It Peace*, 180.
24. See, for example, Homi Bhabha, "Of Mimicry and Man: The Ambivalence of Colonial Discourse," *Discipleship* 28 (1984): 125–133.
25. See, for example, Satia, *Empire of Guns.*
26. Weng Ching, *The Chinese Crisis from Within* (London: Grant Richards, 1901), 12.
27. Brooke to Palmerston. Sarawak, October 1, 1849. HCPP: Correspondence respecting Piracy on the Coast of Borneo, 1852.
28. British merchants and inhabitants of Singapore to Joseph Hume. Singapore, January 1851. HCPP: Correspondence respecting Piracy on the Coast of Borneo, 1852.
29. Brooke to Palmerston. Sarawak, October 1, 1849. HCPP: Correspondence respecting Piracy on the Coast of Borneo, 1852.
30. Raffles to C. Lushington. Singapore, May 20, 1823. NAS: M. 2. Singapore: Letters from Bengal to the Resident. December 1823–March 1824.
31. Owen to William Bentinck. Southampton, Penang, October 16, 1830. Arkib Negara Malaysia, Kuala Lumpur (hereafter ANM): 2014/0012135.
32. J. N. Vosmaers to the Interim General Governor of the Dutch East Indies. Batavia, November 25, 1833. NNA: Ministerie van Kolonien, 1814–1849. No. 4168.
33. "In-Official Part. Batavia, April 23, 1847," *Javasche Courant*, April 24, 1847.
34. Cornets de Groot, *Notices Historiques*, 24.

35. Cornets de Groot, *Notices Historiques*, 33–35. The Rayat, according to Cornets de Groot, inhabited a group of islands north of the Strait of Makassar.
36. Ignacio de Abenia Taure, *Memorias sobre el Riff, su conquista y colonización* (Zaragoza: Imprenta de Antonio Gallifa, 1859), 49.
37. José Manuel Diana, *Un prisionero en el Riff; memorias del ayudante Alvarez* (Madrid: Imprenta Nacional, 1859), 242.
38. Chasteau to Guizot. Tangier, November 7, 1847. Archives Nationales d'Outre-Mer, Aix-en-Provence (hereafter ANOM): Gouvernement Général de l'Algérie. Correspondence Politique Générale. 1E 215. Documents relatifs à Abd el-Kader.
39. The island in question was Donousa. Extract of a report by the Captain of Frigate Lebèque, Commander of the Héron, 1854. Ypourgeio Exoterikon. Archives of the Ministry of Foreign Affairs, Athens (hereafter YE): Central Office, 55/1A (1854–55).
40. Emilio Bernaldez, *Reseña histórica de la guerra al sur de Filipinas, sostenida por las armas españolas contra los piratas de aquel archipiélago, desde la conquista hasta nuestros días* (Madrid: Imprenta del Memorial de Ingenieros, 1857), 224.
41. James F. Jones to H. C. Rawlinson, Political Agent, Arabia. Maghile [Al Maq'il], December 18, 1845. The National Archives, Kew, London (hereafter TNA): Admiralty, 127/51.
42. Jones to Rawlinson. Maghile [Al Maq'il], December 18, 1845. TNA: Admiralty, 127/51.
43. Jones to Commodore J. C. Hawkins. Nitocris, Maghil [Al Maq'il], January 16, 1846. TNA: Admiralty, 127/51.
44. Arnold Burrowes Kemball to Commodore George Robinson. Bushire [Bushehr], January 27, 1855. TNA: Admiralty, 127/58.
45. Lewis Pelly to the Chief Secretary to Government in the Political Department, Bombay. Bushire [Bushehr], April 13, 1868. NAI: Foreign Department. Political-A. Nos. 68/72.
46. Pelly to the Chief Secretary to Government in the Political Department, Bombay. Bushire [Bushehr], April 13, 1868. NAI: Foreign Department. Political-A. Nos. 68/72.
47. Brooke to Palmerston. Sarawak, April 16, 1849. HCPP: Piracy (Borneo). Return to an Address of the Honourable the House of Commons, dated February 5, 1850; for "Copies of Extracts of any Despatches relating to the Suppression of Piracy off the Coast of Borneo."
48. Henry Wise to the Earl of Malmelsbury. Lloyds, London. April 26, 1852. OUWL: Papers of the Brookes of Sarawak. MSS Pac. s. 66.
49. Hume to Messrs. Kerr, Fraser, Guthrie, and fifty other Merchants of Singapore. London, February 24, 1851. HCPP: Correspondence respecting Piracy on the Coast of Borneo, 1852.
50. Brooke to Malmelsbury. United Service Club, November 23, 1852. HCPP: Correspondence respecting Piracy in E. Archipelago, and Proceedings of Sir J. Brooke 1852.

51. Brooke to Malmelsbury. United Service Club, November 23, 1852. HCPP: Correspondence respecting Piracy in E. Archipelago, and Proceedings of Sir J. Brooke 1852.
52. B. U. Vigors to the Editor of the *Illustrated London News*. Sarawak, August 29, 1849. HCPP: Correspondence respecting Piracy on the Coast of Borneo, 1852.
53. Brooke to Palmerston. Sarawak, September 13, 1848. HCPP: Piracy (Borneo). Return to an Address of the Honourable the House of Commons, dated February 5, 1850; for "Copies of Extracts of any Despatches relating to the Suppression of Piracy off the Coast of Borneo."
54. Hume to Lord Wodehouse. Bryanstone Square, March 18, 1853. HCPP: Correspondence with Admiralty respecting alleged Discrepancy between Accounts of Captain Farquhar and Sir J. Brooke, on Action with Pirates of Borneo, 1853.
55. Antonio Caballero to the Minister of Government. Palacio [Madrid], November 1, 1847. AHN: Ultramar, 5159/45.
56. Rear Admiral Owen to John Wilson Croker (Admiralty). Southampton, Penang, October 6, 1830. BL: IOF/F/4/1331/52588.
57. Konemenos to Ali Pacha. Samos, September 25, 1851. BOA: HR.TO 416/5.
58. Fr. Ylario Alcazar to [?]. Tonkin, December 20, 1856. AHN: Ultramar, 5200/21. It is worth noting again that Tu Duc had more reasons to suspect the French as they had previously bombarded the coast of Vietnam in the mid-1840s.
59. W[illiam] D[allas] Bernard, *Narrative of the Voyages and Services of the Nemesis, from 1840 to 1843; and of the Combined Naval and Military Operations in China: Comprising a Complete Account of the Colony of Hong Kong and Remarks on the Character and Habits of the Chinese. From Notes of Commander W[illiam] H[enry] Hall, R.N.* (London: Henry Colburn, 1844), vol. 2, 333.
60. Bernard, *Narrative of the Voyages and Services of the Nemesis.*
61. Scott Beresford, *An Account of the Destruction of the Fleets of the Celebrated Pirate Chieftains Chui-Apoo and Shap-Ng-Tsai, on the Coast of China* (London: Saville and Edwards, 1851), 93.
62. Beresford, *Account of the Destruction of the Fleets.*
63. Lieutenant (W. G.) Willinck to the Captain-Lieutenant at sea, Station's Commander in the Celebes waters. On board His Majesty's screw steamer *Reinier Claeszen*. Makassar Roads, December 26, 1860. NNA: Ministerie van Kolonien, 1814–1849. No. 4168.
64. Willinck to the Captain-Lieutenant at sea, Station's Commander in the Celebes waters. On board His Majesty's screw steamer *Reinier Claeszen*. Makassar Roads, December 26, 1860. NNA: Ministerie van Kolonien, 1814–1849. No. 4168.
65. Layton. "Discourses of Piracy," 84.

66. Amirell, *Pirates of Empire*, 56; and Warren, "In Search of Julano Taupan," 23–24.
67. Drummond Hay to Clarendon. Tangier, June 10, 1856. TNA: Foreign Office, 99/74.
68. Diana, *Un prisionero en el Riff*, 115.
69. Drummond Hay to Clarendon. Tangier, June 10, 1856. TNA: Foreign Office, 99/74.
70. M[elchior-Honoré] Yvan, *De France en Chine* (Paris: Librarie de L. Hachette et Cie., 1855), 377.
71. Evaristo Ventosa, *Españoles y Marroquíes. Historia de la Guerra de África* (Barcelona: Librería de Salvador Manero, 1860), vol. 2, 969.
72. In its issue of December 2, 1859, the writers of the newspaper *La Esperanza*, rejoiced about the "African blood that runs in torrents" and "barbarous Africans who bite the sand in their agony, prisoners of their impotent rage." See also Ioan Serrallonga Urquidi, "La guerra de África, 1859–1860: Una revisión," *Ayer* 29 (1998): 139–159, esp. 151.
73. H. de T. D'Arlach, *Le Maroc en 1856* (Paris: Chez Ledoyen, 1856), 7.
74. D'Arlach, *Le Maroc en 1856*.
75. John Bowring, *A Visit to the Philippine Islands* (London: Smith, Elder, 1859), 109.
76. D'Arlach, *Le Maroc*, 9.
77. Charles Robert Prinsep to the Secretary of the Government of India. Calcutta, January 13, 1855. HCPP: Borneo: Reports of the Commissioners Appointed to Inquire into Certain Matters connected with the Position of Sir James Brooke. Presented to both Houses of Parliament by Command of Her Majesty, 1855.
78. Prinsep to the Secretary of the Government of India. Calcutta, January 13, 1855. HCPP: Borneo: Reports of the Commissioners Appointed to Inquire into Certain Matters connected with the Position of Sir James Brooke. Presented to both Houses of Parliament by Command of Her Majesty, 1855.
79. Norris to Bonham. Penang, June 20, 1838. BL: IOR/F/4/1841/77129.
80. Echagüe to the Minister of War and the Colonies. Manila, October 25, 1862. AHN: Ultramar, 5193/30.
81. Secretary of Ultramar [Juan de Zavala] to the Ministers of War and Marine. Madrid, January 17, 1856. AHN: Ultramar, 5167/13.
82. Captain H. W. Giffard to the Admiral in the Mediterranean [James Dundas]. HMS *Dragon*, Gibraltar, January 22, 1852. TNA: Foreign Office, 99/69.
83. James G. Percival, "Varieties of the Human Race," in J. Goldsmith, *A Geographical View of the World, Embracing the Manners, Customs, and Pursuits, of Every Nation; Founded on The Best Authorities* (New York: E. Hopkins and W. Reed, 1826), 21.
84. W. S. Bridges to H[enry] Labouchere. 46 Picadilly, March 28, 1856. TNA: Colonial Office, 129/61.

85. Count Ludolf to Palmerston. London, June 9, 1838. HCPP: Papers relative to Piracy in Adriatic 1840.
86. Raffles to C. Lushington. Singapore, May 20, 1823. NAS: M. 2. Singapore: Letters from Bengal to the Resident. December 1823–March 1824.
87. Lewis Pelly to the Chief Secretary to Government in the Political Department, Bombay. Bushire [Bushehr], April 13, 1868. NAI: Foreign Department. Political-A. Nos. 68/72.
88. J. N. Vosmaer to the Interim General Governor of the Dutch East Indies. Batavia, November 25, 1833. NNA: Ministerie van Kolonien, 1814–1849. No. 4168. For an in-depth study of Vosmaer's activities during his time in the Dutch navy and, subsequently, as a settler in Sulawesi, see Anita van Dissel, "Pioneering in Southeast Asia in the First Half of the Nineteenth Century," in Catia Antunes and Jos Gommans, eds., *Exploring the Dutch Empire: Agents, Networks and Institutions, 1600–2000* (London: Bloomsbury, 2015), 43–58.
89. "De Zeerovers in den Indischen Archipel," *De Oostpost* (March 16, 1857).
90. "De Zeerovers in den Indischen Archipel."
91. Cornets de Groot, *Notice Historiques*, 40.
92. Alexandre de Miltitz, *Manuel des Consuls* (London: A. Asher, 1838), vol. 2, part 1, 27.
93. Abenia Taure, *Memorias sobre el Riff*, 49.
94. Edwards Judson, *The Life of Adoniram Judson by His Son* (New York: Anson D. F. Randolph, 1883), 93.
95. Charles William Bradley to David Webster. United States Consulate, Amoy, May 25, 1852. National Archives and Records Administration, United States (hereafter NARA): Despatches from U.S. Consuls in Amoy, China, 1844–1906. Volume 1 (October 29, 1844–December 26, 1857).
96. Bradley to Webster. United States Consulate, Amoy, May 25, 1852. NARA: Despatches from U.S. Consuls in Amoy, China, 1844–1906. Volume 1 (October 29, 1844–December 26, 1857).
97. Bowring, *Visit to the Philippine Islands*, 109.
98. John Crawfurd, *A View of the Present State and Future Prospects of the Free Trade and Colonization of India* (London: James Ridgway, 1829), 37.
99. Crawfurd, *View of the Present State*, 37, 67.
100. Crawfurd, *View of the Present State*, 67.
101. See, for instance, "The Bornese Pirates," *Illustrated London News*, May 29, 1852.
102. "Le Riff et le Maroc en 1856," *L'illustration, journal universel* 27, no. 712 (October 18, 1856); and "Chui-A-Poo, the Chinese Pirate," *Illustrated London News*, June 14, 1851.
103. Alfred de Moges, *Recollections of Baron Gros's Embassy to China and Japan in 1857–58* (London: Griffin, Bohn, 1861), 54, 151.

104. de Moges, *Recollections of Baron Gros's Embassy*, 54.
105. Yvan, *De France en Chine*, 353.
106. Yvan, *De France en Chine*, 353.
107. "De Zeerovers in den Indischen Archipel," *De Oostpost* (March 16, 1857).
108. Jose García y Ruiz, "Memorias sobre Filipinas, 1859." Biblioteca Nacional de España, Madrid (hereafter BNE): Manuscritos, MSS 6316.
109. García y Ruiz, "Memorias sobre Filipinas, 1859." BNE: Manuscritos, MSS 6316.
110. Antonio de Mora to the General Commander of the Apostadero. Isabela de Basilán, August 19, 1862. NAP: Piratas, 4.
111. Antonio de Urbiztondo to the Secretary of State and Government. Manila, June 8, 1851. AHN: Ultramar 5162/68.
112. Urbiztondo to [Jan Jacob] Rochussen. Cartier Général de Zamboanga. March 15, 1851. AHN: Ultramar 5167/13.
113. "Antonio Alloy, Master of the Town Felucca Mary (formerly the Sultan) Deposes the Following Facts." Gibraltar, November 11, 1834. TNA: Foreign Office, 174/41.
114. Abenia Taure, *Memorias sobre el Riff*, 49.
115. Commander Maxse to the Senior Officer on the Gibraltar Station. HMS *Ariel*, Gibraltar, June 3, 1856. TNA: Foreign Office, 174/56.
116. Ibbetson to George Swinton. Prince of Wales Island, November 23, 1831. NAS: R. 1. Governor's Letters to Bengal. May 1831–August 1832.
117. On board the HM Brigantine *Dolphin*, off Shark Point, River Congo. Thursday Night, June 24, 1852. Duke University Library, Durham, NC: Appleton Oaksmith Papers. Journal of a voyage, 1851–1852. M-5797.
118. Eusebio Salcedo to Rafael de Echagüe. Manila, October 19, 1862. AHN: Ultramar, 5192/5.
119. "In-Official Part. Batavia, April 23, 1847," *Javasche Courant*, April 24, 1847.
120. Vosmaer to the Interim General Governor of the Dutch East Indies. Batavia, November 25, 1833. NNA: Ministerie van Kolonien, 1814–1849. No. 4168.
121. Mora to the General Commander of the Apostadero. Isabela de Basilán, August 19, 1862. NAP: Piratas, 4.
122. "Letter from the Bombay Government to the Honble Court of Directors No. 7, dated 15th April 1831. Transmitting copy of a report from the Resident in the Persian Gulf containing the result of his Enquiries into the slave trade in that quarter." BL: IOR/F/4/1398/55440.
123. "Letter from the Bombay Government to the Honble Court of Directors No. 7, dated 15th April 1831." BL: IOR/F/4/1398/55440.
124. Pelly to the Chief Secretary to Government in the Political Department, Bombay. Bushire, April 13, 1868. NAI: Foreign Department. Political-A. Nos. 68/72.

125. Pelly to the Chief Secretary to Government in the Political Department, Bombay. Bushire, April 13, 1868. NAI: Foreign Department. Political-A. Nos. 68/72.
126. Osborn, *My Journal in Malayan Waters*, 51.
127. Osborn, *My Journal in Malayan Waters*, 156.
128. Amirell, *Pirates of Empire*, 169.
129. See, for example, Oscar Chapuis, *The Last Emperors of Vietnam: From Tu Duc to Bao Dai* (Westport, CT: Greenwood Press, 2000), 47; and Spencer C. Tucker, *Vietnam* (London: UCL Press, 1999), 27–29.
130. Nguyen Thi My Hanh, "The Anti-piracy Activities of the Nguyen Dynasty in the South China Sea, 1802–1858," *International Journal of Maritime History* 31, no. 1 (2019): 50–80. This article includes a comprehensive and detailed list of maritime raiding events along the coast of Vietnam during the period.
131. Arthur Waley, *The Opium War through Chinese Eyes* (London: George Allen and Unwin, 1958), 44.
132. Waley, *Opium War through Chinese Eyes*, 69.
133. Waley, *Opium War through Chinese Eyes*, 68–69.
134. Waley, *Opium War through Chinese Eyes*, 213.
135. Waley, *Opium War through Chinese Eyes*, 194, 213.
136. Waley, *Opium War through Chinese Eyes*, 29.
137. Waley, *Opium War through Chinese Eyes*, 66.
138. Waley, *Opium War through Chinese Eyes*, 67.
139. Michael Levien, ed., *The Cree Journals: The Voyages of Edward H. Cree, Surgeon R.N. as Related in His Private Journals, 1837–1856* (Exeter: Webb & Bower, 1981), 72.
140. Levien, ed., *Cree Journals*, 58.
141. Viscount Ponsonby to Lord Palmerston. Therapia, December 27, 1840. TNA: Foreign Office, 84/333.
142. "Damning a Brooke." OUWL: Papers of the Brookes of Sarawak. MSS Pac. s. 83. box 9, vol. 35. History of Sarawak. 1841–1968.
143. "Damning a Brooke."
144. "Damning a Brooke."
145. Benton, *They Called It Peace*, 150.
146. Richard Gott, *Britain's Empire: Resistance, Repression and Revolt* (London: Verso, 2011), 358.

Chapter Two. Abolition and the Suppression of Maritime Raiding

1. See, for example, *Trial of the Twelve Spanish Pirates of the Schooner Panda;* and *A Report of the Trial of Pedro Gibert, Bernardo de Soto, Francisco Ruiz, Nicola Costa, Antonio Ferrer, Manuel Boyga, Domingo de Guzman, Juan Antonio Portana, Manuel Castillo, Angel Garcia, Jose Velazquez, and Juan*

Montenegro, alias Jose Basilio de Castro, before the United States Circuit Court, on an Indictment Charging Them with the Commission of an Act of Piracy, on Board the Brig Mexican, of Salem (Boston: Russell, Odiorne & Metcalf, 1834).

2. William Macleay to the Earl of Aberdeen. Havana, April 1, 1829. TNA: Foreign Office, 84/91; Macleay to Aberdeen. Havana, November 30, 1829. TNA: Foreign Office, 84/92; MacLeay to Aberdeen. Havana, September 18, 1830. TNA: Foreign Office, 84/107; Macleay to Palmerston. Havana, February 28, 1831. TNA: Foreign Office, 84/119; Macleay to Palmerston. Havana, October 15, 1831. TNA: Foreign Office, 84/119; Macleay to Palmerston. Havana, July 20, 1832. TNA: Foreign Office, 84/128; Juan Bautista Topete to Nicholas P. Trist. Havana, April 22, 1834. Sterling Memorial Library, Yale University, New Haven (hereafter SML): Macrofilms Collection, US Consular Records. Havana, 1834–35.
3. If we are to believe Nicholas Trist, U.S. consul in Havana, the third mate had been "the instigator of all the robbery of the Mexican." According to conversations he had had with slave traders living in Havana, the third mate had managed to escape soon after arriving at river Nazareth and had made his way back to Cuba, joining the crew of another slave vessel. Trist to John Forsyth. US Consulate, Havana, December 27, 1834. SML: Macrofilms Collection, US Consular Records: Havana, 1834–35.
4. Citizens of Boston and Watertown to the President of the United States. Boston, May 6, 1835. NARA: Records Regarding Privateering and Piracy, 1813–1835. RG 59, box 1, folder 1.
5. Letter signed by James Font, Pedro Martinez & Co., Juan Martinez & Co., George de Alfuria, Marti & Mazon, L. Diego Jimenez, Alejo de Torres, Salvador Samá, and Manuel Pié. Havana, February 10, 1835. New-York Historical Society Library, New York City: Manuscripts Collections. Havana (Cuba) documents, 1835–1864. See also Cándido Pequeño to Trist. Havana, February 5, 1835. NARA: Records Regarding Privateering and Piracy, 1813–1835. RG 59, box 1, folder 2. Pequeño also attached testimonies of several Havana-based slave traders, such as Pedro Martínez, Jose A. Yrigoyen, Joaquín Gómez, as well as those of the consuls of Russia, the Low Countries, Prussia, and Britain in Havana.
6. Alexander Bryson, *Report on the Climate and Principal Diseases of the African Station; Compiled from Documents in the Office of the Director-General of the Medical Department, and from Other Sources, in Compliance with the Directions of the Right Honorable The Lords Commissioners of the Admiralty* (London: William Clowes and Sons, 1847), 200.
7. Enclosure 9 in No. 187. Divisions and Stations of the French Squadron employed in the Suppression of the Slave Trade on the West Coast of Africa, on April 30, 1846. HCPP: Correspondence with British Coms. at Sierra Leone, Havana, Cape of Good Hope, Jamaica, Loanda, and Cape

Verde Islands; Reports from British Vice-Admiralty Courts and Naval Officers on Slave Trade, 1846 (Class A), 337.

8. Joseph Story, *A Charge Delivered to the Grand Jury of the Circuit Court of the United States, at Its First Session in Portland, for the Judicial District of Maine, May 8, 1820* (Portland: A. Shirley, 1820), 8.
9. "Law Declaring the Traffic of Negroes on the Coast of Africa an Act of Piracy. Buenos Ayres, November 15, of 1824." HCPP: Class A. Correspondence with the British Commissioners at Sierra Leone, the Havana, Rio de Janeiro, and Surinam, relating to the Slave Trade, 1840–1841, 258; and "Law of the Congress of Chile, Declaring Slave Trade Piracy. Santiago, October 21, 1842," 198. Lewis Herstlet, compiler, *A Complete Collection of the Treaties and Conventions and Reciprocal Regulations, at Present Subsisting between Great Britain and Foreign Powers* (London: Butterworths, 1856), vol. 9, 198.
10. "Tratado Celebrado entre a Rainha a Senhora Dona Maria II e Victoria I Rainha da Gran-Bretanha, para a Completa Abolição do Trafico da Escravatura, assignado em Lisboa a 3 de Julho de 1842." Collecção dos Tratados, Convenções, *Contratos e Actos Publicos Celebrados entre a Corôa de Portugal e as mais Potencias desde 1640 até ao Presente.* (Lisbon: Imprensa Nacional, 1856–1858). vol. 6, 374–397; and "Decreto, 25 July 1842." Supplemento á Collec*ção dos Tratados*, 28, 630.
11. For an extensive study of this law and its impact on the Brazilian involvement in the slave trade, see Leslie Bethell, *The Abolition of the Brazilian Slave Trade* (Cambridge: Cambridge University Press, 1970), 343–349.
12. The most comprehensive study of this law and its immediate consequences for the slave trade to Brazil to date is Beatriz G. Mamigonian, *Abolição do tráfico de escravos: 170 anos da Lei Eusébio de Queirós* (São Paulo: Companhia das Letras, 2020). See also Bethell, *Abolition of the Brazilian Slave Trade;* and Jaime Rodrigues, *O infame comércio* (Campinas: Editora Unicamp, 2000).
13. "General Treaty with the Arab Tribes of the Persian Gulf. 1820." BL: IOR/H/641.
14. "General Treaty with the Arab Tribes of the Persian Gulf. 1820." BL: IOR/H/641.
15. Thomson, *Mercenaries, Pirates, and Sovereigns*, especially introduction and chapter 1.
16. Articles 9 and 10 in particular referred to these issues. For a study of the role of slavery and the slave trade in the Webster-Ashburton Treaty, see Wilbur Devereux Jones, "The Influence of Slavery on the Webster-Ashburton Negotiations." *Journal of Southern History* 22, no. 1 (1956): 48–58.
17. "Convention between Her Majesty and the King of the French, for the Suppression of the Traffic in Slaves." *British and Foreign Anti-Slavery Reporter* (Wednesday, June 25, 1845), esp. article 8.

18. "The French Treaty with the Imaum of Muscat," *British and Foreign Anti-Slavery Reporter* (Wednesday, July 23, 1845). For an analysis of the agreement between Great Britain and Muscat for the termination of the export of slaves, signed at Zanzibar on October 2, 1845, see Yusuf A. Al Ghailani, "British Early Intervention in the Slave Trade with Oman, 1822–1873," *History Research* 5, no. 4 (2015): 225–238.
19. David Murray, *Odious Commerce: Britain, Spain, and the Abolition of the Cuban Slave Trade* (Cambridge: Cambridge University Press, 1980), 331–4.
20. Jesús Sanjurjo, *In the Blood of Our Brothers: Abolitionism and the End of the Slave Trade in Spain's Atlantic Empire, 1800–1870* (Tuscaloosa: University of Alabama Press, 2021), 117–118.
21. Thomas Fowell Buxton, *The African Slave Trade and Its Remedy* (London: John Murray, 1840), 218–219.
22. Kent, *Commentaries on American Law*, vol. 1, 180. For an extensive examination of Kent's input into discussions around the likening of piracy and slave trade in this period, see Jenny Martinez, *The Slave Trade and the Origins of International Human Rights Law* (Oxford: Oxford University Press, 2012), 65.
23. Kent, *Commentaries on American Law*, vol. 1, 219.
24. Henry James Matson, *Remarks on the Slave Trade and African Squadron* (London: James Ridgway, 1848), 51.
25. Matson, *Remarks on the Slave Trade and African Squadron.*
26. Matson, *Remarks on the Slave Trade and African Squadron*, 65–66.
27. W. M. Gore Ouseley, *Notes on the Slave-Trade with Remarks on the Measures Adopted for Its Suppression* (London: John Rodwell, 1850), 62.
28. Gore Ouseley, *Notes on the Slave-Trade.*
29. These effects have been studied in-depth by Harris, *The Last Slave Ships: New York and the End of the Middle Passage* (New Haven: Yale University Press, 2020); and Mamigonian, *Abolição do tráfico de escravos.*
30. "An Act to Protect the Commerce of the United States and Punish the Crime of Piracy." March 3, 1819, specifically the amendments made in 1820.
31. Sparks, "Blind Justice," 53–79; and Harris, *Last Slave Ships*, esp. 183–234.
32. Manuel Barcia and Effie Kesidou, "Innovation and Entrepreneurship as Strategies for Success among Cuban-Based Firms in the Late Years of the Transatlantic Slave Trade," *Business History* 60, no. 4 (2018): 542–561.
33. For a full examination of Gordon's trial and execution, see "The United States vs. Nathaniel Gordon, October 25, 1860." NARA: Criminal Cases, 1790–1912. RG 21: Records of District Courts of the United States, 1685–2009.
34. Barcia, "Cause and Consequence."
35. *Dying Declaration of Nicholas Fernandez, Who with Nine Others Were Executed in Front of Cadiz Harbour, December 29, 1829. For Piracy and Murder*

on the High Seas (New York: [George Lambert], 1836), 11. See also "Testament of Saint Cyr Barbazán, Natural of Pondesac (France)." Cádiz, January 10, 1830. Archivo Histórico Provincial de Cádiz, Cádiz: Protocolo Notarial de Cádiz (before Juan Manuel Martínez), ff. 22–23.

36. "Prosecutor's Conclusion of the Process Followed against the Crew of the Brazilian Brigantine, Defensor de Pedro, Accused of Piracy and Other Crimes," by Jorge Lasso de la Vega. San Fernando, November 18, 1829. Archivo Histórico General de Marina, Viso del Marqués (hereafter AGMAB): Legajos Ferrol, no. 10924/4.
37. Tomás de Ayalde to the Secretary of State and Marine. San Fernando, May 30, 1828. AGMAB: Legajos Ferrol, no. 10924/4.
38. Lt. Colonel D. Falla to [S. R.] Chapman. Gibraltar, January 18, 1829. Gibraltar National Archives, Gibraltar (hereafter GNA): Despatches from Gibraltar, 1829.
39. Francisco de Quevedo y Bueno to the Secretary of State and Marine. Madrid, February 28, 1830. AGMAB: Corsos y Presas, 5246, no. 1656/1.
40. Manuel González Salmón to the Secretary of Marine. Palace [Madrid], February 2, 1830. AGMAB: Corsos y Presas, 5246, no. 1656/1.
41. González Salmón to the Secretary of Marine. Palace [Madrid], February 2, 1830. AGMAB: Corsos y Presas, 5246, no. 1656/1. See also George Don to George Murray. Gibraltar, January 28, 1830. GNA: General's Don Despatches, 1827–1832.
42. See, for example, the recent books by Michael E. A. Ford, *Hunting the Last Great Pirate: Benito de Soto and the Rape of the Morning Star* (Barnsley: Pen & Sword, 2020); and Sarah Craze, *Atlantic Piracy in the Early Nineteenth Century: The Shocking Story of the Pirates and the Survivors of the Morning Star* (Woodbridge: Boydell Press, 2022).
43. Sidney Henry Ussher to Commodore William Jones. Her Majesty's Sloop *Wasp*, off Lagos. March 5, 1845; Stupart to Ussher. Her Majesty's Sloop *Wasp*, at sea, March 5, 1845; and Ussher to Jones. HM Sloop *Wasp*, at Ascension. April 24, 1845. TNA: Treasury Solicitor, 45/28.
44. [?] to H.J.D. Corry. Lancaster Place, July 30, 1845. TNA: Treasury Solicitor, 45/28. See also "Regina v. Serva and Nine Others. July 24, 25, & 26." *Reports of Cases Argued and Determined in the English Courts of Common Law with Tables of the Cases and Principal Matters* (Philadelphia: T. & J. W. Johnson, 1869), vol. 61, 53–100.
45. "Regina v. Serva and Nine Others. July 24, 25, & 26," vol. 61, 98.
46. "Regina v. Serva and Nine Others. July 24, 25, & 26," vol. 61, 98–99. The conviction was also publicly challenged by others. See, for example, W. B. Hewson, *The Case of the Queen against Serva and Others, Inclusive of the Trial and the Argument before the Judges* (London: William Benning, 1846).
47. Juan José Zangroniz to [?]. Santander, July 23, 1816. AHN: Estado, 8028/1.

48. Deposition of Francisco de Garriaga. Archivo Nacional de Cuba, Havana (hereafter ANC): Real Consulado y Junta de Fomento, 86/3497.
49. Ramón de Bustillo and Mariano de Mendive acknowledging the damages suffered by the insurance company of which they are directors, as a result of the capture of vessels they had insured. ANC: Tribunal de Comercio, 32/10.
50. On the Mixed Commission courts, see Leslie Bethell, "The Mixed Commission for the Suppression of the Transatlantic Slave Trade in the Nineteenth Century," *Journal of African History* 7, no. 1 (1966): 79–93; Luis Martínez-Fernández, "The Havana Anglo-Spanish Mixed Commission for the Suppression of the Slave Trade and Cuba's Emancipados," *Slavery & Abolition* 16, no. 2 (1995): 205–25; Farida Shaikh, "Judicial Diplomacy: British Officials and the Mixed Commission Courts," in Keith Hamilton and Patrick Salmon, eds., *Slavery, Diplomacy, and Empire: Britain and the Suppression of the Slave Trade, 1807–1975* (Brighton: Sussex Academic Press, 2009), 42–64; and Jennifer L. Nelson, "Liberated Africans in the Atlantic World: The Courts of Mixed Commission in Havana and Rio de Janeiro, 1819–1871" (PhD diss., University of Leeds, 2015).
51. "Extrato da 'parte semanal' da escuna portuguesa Relâmpago, de 26 de abril a 2 de maio de 1846, relativo ao cruzeiro entre o Ambriz e o Ambrizete." Arquivo Histórico Ultramarino, Lisbon (hereafter AHU): Angola, Maço 874. Embarcações Apresadas nas Águas Territoriais, 1841–1848.
52. G. M. Hawe to Charles Henry Pennell. St. Helena, April 20, 1846; and Lt. S. Elliot to R. C. Pennell. St. Helena, May 2, 1846. St. Helena Government Archives, Jamestown (hereafter SHGA): Colonial Secretary's Letter Book, 24/1 (1846).
53. John N. Firmin to Pennell. St. Helena, June 4, 1846. SHGA: Colonial Secretary's Letter Book, 24/1 (1846).
54. Firmin to Pennell. St. Helena, September 1, 1845. SHGA: Colonial Secretary's Letter Book, 24/2 (1846–1847).
55. Diogo Ignacio Tavares to the Governor of St. Helena. On board the corvette *Bertioga*, anchored in St. Helena Roads, June 29, 1846. SHGA: Colonial Secretary's Letter Book, 24/1 (1846).
56. John Dodson to Lord Palmerston. Doctors Commons, September 26, 1846. TNA: Colonial Office, 247/53.
57. Dodson to Palmerston. Doctors Commons, September 26, 1846. TNA: Colonial Office, 247/53.
58. Daniel Hamilton to George Canning. Sierra Leone, 20 September 1826. TNA: Foreign Office, 84/48.
59. "Report of the Case of the Spanish Brig 'Formidable,' Manuel Mateu, Master." Sierra Leone, February 10, 1835. HCPP: Class A. Correspondence with British Commissioners at Sierra Leone, Havana, Rio de Janeiro and Surinam on Slave Trade: 1835, 49.

60. N. W. Macdonald to Logan Hook. Secretary's Office. January 31, 1835. Sierra Leone Public Archives, Freetown (hereafter SLPA): Colonial Secretary's Letter Book, January 22, 1835–December 3, 1836.
61. For the case of the *Midas*, see William Macleay to Lord Aberdeen. Havana, July 17, 1829. TNA: Foreign Office, 84/92. For the *Patacho Veiga*, see "Patacho Veiga, January 22, 1850, Resisted Apprehension from the English on the Littoral of Luanda. 623 slaves." AHU: Angola, Correspondencia dos Governadores, 17A. January 7, 1851; and Arquivo Histórico Nacional de Angola, Luanda: Códice C-13-1 (1851).
62. For a study of this case, see Manuel Barcia, "White Cannibalism in the Illegal Slave Trade: The Peculiar Case of the Portuguese Schooner Arrogante in 1837," *Nieuwe West-Indische Gids/New West Indian Guide* 96, nos. 1–2 (2022): 1–28.
63. Milne to the Governor of the Fort of Xagua. HMS *Snake*, off Xagua, November 28, 1837. Alexander Milne Private Letter Book, HMS *Snake*. National Maritime Museum, Greenwich (hereafter NMM): MLN/101/12.
64. "Instructions for Mr. de Trobriand." Saubot, Foubert & Co. [St. Thomas], May 26, 1825. TNA: Foreign Office, 315/55.
65. Thomas C. Matthews to William Smith. Brig Z, detained by HMS *Maidstone*, at Sierra Leone, August 27, 1825. TNA: Foreign Office, 315/55.
66. French Consul in Havana [Marquis de Vins de Peysac] to Le Ministre de la Marine et des Colonies. Havana, April 10, 1829. ANOM: Généralités, 166/1342.
67. Magnan to Vins de Peysac. Matanzas, March 14, 1829. Centre des Archives Diplomatiques, La Corneuve, Paris (hereafter CAD): La Havane. Vol. 8. 1829–1831.
68. Vins de Peysac to the Count of La Ferronays (Foreign Minister). Havana, April 30, 1829. CAD: La Havane. Vol. 8. 1829–1831.
69. Dénis de Trobriand, *Une aventure de Négrier* (Le Havre: Chez J. Morlent, 1836).
70. "Capture of a Slave Ship," *Morning Post*, December 29, 1830.
71. Alexander Findlay and W. M. Smith to Aberdeen. Sierra Leone, October 18, 1830. HCPP: Class A & B. Correspondence with British Coms. at Sierra Leone, Havana, Rio de Janeiro, and Surinam, and with Foreign Powers on Slave Trade, 1830.
72. H[enry] Richton to Lt. Montgomery. Secretary's Office [Freetown], December 6, 1830. SLPA: Colonial Secretary's Letter Book, February 12 1830–May 12, 1832.
73. Charles Jones to G. Elliot. Lancaster Place, [London], February 4, 1831. HCPP: Class A. Correspondence with the British Commissioners, at Sierra Leone, Havana, Rio de Janeiro, and Surinam, relating to the Slave Trade, 1831.
74. William Macleay and Charles Mackenzie to Palmerston. Havana, March 17, 1832. HCPP: Class A & B. Correspondence with British Commis-

sioners at Sierra Leone, Havana, Rio de Janeiro, and Surinam, and with Foreign Powers on Slave Trade, 1832; and Macleay and Schenley to Palmerston. Havana, March 31, 1836. TNA: Foreign Office, 84/196.

75. José Antonio Falp, manual de 1828, September 25, 1828. Arxiu Històric de Protocols de Barcelona, Barcelona: Escribanía de Marina, 289v–290. In this document it was clarified that the vessel was armed for predatory and defensive action. Captain and crew also committed to defend themselves should anyone try to board them.

76. Don to Murray. Gibraltar, April 8, 1829. GNA: Despatches from Gibraltar, 1829.

77. Antonio Constantí to José Martorell y Cía. Gallinas, October 25, 1828. TNA, Foreign Office, 315/75. Multiple letters written by Constantí soon after arriving at Whydah can also be found in the same document. See also, Martin Rodrigo, "El pirata Antonio Constantí y su falucho Despejado," unpublished.

78. For the disappearance of the vessel, see Rodrigo, "El pirata Antonio Constantí."

79. Constantí to Arribas. [Whydah] [1830]; and Francisco Félix de Souza to Arribas. [Whydah], April 24, 1830. Arquivo Nacional do Rio de Janeiro, Rio de Janeiro: Coleções Especiais–III; 33–Comissões Mistas Brasil Grã-Bretanha (tráfico de negros). Lata 10, Maço 2, Embarcação Destemida, 1830–1831.

80. "Atrocious Piracy and Murder," *The Standard* (June 16, 1830); and "Piracy: Sierra Leone, May 14." *Leicester Chronicle* (August 21, 1830).

81. Ana Flavia Cicchelli Pires, "A abolição do Comércio Atlãntico de Escravos e os Africanos Livres no Brasil," in *Los estudios afroamericanos y africanos en América Latina: herencia, presencia y visiones del otro* (Córdoba and Buenos Aires: CLACSO, 2008), 98.

82. "List of Arrivals of Slave Vessels in the Havana from the Coast of Africa, during the Year 1832." HCPP: Class A. Correspondence with British Commissioners at Sierra Leone, Havana, Rio de Janeiro, and Surinam on Slave Trade, 1833.

83. Macleay and Mackenzie to Palmerston. Havana, February 20, 1834. HCPP: Class A. Correspondence with British Commissioners at Sierra Leone, Havana, Rio de Janeiro, and Surinam on Slave Trade, 1834.

84. "List of Vessels Which Have Entered Bahia, from the Coast of Africa, during the Six Months Ending 31st December 1834." HCPP: Class B. Correspondence with Foreign Powers on Slave Trade, 1835.

85. Trist to John Forsyth. U.S. Consulate, Havana, December 27, 1834. SML: Macrofilms Collection. US Consular Records. Havana, 1834–35.

86. [Trist to Forsyth], [Havana], January 5, 1835. SML: Macrofilms Collection. US Consular Records. Havana, 1834–35.

87. Macleay to John Backhouse. Havana, October 4, 1831. TNA: Foreign Office, 84/119.

88. Trist to Forsyth. Consulate of the United States, Havana, April 15, 1835. NARA: Records Regarding Privateering and Piracy, 1813–1835. RG 59, box 1, folder 3, part 2. For an in-depth discussion of the Zangroniz clan and their involvement in various sorts of human trafficking businesses at the time, see Manuel Barcia, " 'Fully Capable of Any Iniquity': The Atlantic Human Trafficking Network of the Zangroniz Family," *The Americas* 73, no. 3 (2016): 303–324.
89. Joaquín José Duarte Silva to Blanco & Carvallo. Havana, November 26, 1838. For the most recent study on the activities of Pedro Blanco and his partner Lino Carvallo, see María del Carmen Barcia, *Pedro Blanco el negrero. Mito, realidad y espacios* (Havana: Ediciones Boloña, 2020).
90. Schenley to Palmerston. Havana, July 30, 1836. TNA: Foreign Office, 84/197.
91. Schenley to Byng. Havana, July 28, 1836. 11 o'clock p.m. TNA: Foreign Office, 84/197.
92. George Jackson to Palmerston. Rio de Janeiro, January 18, 1840. TNA: Foreign Office, 84/313.
93. Beatriz Mamigonian, *Africanos livres: A Abolição do Tráfico de Escravos para o Brasil* (São Paulo: Companhia das Letras, 2017), 182; and Nelson, "Liberated Africans," 133–134.
94. D'Aguilar to Porter. Salvador, April 30, 1848. TNA: Foreign Office, 84/725.
95. Dale Graden and Paulo Cesar Oliveira de Jesus, "The *Bella Miquelina* Affair: The Transatlantic Slave Trade, British Suppression and One African's Quest for Liberty in the Bay of All Saints, Brazil in 1848," *Atlantic Studies* 14, no. 2 (2017): 201.
96. Paulino de Souza to James Hudson. Rio de Janeiro, June 26, 1850. TNA: Foreign Office, 84/804.
97. Herbert Schomberg to Rear Admiral Barrington Reynolds. HMS *Cormorant*, at sea, July 5, 1850. TNA: Foreign Office, 84/804.
98. Robert Smith, *The Lagos Consulate, 1851–1861* (Berkeley: University of California Press, 1979): 26–31.
99. *The Destruction of Lagos* (London: James Ridgway, 1852), 21.
100. For British imperial endeavors in Nigeria after 1861, see Piers M. Wood, *A Microcosm of Imperialism: Lagos, 1861 to 1865* (Madison: University of Wisconsin Press, 1972); and Derek R. Peterson, ed., *Abolitionism and Imperialism in Britain, Africa, and the Atlantic* (Athens: Ohio University Press, 2010).
101. See Roger S. Clark, "British Anti-Slave-Trade Treaties with African and Arab Leaders as Precursors of Modern Suppression Conventions," in Neil Boister, Sabine Gless, and Florian Jessberger, eds., *Histories of Transnational Criminal Law* (Oxford: Oxford University Press, 2021), 128–137.

102. "Attack on Medina, Sierra Leone River," *Illustrated London News*, May 14, 1853, 368.
103. Alfred Burdon Ellis, *A History of the Gold Coast of West Africa* (London: Chapman and Hall, 1893), 160–161.
104. Ibrahim K. Sundiata, *From Slaving to Neoslavery: The Bight of Biafra and Fernando Po in the Era of Abolition, 1827–1930* (Madison: University of Wisconsin Press, 1996).
105. Monleón to the Baron de Mackau. Brig *La Zebre*, Sierra Leone, February 19, 1845. ANOM: Généralités, 166/1341.
106. Rapport sur l'état actuel de la traite des noirs. Gorée, April 3, 1845. ANOM: Généralités, 166/1341.
107. Baudin to the Minister of Marine and Colonies. Gorée docks, November 12, 1844. ANOM: Généralités, 166/1341.
108. Africanus, "Proposed Settlement off the African Coast." *Morning Chronicle* (Liverpool), October 5, 1825, 3; and Edmund Ruffin, "The Colonization Society and Liberia." *De Bow's Review* 27 (1859): 60–62.
109. George Jackson and Edmund Gabriel to Palmerston. Luanda, February 18, 1847. HCPP: Correspondence with British Coms. at Sierra Leone, Havana, Cape of Good Hope, Jamaica, Loanda, and Cape Verde Islands; Reports from British Vice-Admiralty Courts and Naval Officers on Slave Trade: 1847–March 1848 (Class A), 154; and Her Majesty's Commissioners to Palmerston. Luanda, February 5, 1850. HCPP: Correspondence with British Coms. at Sierra Leone, Havana, Cape of Good Hope, Jamaica, Loanda, and Cape Verde Islands; Reports from British Vice-Admiralty Courts and Naval Officers on Slave Trade, 1850–51 (Class A), 59. See also Mariana Candido, *An African Slaving Port and the Atlantic World: Benguela and Its Hinterland* (Cambridge: Cambridge University Press, 2013), 151–152, 160–170.
110. For the Siamese case, which is further discussed in chapter 4 of this book, see "Continuation of Captain H. Burney's Journal of His Mission to the Court of Siam," in *Burney Papers*, vol. 1, 123, 176. For a discussion of the tolerance and even encouragement of the slave trade in Singapore, see "Slave Trade in the Indian Archipelago," *Singapore Free Press and Mercantile Advertiser*, November 8, 1845, 2.
111. In February 1826, Burney managed to obtain the release of 547 enslaved Burmese men, women, and children. See "Continuation of Captain H. Burney's Journal." In *Burney Papers*, vol. 1, 123.
112. *Burney Papers*, vol. 1, 176.
113. *Burney Papers*, vol. 1.
114. Memorial from Captain H. Burney, Envoy to the Court of Siam to the Ministers of the King of Siam. Bangkok, May 9, 1826. *Burney Papers*, vol. 2, 295.
115. John Crawfurd, *Journal of an Embassy from the Governor-General of India to the Courts of Siam and Cochin China; Exhibiting a View of the Actual State of Those Kingdoms* (London: Henry Colburn, 1828), 59.

116. Crawfurd, *Journal of an Embassy.*
117. Maung Htin Aung, *A History of Burma* (New York: Cambridge University Press, 1967), 210–4.
118. Burney often questioned the instructions he received. Multiple examples can be found his *Burney Papers*, vols. 1 and 2.
119. Osborn, *My Journal in Malayan Waters*, 179.
120. Osborn, *My Journal in Malayan Waters*, 179–180.
121. Shawna Herzog, "Domesticating Labor: An Illicit Slave Trade to The British Straits Settlements, 1811–1845." *Journal of World History* 28, nos. 3 & 4 (2017): 348.
122. Herzog, "Domesticating Labor," 369.
123. Butterworth to the Resident Councilor in Singapore. Singapore, December 27, 1843. NAS: Z. 15. Singapore: Letters from Governor. October 1842–February 1844.
124. Testimonies of William Wilson Brereton, Tuanko Serib Hussein, Kossim, and Joseph Middleton. HCPP: Piracy (Borneo). Return to an Address of the Honourable the House of Commons, dated February 5, 1850; for "Copies of Extracts of any Despatches relating to the Suppression of Piracy off the Coast of Borneo."
125. "Extract from the Summary of the Relation between the State of Muscat and the British Government." [1826]. BL: IOR/R/15/1/37.
126. Al Ghailani, "British Early Intervention," 225–238.
127. See, for example, Murray, *Odious Commerce.*
128. Urbiztondo to Jan Jacob Rochussen. Cartier Général de Zamboanga. March 15, 1851. AHN: Ultramar, 5167/13.
129. Urbiztondo to Rochussen. Cartier Général de Zamboanga. March 15, 1851. AHN: Ultramar, 5167/13.
130. Urbiztondo to the Sec. de Estado y del Despacho de Gobernación del Reino. Manila, June 21, 1851. AHN: Ultramar, 5162/68.
131. Luis Martínez-Fernández, "Political Change in the Spanish Caribbean during the United States Civil War and Its Aftermath," *Caribbean Studies* 27, nos. 1 & 2 (1994): 39.
132. Echagüe to the Minister of War and the Colonies. Manila, October 25, 1862. AHN: Ultramar, 5192/18.
133. The files for each of these cases can be found at: NAP: Piratas, Leg. 2.
134. The Sultan de Joló to the Captain General. Joló, September 24, 1849. NAP: Pirates, Leg. 1.
135. Pablo Antonio Sabra to the Captain General. San Pascual, June 20, 1859. NAP: Pirates, Leg. 1.
136. O'Donnell defended the slave trade and slavery multiple times during his time as governor of the island of Cuba (1843–1848). At the beginning of his term as governor, he also unleashed the most severe repression against non-white people ever witnessed on the island to that date, namely, the so-called Conspiracy of La Escalera. Narváez's support for

pro-slavery forces was continuous during the period. As late as in 1866, he ordered the dissolution of the Spanish Abolitionist Society. On O'Donnell and La Escalera, see Robert L. Paquette, *Sugar Is Made with Blood: The Conspiracy of La Escalera and the Conflict between Empires Over Slavery in Cuba* (Middleton, CT: Wesleyan University Press, 1988). On Narváez and the dissolution of the Spanish Abolitionist Society, see Sanjurjo, *In the Blood of Our Brothers*, 167, n. 179.

137. Norzagaray to Charles Ferdinand Pahud. Manila, April 28, 1857. AHN: Ultramar, 5172/10.
138. Maarten Kuitenbrouwer, "The Dutch Case of Antislavery: Late and Elitist Abolition," in Gert Oostindie, ed., *Fifty Years Later: Antislavery, Capitalism and Modernity in the Dutch Orbit* (Pittsburgh: University of Pittsburgh Press, 1996), 77.
139. Smulders to the Governor General of the Dutch Indies. Ceram (Serang), October 16, 1831. NNA: Ministerie van Kolonien, 1814–1849. No. 4168.
140. Warren, *Sulu Zone*, 252.
141. See, for example, the depositions of thirty-six-year-old Lama, twenty-five-year-old Sattong, and fifty-year-old Lakka. Verbal Process. Arsip Nasional Republik Indonesia, Jakarta (hereafter ANRI): Soerabaya, 1427. Openbare Orde, 1850–1851.
142. Wijndham was lucky enough to have the F. C. Rose, adjunct secretary to the government, in Batavia to agree to reimburse him the 650 Spanish reals he had paid to the pirates. Extract from the Register of the Apostillar Disposition of the Minister of State, Governor General of the Netherlands Indies of May 5, 1847. ANRI: Riouw, 150. Aankomende Brieven. 1847.
143. "Further Notes on Piracy in the Dutch East Indies." Batavia, June 4, 1835. NNA: Ministerie van Kolonien, 1814–1849. No. 4168.
144. "Further Notes on Piracy in the Dutch East Indies."
145. "Further Notes on Piracy in the Dutch East Indies."
146. Vogelpoot to Pahud. Batavia, January 9, 1861. "Further Notes on Piracy in the Dutch East Indies." Unlike their Spanish counterparts, some of the Dutch East Indies governors of this period, played an important role in the abolition process within their empire. Pahud, for example, before taking over as governor, had been charged with setting up the State Commission for Slave Emancipation in 1853. Jean-Chrétien Baud, another former governor, was named the chairman of the said commission soon after. See P. J. Horsman, *Archive of the State Commission for Slave Emancipation in the Netherlands Colonies, 1853–1856* (Amsterdam: Moran Micropublications, 2009).
147. Willinck to the Captain-Lieutenant at sea, Station's Commander in the Celebes waters. On board His Majesty's screw steamer *Reinier Claeszen*. Makassar Roads, December 26, 1860. "Further Notes on Piracy in the Dutch East Indies."

148. "Further Notes on Piracy in the Dutch East Indies."
149. "Further Notes on Piracy in the Dutch East Indies." For an extensive discussion on the operations carried out by Lt. Willinck, see chapters 4 and 5.
150. Three of the governors of Macau during these years had been previously governors of Angola. They were Pedro Alexandrino da Cunha, António Sérgio de Sousa, and José Rodrigues Coelho do Amaral. Another one, Francisco António Gonçalves Cardoso, had been the commander of the Anti-Slave Trade Squadron in West Africa, and Bernardo José de Sousa Soares de Andrea had been governor of São Tomé e Príncipe before being appointed to the governorship of Macau.
151. Draft of a Proclamation (to be) issued in the name of the Governor [1855]. Correspondência Macau, Timor. 1856. AHU: ACL/SEMU/DGU, 005, Cx. 22.
152. Julião Jozé da Silva Vieira to Manoel Pereira da Costa. Dili, Timor, October 2, 1845. AHU: ACL/SEMU/DGU, 005, Cx. 15.
153. The British anti-piracy campaign of 1836, led by Chads and George Bonham, is extensively discussed in chapters 3 and 4 of this book.
154. "Notes on the Mozambique, 1847." OWBL, Montagu Burrows. MSS Afr. R. 7.
155. "Notes on the Mozambique, 1847."
156. Barcia, "White Cannibalism," 20.

Chapter Three. Commerce and the Suppression of Maritime Raiding

1. "Prince Adalbert of Prussia's Expedition to Tres Forcas. August 7, 1856." Geheimen Staatsarchives, Berlin: BPH, Rep. 58 III, No. 82.
2. "Prince Adalbert of Prussia's Expedition to Tres Forcas. August 7, 1856."
3. "Prince Adalbert of Prussia's Expedition to Tres Forcas. August 7, 1856."
4. "Prince Adalbert of Prussia's Expedition to Tres Forcas. August 7, 1856."
5. Hore to Rear Admiral Lord Lyons. HMS *Vesuvius*, Gibraltar, August 8, 1856. TNA: Foreign Office, 99/81.
6. Hore to Lyons. HMS *Vesuvius*, Gibraltar, August 8, 1856. TNA: Foreign Office, 99/81.
7. "Notes of the Week," *Illustrated London News*, August 25, 1856, 189.
8. The year before these events unfolded, the British consul in Tangier, John Drummond Hay, recalled a number of "pirate" attacks that had taken place in these waters since at least 1846. Drummond Hay to the Earl of Clarendon. Tangier, August 29, 1853. TNA: Foreign Office, 99/69.
9. See, for example, the concerns expressed in 1852 by the governor of Gibraltar, Robert Gardiner. Gardiner to Lord Grey. Gibraltar, January 18, 1852. TNA: Foreign Office, 99/69.

10. Chasteau to Guizot. Tangier, November 7, 1847; Chasteau to Guizot. Tangier, December 10, 1847; and Lamoricière to the Duke of Oumale. Nemours, November 21, 1847. See also, M. Béchameil to the Minister of the Navy. Orénoque, October 14, 1847. ANOM: Gouvernement Général de l'Algérie. Correspondence Politique Générale. 1E 215. Documents relatifs à Abd el-Kader.
11. See, for example, Jean Jules Henri Mordacq, *La guerre au Maroc: Enseignements tactiques des guerres franco-marocaine (1844) et hispano-marocaine (1859–1860)* (Paris: Charles-Lavauzelle, 1904); and Jean-Pierre Bois, *La campagne de Louis-Philippe au Maroc, 1844* (Paris: Economica, 2013).
12. Rafael del Castillo, *España y Marruecos: Historia de la Guerra de África, escrita desde el campamento por Don Rafael del Castillo* (Madrid: Jesús Gracia, 1859), 42–45.
13. On protection and empire, see Lauren A. Benton, Adam Clulow, and Bain Attwood, eds., *Protection and Empire: A Global History* (Cambridge: Cambridge University Press, 2017), especially the essays in parts 4 and 5.
14. See, for example: John Vincent Nye, "The Myth of Free-Trade Britain and Fortress France: Tariffs and Trade in the Nineteenth Century," *Journal of Economic History* 51, no. 1 (1991): 23–46.
15. John Gallagher and Ronald Robinson, "The Imperialism of Free Trade," *Economic History Review* 6, no. 1 (1953): 1–15.
16. John A. Hobson, *Imperialism: A Study* (New York: John Potts, 1902); and Vladimir Ilich Lenin, *Imperialism, the Highest State of Capitalism* (Petrograd: Жизнь и Знание, 1917). For contemporary witnesses and critics see below.
17. Risso, "Cross-Cultural Perceptions," 296.
18. William Huskisson, *Free Trade: Speech of the Right. Hon. W. Huskisson in the House of Commons, Thursday 23d of February, 1826* (London: J. Hatchard, 1826), 49.
19. Engels, "Preface" to Karl Marx, *Free Trade: A Speech Delivered before the Democratic Club, Brussels, Belgium, Jan. 9, 1848* (Boston: Lee and Shepard, 1888), 10.
20. Nye, "Myth of Free-Trade."
21. Benton, *They Called in Peace*, 19.
22. Benton, *They Called in Peace*, 152.
23. L. Allatini, J. Mochano, and S. Allatini to Charles Blunt. Thessaloniki, March 6, 1850. BOA: HR.TO 213/31.
24. Memorial of the undersigned merchants and inhabitants of Singapore to the Right Honorable, the Governor General in Council, [at] Fort William. Singapore, April 24, 1835. BL: IOF/F/4/1724/69433.
25. Memorial of the undersigned merchants and inhabitants of Singapore to the Right Honorable, the Governor General in Council, [at] Fort William. Singapore, April 24, 1835. BL: IOF/F/4/1724/69433.
26. Arrival of Captain Chads in Singapore on board HMS *Andromache*, Singapore, June 20, 1836. ANM: 2014/0012139.

27. Memorial of the undersigned merchants, traders, and other inhabitants of Singapore to the Governor General of India in Council. Singapore, May 25, 1855. NAS: W. 21. Governor: Miscellaneous Letters In. January 1855–December 1855.
28. Memorial of the undersigned merchants, traders, and other inhabitants of Singapore to the Governor General of India in Council. Singapore, May 25, 1855. NAS: W. 21. Governor: Miscellaneous Letters In. January 1855–December 1855.
29. Drummond Hay to Clarendon. Tangier, June 10, 1856. TNA: Foreign Office, 99/74.
30. Jervois to [Henry Pelham] the Duke of Newcastle. Victoria, Hong Kong, April 18, 1853. TNA: Colonial Office, 129/42.
31. Nolloth to Mercer. HMS *Princess Charlotte*, Hong Kong, October 27, 1865. TNA: Colonial Office, 129/107.
32. Nolloth to Mercer. HMS *Princess Charlotte*, Hong Kong, October 27, 1865. TNA: Colonial Office, 129/107.
33. Nolloth to Mercer. HMS *Princess Charlotte*, Hong Kong, October 27, 1865. TNA: Colonial Office, 129/107.
34. A. J. van Olpen to Cleerens. Manado, March 14, 1846. See also the complaints received by van Olpen from a local Dutch merchant a few months earlier: L. A. Weintre to van Olpen. Amerang, November 28, 1845. ANRI: K. 42. Ambon 1264.
35. Roberts to the Secretary of State. Batavia, March 31, 1848. NARA: Despatches from U.S. Consuls in Batavia, Java, Netherlands East Indies, 1818–1906. Vol. 2 (July 31–August 26, 1850).
36. Roberts to the Secretary of State. Batavia, March 31, 1848. NARA: Despatches from U.S. Consuls in Batavia, Java, Netherlands East Indies, 1818–1906. Vol. 2 (July 31–August 26, 1850).
37. Eduardo Carratalá to [the Secretary of Government]. Manila, November 21, 1863. NAP: Piratas, Leg. 2.
38. Carratalá to [the Governor of Mindanao]. Manila, November 25, 1863. NAP: Piratas, Leg. 2.
39. Forth-Rouen to Mavrokordatos. Athens, November 29, 1854. YE: Central Office, 55/1A (1854–55).
40. Mavrokordatos to Forth-Rouen. Athens, December 8, 1854. YE: Central Office, 55/1A (1854–55).
41. Forth-Rouen to Mavrokordatos. Athens, December 10, 1854. YE: Central Office, 55/1A (1854–55).
42. Forth-Rouen to Mavrokordatos. Athens, December 22, 1854. YE: Central Office, 55/1A (1854–55).
43. Lloyd to Captain George King (at HMS *Leander*). HMS *Triton*, Piraeus, June 29, 1854. YE: Central Office, 55/1A (1854–55).
44. Lloyd to King (at HMS *Leander*). HMS *Triton*, Piraeus, June 29, 1854. YE: Central Office, 55/1A (1854–55).

45. Wise to Mavrokordatos. Athens, August 30, 1854. YE: Central Office, 55/1A (1854–55).
46. Wise to Mavrokordatos. Athens, August 30, 1854. YE: Central Office, 55/1A (1854–55).
47. Wise to Mavrokordatos. Athens, August 30, 1854. YE: Central Office, 55/1A (1854–55).
48. Wise to Mavrokordatos. Athens, August 30, 1854. YE: Central Office, 55/1A (1854–55).
49. Wise to Mavrokordatos. Athens, April 11 and April 21, 1855. YE: Central Office, 55/1 A-B (1854–55).
50. Wise to Mavrokordatos. Athens, April 11, 1855. YE: Central Office, 55/1 A-B (1854–55).
51. Wise to Argyropoulos. Athens, September 22, 1855. YE: Central Office, 55/1 A-B (1854–55).
52. Wise to Argyropoulos. Athens, September 22, 1855. YE: Central Office, 55/1 A-B (1854–55).
53. M. Von Wallenburg to Konstantinos Zographos. Athens, April 20, 1840. YE: Central Office, 55/1 (1840); and Clement Solar de la Marguerite to the Chargé d'Affaires of Sweden in Athens. Turin, October 3, 1842. YE: Central Office, 55/1 (1842).
54. Morris to Ali Pacha. [Constantinople], March 6, 1862. BOA: HR.TO 146/97.
55. Morris to Ali Pacha. Constantinople, July 5, 1862. BOA: HR.TO 146/100.
56. Morris to Ali Pacha. Constantinople, July 5, 1862. BOA: HR.TO 146/100.
57. "Correspondance du Maroc," *Revue Orientale et Algérienne* (Paris: Gide et. J. Baudry, 1852), vol. 1, 504.
58. Ventosa, *Españoles y Marroquíes*, 816.
59. Charles Napier to Lord Palmerston. Gibraltar, March 15, 1849; and Robert Gardiner to Drummond Hay. Gibraltar, October 21, 1851. TNA: Foreign Office, 174/56.
60. Drummond Hay to Clarendon. Tangier, September 22, 1856. TNA: Foreign Office, 88/91. See also Drummond Hay to Clarendon. Tangier, May 30, 1856. TNA: Foreign Office, 99/74.
61. Drummond Hay to Clarendon. Tangier, April 21, 1857. TNA: Foreign Office, 88/91.
62. Drummond Hay to Clarendon. Tangier, April 21, 1857. TNA: Foreign Office, 88/91.
63. Drummond Hay to Seed Mohamed Khateeb. [Tangier], April 18, 1857. TNA: Foreign Office, 88/91.
64. Drummond Hay to Seed Mohamed Khateeb. [Tangier], April 18, 1857. TNA: Foreign Office, 88/91. It is worth noting that just a few months earlier, Drummond Hay and Khateeb had signed a bilateral treaty by which the

British had acquired several privileges from the sultan. See "Convention of Commerce and Navigation between Her Majesty and the Sultan of Morocco. Signed, in the English and Arabic languages, at Tangier, December 9, 1856," in Leone Levi, *Annals of British Legislation: Being a Classified and Analysed Summary of Public Bills, and of Sessional Papers Generally, of the Houses of Lords and Commons* (London: Smith, Elder, 1858), vol. 3, 177–180.

65. The Sultan of Sumenep to van den Bosch. Sumenep, November 1, 1830. NNA: Ministerie van Kolonien, 1814–1849. No. 4168.
66. The Sultan of Sumenep to van den Bosch. Sumenep, November 1, 1830. NNA: Ministerie van Kolonien, 1814–1849. No. 4168.
67. Cornets de Groot to Goldman. [Batavia], March 16, 1837. NNA: Ministerie van Kolonien, 1814–1849. No. 4168.
68. Cornets de Groot to Goldman. [Batavia], March 16, 1837. NNA: Ministerie van Kolonien, 1814–1849. No. 4168.
69. The Assistant Resident at Siak to the Resident at Riau (Tobias). Bengkalies, June 6, 1860. ANRI: Riouw 163. Aankomende brieven, 1860.
70. A. Rutering to Tobias. Batavia, February 10, 1860. ANRI: Riouw 163. Aankomende brieven, 1860.
71. "A Reminder of a Previous Notice Dated 13 January 1828." Issued in Batavia, July 17, 1835. ANRI: K. 42. Ambon, 1119. 1835.
72. Eduardo Scarnichia and João da Silva Carvalho to Isidoro Francisco Guimaraes. On board the Amazona, July 25, 1855. Arquivo de Macau, Macau (hereafter AM): MO/AH/SA/01/00089.
73. See, for example, Isidoro Francisco Guimaraes to the Ministro Secretario de Estado dos Negocios da Marinha e Ultramar. Macau, July 19, 1854. AHU: ACL/SEMU/DGU, 005. Cx. 21. Correspondência Macau, Timor, 1854–1855; and The Council of Government of Macau to the Ministro Secretario de Estado dos Negocios da Marinha e Ultramar. Macau, December 12, 1858. AHU: ACL/SEMU/DGU, 005. Cx. 24. Correspondência Macau, Timor, 1858.
74. Tavares to the Ministro Secretario de Estado dos Negocios da Marinha e Ultramar. Brig Mondego, at rive de Macau, August 21, 1858. Arquivo Histórico da Marinha, Lisbon: Documentação avulse, Cx. 471 (documentação de 1836–1860); Livro de Registro de Oficios e Ordens para os Brigues Mondego e D. Pedro, de 1845–1859.
75. These measures were eventually reversed after Ferdinand VII was crowned as king, shortly after the defeat of France at the hands of a coalition of European nations. See, for example, Regina Grafe and Maria Alejandra Irigoin, "The Spanish Empire and Its Legacy: Fiscal Re-Distribution and Political Conflict in Colonial and Post-Colonial Spanish America," *Working Papers of the Global Economic History Network*, no. 23/06 (2006); and Sanjurjo, *In the Blood of Our Brothers*, 58–60.
76. Bocalán to Mohammad Pulalun. Frigate *Esperanza*, at Joló. April 9, 1845. NAP: Administración Civil. Leg. 1.

77. Bocalán to Mohammad Pulalun. Frigate *Esperanza*, at Joló. April 9, 1845. NAP: Administración Civil. Leg. 1.
78. Emilio Castelar, D. F. de Paula Canalejas, D. G. Cruzada Villamil, and Miguel Morayta, *Crónica de la Guerra de África* (Madrid: Imprenta de V. Maytute y B. Compagni, 1859), vol. 1, chapter 1.
79. Thomas Cole to D. Coker. Liberated African Department, Freetown, June 9, 1831. SLPA: Liberated African Department: Letter books, 1831–34.
80. Macdonald to Bocarree Sillee. Secretary's Office [Freetown], December 31, 1844. SLPA: Colonial Secretary's Letter Book. November 11, 1844–September 29, 1845.
81. Macdonald to Bocarree Sillee. Secretary's Office [Freetown], December 31, 1844. SLPA: Colonial Secretary's Letter Book. November 11, 1844–September 29, 1845.
82. *Burney Papers*, vol. 1, 166.
83. Draft of a letter to the Siamese Minister, signed by George Swinton [1823]. NAS: L. 20. Bengal: Letters from Raffles, etc. January 1823–August 1823.
84. *Burney Papers*, vol. 1, 166.
85. David Todd, "John Bowring and the Global Dissemination of Free Trade," *Historical Journal* 51, no. 3 (2008): 393.
86. B. J. Terwiel, "The Bowring Treaty: Imperialism and the Indigenous Perspective," *Journal of the Siam Society* 79, no. 2 (1991): 40–47.
87. Blane to John Pepper. Bushire Residency, May 31, 1833. TNA: Admiralty, 127/48.
88. Norris to Blane. Bombay, March 7, 1834. BL: IOR/R/15/1/65.
89. Wilson to J. M. Guy. Bushire, January 5, 1829. TNA: Admiralty, 127/48.
90. Hennell to Brucks. Karrak, February 12, 1841. BL: IOR/R/15/1/92.
91. Porter to Lt. J. S. Draper. HMS *Euphrates*, off Sharjah, November 9, 1843. TNA: Admiralty, 127/51.
92. Castelar, Canalejas, Cruzada Villamil, and Morayta, *Crónica de la Guerra de África*, vol. 1, 48. On calls for revenge and violence in Spain against the inhabitants of the Riff, see, among others, Ventosa, *Españoles y Marroquíes*, 881.
93. For a discussion of the role of the Dutch navy in the processes of intimidation and suppression of maritime communities in the East Indies, see van Dissel, "Grensoverschrijdend," 151–169; and, more broadly G. Teitler, A. M. C. van Dissel and J. N. F. M. à Campo, eds., *Zeeroof en zeeroofbestrijding in de Indische archipel (19de eeuw)*. (Amsterdam: Uitgeverij De Bataafsche Leeuw, 2005).
94. Prince to John Anderson. Batavia, November 24, 1827. BL: IOR/F/4/1282. Prince had left from Singapore just a weeks earlier, leaving the assistant resident councilor, Edward Presgrave, in charge of the Residency. NAS: N. 3: Singapore: Resident's Diary, 251.

95. Prince to John Anderson. Batavia, November 24, 1827. BL: IOR/F/4/1282.
96. Matthew C. Perry, *Narrative of the Expedition of an American Squadron to the China Seas and Japan, Performed in the Years 1852, 1853, and 1854* (New York: D. Appleton, 1856), 261–77.
97. Treaty of Kanagawa. Signed at Kanagawa, March 31, 1854. NARA: General Records of the United States Government, 1778–2006. RG 11. Series: Perfected Treaties, 1778–1845.
98. On the Treaty of Shimoda, see Hiroshi Kimura, *The Kurillian Knot: A History of Japanese-Russian Border Negotiations* (Stanford: Stanford University Press, 2008), 21–32.
99. See, for example, Jérôme Félix de Monleón to the Baron de Mackau. Brig *La Zèbre*, Sierra Leone, February 19, 1845. ANOM: Généralités, 166/1341.
100. Charles Baudin to [?]. Gorée, April 3, 1845. ANOM: Généralités, 166/1341.
101. Charles Mackenzie, *Notes on Haiti: Made during a Residence in that Republic* (London: H Colburn and R. Bentley, 1830), vol. 2, 87.
102. See, for example, Jean-François Brière, "La France et la reconnaissance de l'indépendance Haïtienne: Le débat sur l'Ordonnance de 1825," *French Colonial History* 5 (2004): 125–138; and Brière, "L'Emprint de 1825 dans la dette de l'indépendance haitienne envers la France," *Journal of Haitian Studies* 12, no. 2 (2006): 126–134. For a full reproduction of its text, see "Ordonnance de Charles X," in Thomas Madiou, *Historie d'Haïti, 1819–1826* (Port-au-Prince: Editions Henri Deschampes, 1826), vol. 6, 448.
103. Mackenzie, *Notes on Haiti*, vol. 2, 87.
104. Comte de Chabrol to Pierre Roch Jurien de la Gravière (Very secret). Paris, April 17, 1825. In Jean-François Brière, *Haïti et la France, 1804–1848: Notices Histo*brisé (Paris: Karthala, 2008), 328–329.
105. Madiou, *Historie d'Haïti: 1819–1826*, vol. 6, 44.
106. Guive Mirfendereski, *A Diplomatic History of the Caspian Sea: Treaties, Diaries, and Other Stories* (London: Palgrave, 2001), 31–40; and Edward G. Browne, *A Year amongst the Persians: Impressions as to the Life, Character, and Thought of the People of Persia, Received during Twelve Months' Residence in That Country in the Years 1887–8* (London: Adam and Charles Black, 1893), 568–569.
107. Ram Rahul, *Central Asia: An Outline History* (New Delhi: Concept Publishing, 1997), 131; and Rudi Matthee, "Facing a Rude and Barbarous Neighbor: Iranian Perceptions of Russia and the Russians from the Safavids to the Qajars," in Abbas Amanat and Farzin Vejdani, eds., *Iran Facing Others: Identity Boundaries in a Historical Perspective* (London: Palgrave Macmillan, 2012), 112.
108. These gunboats were built by the firm of Rennie expressly for the Russian government. See John Timbs, *The Industry, Science, and Art of the*

Age: or The International Exhibition of 1862 (London: Lockwood, 1863), 129.

109. Harold N. Ingle, *Nesselrode and the Russian Rapprochement with Britain, 1836–1844* (Berkeley: University of California Press, 1976), 152; and Aleksandr Mikhailovich Prokorov, *Great Soviet Encyclopedia* (London: Macmillan, 1973), vol. 21, 363.
110. *Colburn's United Service Magazine, and Naval and Military Journal* (London: Hurst and Blackett, 1857), part I, 298.
111. José Montero y Vidal, *Historia de la piratería malayo-mahometana en Mindanao, Joló y Borneo* (Madrid: Imprenta y Fundición de Manuel Tello, 1888), vol. 1, 375.
112. Echagüe to the Minister of War and the Colonies. Manila, October 25, 1862. AHN: Ultramar, 5193/30.
113. Cornets de Groot, *Notices Historiques*, 42–43. See also *"Further Notes on Piracy in the Dutch East Indies."* NNA: Ministerie van Kolonien, 1814–1849. No. 4168.
114. Cornets de Groot, *Notices Historiques*, 58.
115. "The War in Morocco," *Illustrated London News*, August 24, 1844, 121–122.
116. "Correspondance du Maroc," vol. 1, 501.
117. *Expedition du Maroc. Bombardement de Salé et de Rabat. Extrait du Rapport de M le Contre-Amiral Dubordieu, commandant en chef de la division navale expeditionnaire du Maroc* (St. Lo: A. Jacqueline, 1851).
118. M. Léon Godard, *Description et Histoire du Maroc* (Paris: Ch. Tanera, 1860), 622.
119. Godard, *Description et Histoire du Maroc*, 622–623; *Expedition du Maroc*, 3.
120. John M. Belohlavek, "Andrew Jackson and the Malaysian Pirates: A Question of Diplomacy and Politics," *Tennessee Historical Quarterly* 36, no. 1 (1977): 19–29.
121. Shubrick to John Downes. US Ship *Potomac*, off the Town of Quallah-Battoo, February 6, 1832. In Jeremiah N. Reynolds, *Voyage of the United States Frigate Potomac. Under the Command of Commodore John Downes, during the Circum-navigation of the Globe, in the Years 1831, 1832, 1833, and 1834* (New York: Harper & Brothers, 1835), vol. 1, 536.
122. A. Van Yseghem to John Revely. Penang, October 12, 1838. NARA: Despatches from U.S. Consuls in Singapore, Straits Settlements, 1833–1906. Volume 1 (October 31, 1833–December 4, 1846).
123. William Meacham Murrell, *Cruise of the Frigate Columbia around the World, under the Command of Commodore George C. Read, in 1838, 1839, and 1840* (Boston: Benjamin B. Mussey, 1840), 103–116, esp. 111.
124. Joseph Balestier to John Forsyth. United States Consulate, Singapore, June 20, 1839. NARA: Despatches from U.S. Consuls in Singapore, Straits Settlements, 1833–1906. Volume 1 (October 31, 1833–December 4, 1846).

125. W. W. Shaw to Daniel Webster. Consulate of the United States of America. Singapore, June 15, 1851. NARA: Despatches from U.S. Consuls in Singapore, Straits Settlements, 1833–1906. Volume 2 (January 1, 1847–December 20, 1851).
126. Shaw to Webster. Consulate of the United States of America. Singapore, June 15, 1851. NARA: Despatches from U.S. Consuls in Singapore, Straits Settlements, 1833–1906. Volume 2 (January 1, 1847–December 20, 1851).
127. Shaw to Webster. Consulate of the United States of America. Singapore, June 15, 1851. NARA: Despatches from U.S. Consuls in Singapore, Straits Settlements, 1833–1906. Volume 2 (January 1, 1847–December 20, 1851).
128. John Ross, *History of Korea, Ancient and Modern with Description of Manners and Customs, Language and Geography* (London: Elliot Stock, 1891), 294.
129. William Elliot Griffis, *Corea, the Hermit Nation* (New York: Charles Scribner's Sons, 1882), 391–395.
130. Griffis, *Corea, the Hermit Nation*, 394.
131. "Corea," *Hawaiian Gazette* (Honolulu, HI), May 13, 1868.
132. Keppel to William Parker. HMS *Dido*, Sarawak, May 17, 1843. HCPP: Despatches from Naval Officers on China Station relative to Attacks on Natives of Borneo, 1842–49.
133. Keppel to William Parker. HMS *Dido*, Sarawak, May 17, 1843. HCPP: Despatches from Naval Officers on China Station relative to Attacks on Natives of Borneo, 1842–49.
134. J. Barrow to [Admiral William] Parker. Admiralty, January 6, 1844. HCPP: Despatches from Naval Officers on China Station relative to Attacks on Natives of Borneo, 1842–49.
135. Parker to the Sec. of the Admiralty. HMS *Cornwallis*, at Hong Kong, July 13, 1843. HCPP: Despatches from Naval Officers on China Station relative to Attacks on Natives of Borneo, 1842–49.
136. Kemball to Ethersay. Bushire, August 6, 1855; see also Kemball to Ethersay. Bushire, June 29, 1855. TNA: Admiralty, 127/58.
137. Kemball to Ethersay. Bushire, August 6, 1855. TNA: Admiralty, 127/58.
138. Ethersey to Kemball. H. C. Clive, off Ras el Khymah, September 10, 1855. TNA: Admiralty, 127/61.
139. Ethersey to Kemball. H. C. Clive, off Ras el Khymah, September 10, 1855. TNA: Admiralty, 127/61.
140. Ethersey to Kemball. H. C. Clive, off Ras el Khymah, September 10, 1855. TNA: Admiralty, 127/61.
141. Disbrowe to Ethersey. Bushire, September 24, 1855. TNA: Admiralty, 127/58.
142. "The Pirates of the Persian Gulf," *Illustrated London News*, November 28, 1868, 526.

143. "Pirates of the Persian Gulf."
144. "(1) Disturbances in Persian Gulf. (2) Violation of the Maritime Truce by the Chiefs of Bahrein and Abuthabi. (3) Ali-bin-Khalifa Made Chief of Bahrein, 1867–68," *Persian Gulf Gazetteer*, part 1, Historical and Political Materials, Précis of Bahrein [Bahrain] Affairs, 1854–1904, 13–19. BL: IOR/R/15/1/722.
145. Levien, ed., *Cree Journals*, 73.
146. See, in particular, "Ching Kiang Foo: A Chamber of Horrors. July 22, 1842," and "A Street in Ching Kiang Foo. July 23, 1842." Private Illustrated Journal of Dr. E. H. Cree, vol. 6, 1842. NMM: CRJ/6.
147. Ting Man Tsao, "Ho! For China: Piratical Incursions, Free Trade Imperialism and Modern Chinese History, c. 1832–1834," in Grace Moore, ed., *Pirates and Mutineers of the Nineteenth Century: Swashbucklers and Swindlers* (London: Routledge, 2011), 60.
148. Chappell. "Maritime Raiding," 474.
149. Laai, *Part Played by the Pirates*, 74–76.
150. John C. Dalrymple-Hay to Admiral Collier. Her Majesty's Sloop *Columbine*, Typoung Bay, September 30, 1849. In Beresford, *Account of the Destruction*, 51.
151. *China Mail*, October 4, 1849. Beresford, *Account of the Destruction, 65.*
152. Levien, ed., *Cree Journals*, 202.
153. Levien, ed., *Cree Journals.*
154. Levien, ed., *Cree Journals.*
155. Arthur to Captain J[ames] J. McCleverty. HMS *Nimrod*, Tanne Bay, December 16, 1860. TNA: Colonial Office, 129/78.
156. "Notes by Bonham." Singapore, June 20, 1836. Appendix to the secret proceedings of the Correspondence for the Suppression of Piracy. 1836. ANM: 2014/0012139.
157. "Notes by Bonham." Singapore, June 20, 1836. ANM: 2014/001 2139.
158. "Notes by Bonham." Singapore, June 20, 1836. ANM: 2014/0012139.
159. Colin MacKenzie, *Storms and Sunshine of a Soldiers Life* (Edinburgh: David Douglas, 1884), vol. 1, 65. For a discussion of other actions undertaken by Chads on the *Andromache*, see, among others, Carl A. Trocky, *Prince of Pirates: The Temenggongs and the Development of Johor and Singapore, 1784–1885* (Singapore: NUS Press, 1979), 81; and Richard Gott, *Britain's Empire: Resistance, Repression and Revolt* (London: Verso, 2022), 287–288.
160. MacKenzie, *Storms and Sunshine of a Soldiers Life.*
161. MacKenzie, *Storms and Sunshine of a Soldiers Life.*
162. Lord Auckland to Dominique Jacques de Eerens. Fort William, September 7, 1836. BL: IOF/F/4/1724/69433.
163. In fact, in September 1836, HMS *Wolf* had been tasked with taking three brass guns from Malacca to Singapore, so that new gunboats could

be armed. Chads to Samuel Gatling. HMS *Andromache*, Malacca, September 15, 1836. BL: IOF/F/4/1724/69433.

164. Stanley to Bonham. Tungannee, May 20, 1838. BL: IOR/F/4/1841/77129.
165. Congalton to J. Church. Singapore, May 25, 1838. BL: IOR/F/4/1841/77129.
166. Antonio de Mora to the Comandante General del Apostadero. Isabela de Basilan, August 19, 1862. NAP: Piratas, Leg. 4.
167. Warren, *Sulu Zone*, 105.
168. Colebrook to Aberdeen. Nassau, April 23, 1835. TNA: Colonial Office, 23/93.
169. On the Commission of Eastern Enquiry, see Zoë Laidlaw, "Investigating Empire: Humanitarians, Reform and the Commission of Eastern Enquiry," *Journal of Imperial and Commonwealth History* 40, no. 5 (2012): 749–68.
170. Laidlaw, "Investigating Empire."
171. Benton, *They Called It Peace*, 152.
172. For the French attack on Kangwha Island, see Daniel C. Kane, "Bellonet and Roze: Overzealous Servants of Empire and the 1866 French Attack on Korea," *Korean Studies* 23 (1999): 1–23; and Carter J. Eckert, *Park Chung Hee and Modern Korea: The Roots of Militarism, 1866–1945* (Cambridge, MA: Harvard University Press, 2016), 15, 21–23.
173. Benton, *They Called It Peace*, 180.
174. Achile Mbembe, *Necropolitics* (Durham, NC: Duke University Press, 2019), 19.
175. Palmerston to Brooke. Foreign Office, April 23, 1850. HCPP: Correspondence respecting Piracy in E. Archipelago, and Proceedings of Sir J. Brooke 1852.

Chapter Four. Proto-Colonial Expansion and the Suppression of Maritime Raiding

1. See, for example, Michael Dent Eiland, "Dragon and Elephant: Relations between Viet Nam and Siam, 1742–1847" (PhD diss., George Washington University, 1989), 122–170.
2. Balestier to Forsyth. Consulate of the United States, Singapore, August 3, 1837. NARA: Despatches from U.S. Consuls in Singapore, Straits Settlements, 1833–1906. Volume 1 (October 31, 1833–December 4, 1846).
3. Balestier to Forsyth. Consulate of the United States, Singapore, August 3, 1837. NARA: Despatches from U.S. Consuls in Singapore, Straits Settlements, 1833–1906. Volume 1 (October 31, 1833–December 4, 1846).
4. Before using a large fleet to capture Kedah in 1821, Siam also used forty-two of these ships to blockade of the rebels in Kedah in 1832. "Penang," *Asiatic Journal and Monthly Register* 8 (May 1832): 26–27. See also [?] to

Chao Phraya Yommarat. Bangkok, 1839. National Library of Thailand, Bangkok (hereafter NLT): JS., 1201/1839.

5. "List of Vessels Built in Siam," in Samuel J. Smith, *Siam Repository* 1, no. 4 (1869): 328. See also Frederick Arthur Neale, *Narrative of a Residence in Siam* (London: Office of the National Illustrated Library, 1852), 44.
6. Balestier to Forsyth. Consulate of the United States, Singapore, August 3, 1837. NARA: Despatches from U.S. Consuls in Singapore, Straits Settlements, 1833–1906. Volume 1 (October 31, 1833–December 4, 1846).
7. Syril Skinner, trans., and Justin Corfield, ed., *Rama III and the Siamese Expedition to Kedah in 1839: The Dispatches of Luang Udosombat* (Melbourne: Monash University Centre of Southeast Asian Studies, 1993), 57.
8. Skinner, trans., and Corfield, ed., *Rama III and the Siamese Expedition*, 236.
9. Skinner, trans., and Corfield, ed., *Rama III and the Siamese Expedition*, 257.
10. Skinner, trans., and Corfield, ed., *Rama III and the Siamese Expedition.*
11. Mr. James Richardson Logan's intervention in Tunku Mohamed Saad trial. "Trial of Tuanku Mahomed Saad and Others for Piracy. Held in the Court of Judicature of Prince of Wales Island, Singapore and Malacca. At Prince of Wales Island. On Monday the 26th and Thursday the 29th October, and Monday the 2nd of November 1840" (Penang: Printed at the Gazette and Chronicle Office, 1840). BL: IOR/F/4/1920.
12. Howard Malcolm, *Travels in South-eastern Asia, Embracing Hindustan, Malaya, Siam, and China* (Boston: Gould, Kendall, and Lincoln, 1839), vol. 1, 106.
13. Francis R. Bradley, "Siam's Conquest of Patani and the End of Mandala Relations, 1786–1838," in Patrick Jory, ed., *Ghosts of the Past in Southern Thailand: Essays on the History and Historiography of Patani* (Singapore: NUS Press, 2013), 159.
14. See, for example, Chao Phraya Akkramaha-senabodi to Chao Phraya Yomraj and Phraya Sipipat. Sunday of the second waning moon of the 2nd month. NLT: J.S., 1201/1839.
15. Barnett, *Empire of Humanity*, 30.
16. Laidlaw, "Investigating Empire"; and Felicity Jenz, *Missionaries and Modernity: Education in the British Empire, 1830–1910* (Manchester: Manchester University Press, 2022), 82.
17. Pitts, *Boundaries of the International*, 3.
18. Amirell, *Pirates of Empire*, 3.
19. Ibbetson to George Swinton. Prince of Wales Island, November 23, 1831. NAS: R. 1. Governor's Letters to Bengal. May 1831–August 1832.
20. Ibbetson to Swinton. Prince of Wales Island, November 23, 1831. NAS: R. 1. Governor's Letters to Bengal. May 1831–August 1832.
21. Ibbetson to Swinton. Prince of Wales Island, November 23, 1831. NAS: R. 1. Governor's Letters to Bengal. May 1831–August 1832.

22. Ibbetson to George Swinton. Prince of Wales Island, November 23, 1831. NAS: R. 1. Governor's Letters to Bengal. May 1831–August 1832.
23. Hannah Arendt, *The Origins of Totalitarianism* (San Diego: Harcourt Brace & World, 1967), part 3, 192.
24. Entry for October 4, 1828. NAS: N. 4. Singapore: Resident's Diary. January 1828–December 1828.
25. See, for example, Emrys Chew, *Arming the Periphery;* Amirell, *Pirates of Empire,* 119–120; and Abel, "Asian Seafaring Communities," 39–41.
26. Moges, *Recollections of Baron Gros's Embassy,* 79.
27. Moges, *Recollections of Baron Gros's Embassy.*
28. Moges, *Recollections of Baron Gros's Embassy,* 60.
29. The American were said to have sold over thirty thousand firearms along the Pepper Coast of Sumatra and in Siam during the 1820s. See Crawfurd, *Journal of an Embassy,* 373.
30. Todd, *Velvet Empire,* 73.
31. Alan Lester, Kate Boehme, and Peter Mitchell, *Ruling the World: Freedom, Civilisation and Liberalism* (Cambridge: Cambridge University Press, 2020), 9.
32. Mbembe, *Necropolitics,* 19.
33. Abenia Taure, *Memorias,* 16. See also "Le Riff et le Maroc en 1856," *L'illustration: journal universel* 25 (October 18, 1856): 245; and Ruperto de Aguirre, *Espedicion al Riff: Su importancia, necesidad y conveniencia* (Madrid: Imprenta de José María Ducazcal, 1858), 5.
34. Abenia Taure, *Memorias,* 49.
35. For example, a French expedition reportedly attacked the Riff peoples in late 1851 or early 1852, subjecting them to a "vigorous repression." "Faits divers," *Le Corsaire* (May 21, 1852): 1. See also "Bulletin du jour," *La Presse,* April 29, 1852, 1.
36. Robert Gardiner to Lord Grey. Gibraltar, January 18, 1852; and Captain H[enry] W. Giffard to the Admiral in the Mediterranean [James Dundas]. HMS *Dragon,* Gibraltar, January 22, 1852. TNA: Foreign Office, 99/69.
37. Drummond Hay to the Earl of Clarendon. Tangier, August 8, 1854. TNA: Foreign Office, 99/69.
38. Drummond Hay to Clarendon. Tangier, August 8, 1854. TNA: Foreign Office, 99/69.
39. Henry W. Giffard to the Admiral in the Mediterranean. HMS *Dragon,* Gibraltar, January 22, 1852. TNA: Foreign Office, 99/69.
40. Giffard to the Admiral in the Mediterranean. HMS *Dragon,* Gibraltar, January 22, 1852. TNA: Foreign Office, 99/69. In May 1855, Drummond Hay once again proposed an armed expedition against the Riff. Drummond Hay to the Earl of Clarendon. Tangier, May 24, 1855. TNA: Foreign Office, 99/69.
41. *Destruction of Lagos,* 21.
42. Baudin to the Minister of Marine and Colonies. Gorée docks, November 12, 1844. ANOM: Généralités, 166/1341.

43. For a description of the French forts at Grand Bassam and Assinoé during this period, see: Horatio Bridge, *Journal of an African Cruiser. Comprising Sketches of the Canaries, the Cape de Verds, Liberia, Madeira, Sierra Leone, and Other Places of Interest on the West Coast of Africa* (London: Wiley and Putnam, 1845), chapter 16.
44. Baudin to the Minister of Marine and Colonies. Gorée docks, November 12, 1844. ANOM: Généralités, 166/1341.
45. Baudin to the Minister of Marine and Colonies. Gorée docks, November 12, 1844. ANOM: Généralités, 166/1341.
46. Baudin to the Minister of Marine and Colonies. Gorée docks, November 12, 1844. ANOM: Généralités, 166/1341.
47. J. de Wal to P. J. B. de Perez. Surabaya, December 12, 1850. ANRI: Soerabaya, 1427. Openbare Orde, 1850–1851.
48. de Wal to de Perez. Surabaya, December 12, 1850. ANRI: Soerabaya, 1427. Openbare Orde, 1850–1851.
49. B. R. Pearn, "Erskine Murray's Fatal Adventure in Borneo, 1843–44," *Indonesia* 7 (1969): 20–32; and Graham Saunders, "James Erskine Murray's Expeditions to Kutei, 1843–1844," *Brunei Museum Journal* 6 (1986): 91–115. For Dutch claims on this part of eastern Borneo, see Ian Black, "The 'Lastposten': Eastern Kalimantan and the Dutch in the Nineteenth and Early Twentieth Centuries," *Journal of South East Asian Studies* 16, no. 2 (1985): 281–291.
50. Black, "'Lastposten.' "
51. "In-Official Part. Batavia, February 18, 1845," *Javasche Courant*, February 19, 1845, 2.
52. "In-Official Part. Batavia, February 18, 1845."
53. "In-Official Part. Batavia, February 18, 1845."
54. Warren, *Sulu Zone*; Amirell, *Pirates of Empire*.
55. A case in question is the treaty signed by the Spanish and the sultan of Joló in April 1851, in the aftermath of the expedition directed against the sultanate earlier in the year. The Spanish and Sulu versions of the treaty differed significantly—the wording in the former suggested that Joló would be "incorporated to the Spanish crown," while the wording in the latter referred to a "union and friendship," between Joló and Spain instead. See Marqués de Olivart, *Colección de los tratados, convenios y documentos internacionales*, vol. 2, 120; and Najeeb M. Saleeby, *The History of Sulu* (Manila: Bureau of Public Printing, 1908), 210–214.
56. "Capitulaciones de paz, protección y comercio." Palace of Joló, September 23, 1836. NAP: Administración Civil, Leg. 1.
57. "Capitulaciones de paz, protección y comercio." Palace of Joló, September 23, 1836. NAP: Administración Civil, Leg. 1.
58. "Capitulaciones de paz, protección y comercio." Palace of Joló, September 23, 1836. NAP: Administración Civil, Leg. 1.
59. "Capitulaciones de paz, protección y comercio." Palace of Joló, September 23, 1836. NAP: Administración Civil, Leg. 1.

60. C. F. Goldman to the Governor General of the Dutch East Indies. Lingga, July 3, 1837. NNA: Ministerie van Kolonien, 1814–1849. No. 4168.
61. William Barrow to [the Government of India]. Calcutta, April 14, 1836. BL: IOF/F/4/1724/69433.
62. Murchison to Chads and Bonham. Prince of Wales Island, August 12, 1836. BL: IOF/F/4/1724/69433.
63. Murchison to Chads and Bonham. Prince of Wales Island, August 12, 1836. BL: IOF/F/4/1724/69433.
64. Chads to Bladen. HMS *Andromache*, off Galang, June 29, 1836. BL: IOF/F/4/1724/69433.
65. Davis to Cochrane. Victoria House, Victoria, January 25, 1845. TNA: Admiralty, 125/145.
66. Davis to Cochrane. Victoria House, Victoria, January 25, 1845. TNA: Admiralty, 125/145.
67. Chads to Parker. HMS *Cumbrian*, July 1, 1843. TNA: Colonial Office, 129/4.
68. Pottinger to Parker. Government House, Victoria, Hong Kong, August 1, 1843. TNA: Colonial Office, 129/4.
69. Parker to Pottinger. Cornwallis at Hong Kong, August 12, 1843. TNA: Colonial Office, 129/4.
70. Alemany to [Clavería]. Manila, December 3, 1849. NAP: Piratas, Leg. 1.
71. Alemany to [Clavería]. Manila, December 3, 1849. NAP: Piratas, Leg. 1.
72. Elphinstone to Rahmah Bin Jabeer. [Bombay], January 16, 1826. BL: IOR/R/15/1/37.
73. Elphinstone to Rahmah Bin Jabeer. [Bombay], January 16, 1826. BL: IOR/R/15/1/37.
74. "Supplementary Treaty between Her Majesty and the Emperor of China." Signed at Hoomun-Chae, October 8, 1843. TNA: Colonial Office, 129/1.
75. Brooke to the Earl of Mamelsbury. United Service Club, November 23, 1852. HCPP: Correspondence respecting Piracy in E. Archipelago, and Proceedings of Sir J. Brooke, 1852.
76. Hume to the Earl of Mamelsbury. 6 Bryanstone Square, April 7, 1852. HCPP: Correspondence respecting Piracy on the Coast of Borneo, 1852.
77. Testimony of Dave. HCPP: Borneo: Reports of the Commissioners Appointed to Inquire into Certain Matters connected with the Position of Sir James Brooke. Presented to both Houses of Parliament by Command of Her Majesty, 1855.
78. Testimonies of Kaek and Moses. HCPP: Borneo: Reports of the Commissioners Appointed to Inquire into Certain Matters connected with the Position of Sir James Brooke. Presented to both Houses of Parliament by Command of Her Majesty, 1855.

79. Testimony of Henry. HCPP: Borneo: Reports of the Commissioners Appointed to Inquire into Certain Matters connected with the Position of Sir James Brooke. Presented to both Houses of Parliament by Command of Her Majesty, 1855.
80. Testimonies of Guthrie and Henry. HCPP: Borneo: Reports of the Commissioners Appointed to Inquire into Certain Matters connected with the Position of Sir James Brooke. Presented to both Houses of Parliament by Command of Her Majesty, 1855.
81. Testimony of Crane. HCPP: Borneo: Reports of the Commissioners Appointed to Inquire into Certain Matters connected with the Position of Sir James Brooke. Presented to both Houses of Parliament by Command of Her Majesty, 1855.
82. Saunders, *History of Brunei*, 75.
83. Graham Irwin, *Nineteenth-Century Borneo: A Study in Diplomatic Rivalry* (Leiden: Brill, 1955): 120–127.
84. Private Illustrated Journal of Dr. E. H. Cree, vol. 9, 1845. Sunday, August 10, 1845. NMM: CRJ/9.
85. Private Illustrated Journal of Dr. E. H. Cree, vol. 9, 1845. Sunday, August 10, 1845. NMM: CRJ/9.
86. Bianca M. Gerlich, *Marudu 1845: The Destruction and Reconstruction of a Coastal State in Borneo* (Hamburg: Abera, 2003); and "Thus Has Marudu Ceased to Exist: The Rise and Fall of a North Bornean Kingdom," *Sabah Society Journal* 29 (2012): 19–55.
87. Drinkwater Bethune, *Views in the Eastern Archipelago, Borneo, Sarawak, Labuan, from Drawings Made on the Spot by Capt. Bethune, R.N., Commr. Heath, R.N., and others* (London: McLean, 1847), n.p.
88. Bethune, *Views in the Eastern Archipelago.*
89. Hume to the Earl of Malmesbury. Bryanstone Square, June 7, 1852. HCPP: Correspondence respecting Piracy on the Coast of Borneo, 1852. For a description of this attack, see Cochrane to the Secretary of the Admiralty. *Spiteful,* off the City of Bruné, Borneo Proper, July 9, 1846. HCPP: Despatches from Sir T. Cochrane to Admiralty, reporting Capture of Brunei; Despatch on Piracy in E. Archipelago, 1852.
90. Charles B. Wells to John M. Clayton, Secretary of State. [Batavia, August, 1850]. NARA: Despatches from U.S. Consuls in Batavia, Java, Netherlands East Indies, 1818–1906. Volume 2 (July 31, 1836–August 26, 1850).
91. Deborah A. Logan, *Harriet Martineau, Victorian Imperialism, and the Civilizing Mission* (London: Routledge, 2016), 173–174.
92. W. Travis Hanes III and Frank Sanello, *The Opium Wars: The Addiction of One Empire and the Corruption of Another* (Naperville, IL: Sourcebooks, 2002), 175–210; and Robert Bickers, *The Scramble for China: Foreign Devils in the Qing Empire, 1800–1914* (London: Allen Lane, 2011).
93. "Memorandum on the Kowloong Peninsula Question." TNA: Colonial Office, 129/79.

94. Eduardo Scarnichia and João da Silva Carvalho to Isidoro Francisco Guimarães. On board the *Amazona*, Kowloon Canal, June 18, 1855. AM: MO/AH/AC/SA/01/00089.
95. "Memorandum on the Kowloong Peninsula Question." TNA: Colonial Office, 129/79.
96. "Memorandum on the Kowloong Peninsula Question." TNA: Colonial Office, 129/79.
97. "Memorandum on the Kowloong Peninsula Question." TNA: Colonial Office, 129/79.
98. "Memorandum on the Kowloong Peninsula Question." TNA: Colonial Office, 129/79.
99. "Memorandum on the Kowloong Peninsula Question." TNA: Colonial Office, 129/79.
100. Hope to Robinson. Hong Kong, March 23, 1860. TNA: Colonial Office, 129/77.
101. Robinson to Hope. Government Offices, Victoria, Hong Kong, March 17, 1860. TNA: Colonial Office, 129/77.
102. Robinson to Hope. Government Offices, Victoria, Hong Kong, March 17, 1860. TNA: Colonial Office, 129/77.
103. Robinson to Hope. Government Offices, Victoria, Hong Kong, March 17, 1860. TNA: Colonial Office, 129/77.
104. Drummond Hay to the Earl of Clarendon. Tangier, April 2, 1856. TNA: Foreign Office, 99/74.
105. "Copy of Mr. Drummond Hay's Diary during His Cruize to the Reef Coast on Board H.M.S. Miranda." TNA: Foreign Office, 99/74.
106. "Copy of Mr. Drummond Hay's Diary during His Cruize to the Reef Coast on Board H.M.S. Miranda." TNA: Foreign Office, 99/74.
107. Drummond Hay to the Earl of Clarendon. Tangier, May 14, 1857. TNA: Foreign Office, 99/81.
108. Diana, *Un prisionero en el Riff*, 115; Serrallonga Urquidi, "La guerra de África," 151.
109. Urbiztondo to the President of the Council of State and Ministers. Manila, June 14, 1852. AHN: Ultramar, 5163/6.
110. Albi de la Cuesta, *Moros*, 412–419.
111. Norzagaray to the Minister of States and Overseas. Manila, May 30, 1857. AHN: Ultramar, 5172/10.
112. Norzagaray to the Minister of States and Overseas. Manila, May 30, 1857. AHN: Ultramar, 5172/10.
113. In this case, the supposed pirates had raided some plantations near the beach, stealing bananas and coconuts. The Spanish response was swift and overwhelming, sending some cañoneras after them and bombing them until nightfall, when they were finally able to escape. [José Velasco] to Marcelino de Oraá. Albay, December 13, 1841. NAP: Erección de Pueblos, 9, Albay (1841–1894).

114. "British and Dutch Expeditions against Pirates, 1859." AHN: Ultramar, 5174/6. See also Sirtjo Koolhof and Roger Tol, "The Delight of the Dutch Compagnie: On the Toloqna Musuq Boné by Daéng ri Aja," *Jambatan* 11, no. 3 (1993): 99–108.
115. G. Vogelpoot (Commander of the East Indies Maritime Forces and Marine Inspector) to Pahud. Batavia, January 9, 1861. NNA: Ministerie van Kolonien, 1814–1849. No. 4168.
116. Extract from the Register of Decrees of the Governor General of the Netherlands Indies. Batavia, March 25, 1861. NNA: Ministerie van Kolonien, 1814–1849. No. 4168.
117. Siedenburg to the Governor of the Celebes (Albert Jacques Frederic Jansen). Aboard Steamer *Gedeh*, Macassar Roads. February 6, 1861; and Willinck to the Commander of the Celebes Station (Siedenburg). On board Steamer *Reinier Claeszen*. Makassar Roads, December 26, 1860. NNA: Ministerie van Kolonien, 1814–1849. No. 4168.
118. J. A. de Moor, *Warmakers in the Archipelago: Dutch Expeditions in Nineteenth Century Indonesia* (London: Routledge, 2001), 59.
119. Cornets de Groot to the Resident at Riouw. [Batavia], March 16, 1837. NNA: Ministerie van Kolonien. 1841–1849. No. 4168.
120. Moor, *Warmakers*, 55.
121. Koolhof and Tol, "Delight of the Dutch Compagnie," 99.
122. M. T. H. Perelaer, *De Bonische Expeditiën. Krijgsgebeurtenissen op Celebes in 1859 en 1860* (Leiden: Gualth, Kolff, 1872), 72.
123. Koolhof and Tol, "Delight of the Dutch Compagnie," 102–103.
124. Koolhof and Tol, "Delight of the Dutch Compagnie," 106.
125. Hume to Messrs. Kerr, Fraser, Guthrie, and fifty other Merchants of Singapore. London, February 24, 1851. HCPP: Correspondence respecting Piracy on the Coast of Borneo, 1852.
126. Hume to Malmesbury. Bryanstone Square, June 22, 1852. HCPP: Correspondence respecting Piracy on the Coast of Borneo, 1852.
127. Miller to Hume. Melbourne, May 31, 1851. HCPP: Correspondence respecting Piracy on the Coast of Borneo, 1852.
128. Miller to Hume. Melbourne, May 31, 1851. HCPP: Correspondence respecting Piracy on the Coast of Borneo, 1852.
129. Miller to Hume. Melbourne, May 31, 1851. HCPP: Correspondence respecting Piracy on the Coast of Borneo, 1852.
130. V. Urban Vigors, "Sketches from Borneo," *Illustrated London News*, November 10, 1849, 312–314.
131. Brooke to Palmerston. Labuan, February 2, 1850. HCPP: Piracy (Borneo). Return to an Address of the Honourable the House of Commons, dated February 5, 1850; for "Copies of Extracts of any Despatches relating to the Suppression of Piracy off the Coast of Borneo."
132. Brooke to Palmerston. Labuan, February 2, 1850. HCPP: Piracy (Borneo). Return to an Address of the Honourable the House of Commons, dated February 5, 1850.

133. Palmerston to Brooke. Foreign Office, April 23, 1850. HCPP: Correspondence respecting Piracy in E. Archipelago, and Proceedings of Sir J. Brooke 1852.
134. Urbiztondo to the Secretary of State and Government. Manila, June 21, 1851. AHN: Ultramar, 5162/68.
135. Antonio Giménez to Urbiztondo. Culion, May 19, 1851. AHN: Ultramar, 5162/68.
136. Giménez to Urbiztondo. Culion, May 19, 1851. AHN: Ultramar, 5162/68.
137. Giménez to Urbiztondo. Culion, May 19, 1851. AHN: Ultramar, 5162/68.
138. Giménez to Urbiztondo. Culion, May 19, 1851. AHN: Ultramar, 5162/68.
139. Urbiztondo to the Secretary of State and Government. Manila, June 8, 1851. AHN: Ultramar, 5162/68.
140. Urbiztondo to the Secretary of State and Government. Manila, June 8, 1851. AHN: Ultramar, 5162/68.
141. Urbiztondo to the Secretary of State and Government. Manila, June 8, 1851. AHN: Ultramar, 5162/68.
142. Urbiztondo to the Secretary of State and Government. Manila, June 21, 1851. AHN: Ultramar, 5162/68.
143. Urbiztondo to the Secretary of State and Government. Manila, June 21, 1851. AHN: Ultramar, 5162/68.
144. Lemery to the Secretary of States and the Colonies. Manila, June 19, 1861. AHN: Ultramar, 5182/3.
145. Years later, in 1876, Malcampo was one of the main protagonists of a new attack again Joló, which also resulted in a bloodshed.
146. Salcedo to Lemery. Manila, June 19, 1861. AHN: Ultramar, 5182/3.
147. Salcedo to Lemery. Manila, June 19, 1861. AHN: Ultramar, 5182/3.
148. Salcedo to Lemery. Manila, June 19, 1861. AHN: Ultramar, 5182/3.
149. Salcedo to Lemery. Manila, June 19, 1861. AHN: Ultramar, 5182/3.
150. Salcedo to Lemery. Manila, June 19, 1861. AHN: Ultramar, 5182/3. See also a report of this event published in *El Panorama Universal. El Mundo Militar*, September 15, 1861, 294. For an engraving depicting the action see page 289.
151. Salcedo to Lemery. Manila, July 2, 1861. AHN: Ultramar, 5182/3.
152. Salcedo to Lemery. Manila, July 2, 1861. AHN: Ultramar, 5182/3.
153. Salcedo to Lemery. Manila, July 2, 1861. AHN: Ultramar, 5182/3.
154. Eusebio Lestrada to the Governor of the Philippines. Manila, August 24, 1861. NAP: Piratas, Leg. 4.
155. Lemery to the Governor of the Visayas. Manila, July 19, 1861. NAP: Piratas, Leg. 4.
156. Beresford, *Account of the Destruction*, 9.
157. "Chui-A-Poo, the Chinese Pirate," *Illustrated London News*, June 14, 1851, 548.

158. Private Illustrated Journal of Dr. E. H. Cree, vol. 12, 1849. October 1, 1849. NMM: CRJ/12.
159. "Chui-A-Poo, the Chinese Pirate."
160. "Chui-A-Poo, the Chinese Pirate."
161. Private Illustrated Journal of Dr. E. H. Cree, vol. 12, 1849. October 13, 1849. NMM: CRJ/12.
162. Dalrymple-Hay to Collier. HMS *Columbine*, Cochin China, October 23, 1849. TNA: Admiralty, 125/145.
163. Dalrymple-Hay to The Illustrious Ho, Governor General of Hainan and Eleven Provinces. HMS *Columbine*, off Hoi-How, October 25, 1849. TNA: Colonial Office, 129/30.
164. Dalrymple-Hay to Ho. HMS *Columbine*, off Hoi-How, October 25, 1849. TNA: Colonial Office, 129/30.
165. Cree also agreed with Dalrymple-Hay's calculation about the number of Chinese killed, which, in his opinion, amounted to 1,700. Private Illustrated Journal of Dr. E. H. Cree, vol. 12, 1849. October 21–23, 1849. NMM: CRJ/12.
166. William Mould to Edward Troubridge. HMS *Amazon*, Hong Kong. September 16, 1849. TNA: Colonial Office, 129/30.
167. James W. Morgan to William N. L. Lockyer. HMS *Hastings*, at Hong Kong, March 4, 1850. TNA: Admiralty, 125/145.
168. Lockyer to Morgan. HMS *Medea*, Mirs Bay, March 5, 1850. TNA: Admiralty, 125/145.
169. Lockyer to Morgan. HMS *Medea*, Mirs Bay, March 5, 1850. TNA: Admiralty, 125/145.
170. Arthur to Captain J. J. Cleverly. HMS *Nimrod*, Tanne Bay, December 16, 1860. TNA: Colonial Office, 129/78.
171. Arthur to Captain J. J. Cleverly. HMS *Nimrod*, Tanne Bay, December 16, 1860. TNA: Colonial Office, 129/78.
172. See, for example, the joint Franco-British expedition against a group of slave traders and pirates who had seized the British merchant ship *Grant* near the Balanta Coast in today's Guinea Bissau. C[laude] H. M. Buckle to Commodore A[rthur] Fanshawe. H.M. Steam Ship *Centaur*, 6 miles north of Kellets Island, Balantes Bay, December 13, 1849. West Sussex Record Office, Chichester (hereafter WSRO): Buckle Papers, MSS 2558.
173. Amy Van Natter, "The Mary Carver Affair: United States Foreign Policy and the Africa Squadron, 1841–1845" (PhD diss., City University of New York, 2010), 268–270.
174. Van Natter, "Mary Carver Affair," 216.
175. Van Natter, "Mary Carver Affair," 216.
176. Perry to Upshur. USS *Saratoga*, Porto Grande, Island of St. Vincent, September 23, 1843. Yale University, Beinecke Library Special Collections, New Haven (hereafter YUBL): African Squadron Letters. Vol. 5. 1843–1845.

177. Perry to Upshur. USS *Saratoga*, Porto Grande, Island of St. Vincent, September 23, 1843. YUBL: African Squadron Letters. Vol. 5. 1843–1845.
178. Van Natter, "Mary Carver Affair," 258.
179. Van Natter, "Mary Carver Affair," 258.
180. Eugene S. van Sickle, "Reluctant Imperialists: The U.S. Navy and Liberia, 1819–1845," *Journal of the Early Republic* 31, no. 1 (2011): 122.
181. Van Natter, "Mary Carver Affair," 303.
182. Van Natter, "Mary Carver Affair," 303.
183. Van Natter, "Mary Carver Affair," 306.
184. Van Natter, "Mary Carver Affair," 306.
185. Van Natter, "Mary Carver Affair," 306.
186. Jabez C. Rich "Commodore Perry's Expedition to the Coast of Africa," *Spirit of the Times*, June 21, 1845, 195–196.
187. Bridge, *Journal of an African Cruiser*, 83.
188. Perry to Upshur. USS *Saratoga*, Mesurado Roads, Monrovia, August 3, 1843. YUBL: African Squadron Letters. Vol. 5. 1843–1845.
189. Perry to Henshaw. US Frigate *Macedonian*, at sea off the West Coast of Africa, January 29, 1844. YUBL: African Squadron Letters. Vol. 5. 1843–1845.
190. Perry to Upshur. USS *Saratoga*, Porto Grande, Island of St. Vincent, September 5, 1843. YUBL: African Squadron Letters. Vol. 5. 1843–1845.
191. Perry to Upshur. USS Saratoga, Porto Grande, Island of St. Vincent, September 5, 1843. YUBL: African Squadron Letters. Vol. 5. 1843–1845.
192. *The Times*, December 22, 1849, 4.
193. Anita van Dissel, "Pioneering in Southeast Asia in the First Half of the Nineteenth Century," in Catia Antunes and Jos Gommans, eds., *Exploring the Dutch Empire: Agents, Networks and Institutions, 1600–2000* (London: Bloomsbury, 2015), 49.
194. Van Dissel, "Pioneering in Southeast Asia," 48–49.
195. Labouchère, *Brown Man's Burden.*

Chapter Five. Inter-imperial Cooperation and Conflict around the Suppression of Maritime Raiding

1. The Council of Government of the Province of Macau, Timor, and Solor to the Minister of State for the Navy and Overseas. Macau, August 27, 1849. AHU: ACL/SEMU/DGU, 005, Cx. 17.
2. Austin Coates, *A Macau Narrative* (Hong Kong: Hong Kong University Press, 2009), 122–125.
3. Xu to Bonham. [Canton], August 29, 1849. TNA: Foreign Office, 682/1982/37.

4. Xu to Bonham. [Canton], August 29, 1849. TNA: Foreign Office, 682/1982/37.
5. Jose Bernardo Goularte e Pereira, Joze Francisco de Oliveira, Thomas Jose de Freitas, and Manoel Pereira to the Ministro Secretario de Estado dos Negocios da Marinha e Ultramar. Macau, [Senate] Session of June 18, 1849. AHU: ACL/SEMU/DGU, 005, Cx. 17.
6. Amaral to the Secretario d'Estado dos Negocios da Marinha e Ultramar. Macau, February 27, 1847; and Amaral to the Ministro Secretario d'Estado dos Negocios da Marinha e Ultramar. April 21, 1847. AHU: ACL/SEMU/DGU, 005, Cx. 15.
7. See, for example Xu to Bonham. [Canton], August 12, 1849, describing such tripartite hydrarchic collaboration among the Chinese, the Portuguese, and the British. TNA: Foreign Office, 682/1982/31.
8. Carlos Augusto Montalto de Jesus, *Historic Macao* (Oxford: Oxford University Press, 1984), 347–348. For a report of the news in the French press, including the role of Forth-Rouen and the men of *La Bayonnaise*, see "Chine," *La Presse*, December 2, 1849, 2.
9. *O Patriota*, February 1, 1850, 1. There seems to be some semblance of truth in this fear. The Spanish certainly were interested and had internal discussions on the topic in late 1849 and early 1850. See Possible cesión portuguesa de Macao a España. AHN: Ultramar, 5166/34.
10. Silver to Clayton. Consulate of the United States of America, Macau, August 27, 1849. NARA: Despatches from U.S. Consuls in Macao, China, 1849–1869. Vol. 1: June 18, 1849–December 31, 1863.
11. Jozé Bernardo Goularte, Lourenço Pereira, Antonio Carlos Brandão, Thomas Jozé de Freitas, Jozé Francisco de Oliveira, and Manoel Pereira to the Minister of State for the Navy and Overseas. Macau, October 26, 1849. AHU: ACL/SEMU/DGU, 005, Cx. 17.
12. Xu to Bonham. Tan Kwang, September 17, 1849. TNA: Foreign Office, 682/1982/42.
13. Despatch from Seu (Xu) to the Council of Government of Macao. Tau Kwang, December 19, 1849. TNA: Foreign Office, 17/165. See also the confession of Chang-Asin, alias Chou-Asin, the surviving member of this group of three. TNA: Foreign Office, 17/165.
14. Xu to Bonham. Tan Kwang, October 11 and October 14, 1849. TNA: Foreign Office, 682/1982/46. See also Xu to Bonham. Tan Kwang, October 15, 1849. TNA: Colonial Office, 129/30.
15. Bonham to Palmerston. Victoria, Hong Kong, January 26, 1850. TNA: Foreign Office, 17/165.
16. Amirell, *Pirates of Empire*, 103–104.
17. Osborn, *My Journal in the Malayan Waters*, 184.
18. Vaillant to Napoleon III. Paris, June 16, 1854. In *Tableau de la situation des établissements Français dans l'Algerie, 1852–1854: Première Partie* (Paris: Imprimerie Impériale, 1856), 83.

19. Ruiz de Lanzarote to Norzagaray. Manila, September 1, 1858. AHN: Ultramar, 5200/21.
20. Ruiz de Lanzarote to Norzagaray. Manila, September 1, 1858. AHN: Ultramar, 5200/21.
21. "Cronique religieuse du mois." *L'observateur du Dimanche* 6, no. 59 (December 1858): 333.
22. "Cronique religieuse du mois." See also "L'Archipel des Philippines et la domination Espagnole," *Revue des deux* Mondes, 27 (Paris: Bureau de la Revue des deux Mondes, 1860), 927.
23. M. Yvan, "The French in the South Seas." In *Littell's The Living Age*, 2nd ser., 2 (July, August, September, 1853): 608.
24. Benton, *They Called It Peace*, 101.
25. García y Ruiz, "Memorias sobre Filipinas, 1859." BNE: Manuscritos, MSS 6316.
26. Cañete y Moral to Norzagaray. Macau, September 26, 1859. AHN: Ultramar, 438/3.
27. Cañete y Moral to Norzagaray. Macau, September 26, 1859. AHN: Ultramar, 438/3.
28. *The Times*, December 22, 1849, 4.
29. Bridges to Labouchère. 46 Piccadilly, London. March 28, 1856. TNA: Colonial Office, 129/61.
30. Levien, ed., *Cree Journals*. Entry for January 14, 1841, 72.
31. Bonham to Palmerston. Victoria, Hong Kong, November 21, 1849. TNA: Foreign Office, 12/159.
32. Bonham to Palmerston. Victoria, Hong Kong, November 21, 1849. TNA: Foreign Office, 12/159.
33. James F. Wardlaw to José Rodriguez Coello de Amaral (Governor of Macao). Amoy, May 25, 1865. AM: MO/AH/AC/SA/01/0002.
34. Wardlaw to Rodriguez Coello de Amaral. Amoy, May 25, 1865. AM: MO/AH/AC/SA/01/0002.
35. Pedder to the Colonial Secretary at Hong Kong. British Consulate, Amoy, May 26, 1865. TNA: Colonial Office, 129/106.
36. J. H. P. E. Kniphorst, "Historische schets van den Zeeroof in den Oost-Indischen Archipel–Middelen, ook aanverwante, ter bestrijding," *Tijdschrift voor Nederlandsch Indië* (1875–1881): 38.
37. Kniphorst, "Historische schets van den Zeeroof," 572.
38. D'Arlach, *Le Maroc in 1856*, 9.
39. On the American and French anti-slave trade West African fleets in the 1840s, see Leonardo Marques, *The United States and the Transatlantic Slave Trade to the Americas, 1776–*1867 (New Haven: Yale University Press, 2016), 137; and Barcia, *Yellow Demon of Fever*, 96–97.
40. Fanshawe to Claud Henry Mason Buckle. Centaur, Balantes Bay, December 11, 1849. WSRO: Buckle Papers, MSS 158.

41. Buckle to Fanshawe. H.M. Steam Ship *Centaur*, 6 miles north of Kellets Island, Balantes Bay, December 13, 1849. WSRO: Buckle Papers, MSS 158. See also HMS *Teazer* ship log, September 21, 1849–January 17, 1850. TNA: Admiralty, 53/1574; and HMS *Centaur* ship log, September 6, 1849–January 1, 1850. TNA: Admiralty, 53/3515.
42. Falla to Chapman. Gibraltar, January 18, 1829. GNA: Despatches from Gibraltar, 1829.
43. González Salmón to the Secretary of Marine. Palace, February 2, 1830. AGMAB: Corsos y Presas, 5246, no. 1656, folder 1.
44. González Salmón to the Secretary of Marine. Palace, December 23, 1828. AGMAB: Corsos y Presas, 5246, no. 1656, folder 1.
45. González Salmón to the Secretary of Marine. Palace, January 14, 1829. AGMAB: Corsos y Presas, 5246, no. 1656, folder 1.
46. González Salmón to the Secretary of Marine. Palace, January 14, 1829. AGMAB: Corsos y Presas, 5246, no. 1656, folder 1.
47. Raffles to Charles Lushington. Singapore, May 20, 1823. NAS: M. 2. Singapore: Letters from Bengal to the Resident. December 1823–March 1824.
48. Raffles to Lushington. Singapore, May 20, 1823. NAS: M. 2. Singapore: Letters from Bengal to the Resident. December 1823–March 1824.
49. Osborn, *My Journal in Malayan Waters*, 23.
50. "Trial of Tunkoo Mahomed Saad, Tunkoo Mahomed Snawee and Tunkoo Mahomed Taheb and Ten of Their Followers for Piracy; before the Court in Its Admiralty Jurisdiction Holden at Prince of Wales Island on Monday the 26th and Thursday the 29th of October, and Monday the 2d of November 1840." BL: IOR/F/4/1920.
51. "Trial of Tunkoo Mahomed Saad, Tunkoo Mahomed Snawee and Tunkoo Mahomed Taheb and Ten of Their Followers for Piracy; before the Court in Its Admiralty Jurisdiction Holden at Prince of Wales Island on Monday the 26th and Thursday the 29th of October, and Monday the 2d of November 1840." BL: IOR/F/4/1920.
52. Ibbetson to George Swinton. Prince of Wales Island, June 8, 1831. NAS: R. 1. Governor's Letters to Bengal. May 1831–August 1832.
53. Ibbetson to George Swinton. Prince of Wales Island, June 8, 1831. NAS: R. 1. Governor's Letters to Bengal. May 1831–August 1832.
54. Bonham to T. H. Maddock. Prince of Wales Island, February 27, 1841. NAS: R. 6. Governor's Letters to Bengal. January 1840–February 1841.
55. Rochussen to Urbiztondo. Batavia, April 22, 1851. AHN: Ultramar, 5167/13.
56. Rochussen to Urbiztondo. Batavia, April 22, 1851. AHN: Ultramar, 5167/13.
57. Osborn, *My Journal in the Malayan Waters*, 179.
58. Osborn, *My Journal in the Malayan Waters*, 179–180.

59. Silva Vieira to Jozé Pereira Pestana. Dili, Timor, October 3, 1845. AHU: ACL/SEMU/DGU, 005, Cx. 15. 1847.
60. Silva Vieira to Jozé Pereira Pestana. Dili, Timor, October 3, 1845. AHU: ACL/SEMU/DGU, 005, Cx. 15. 1847.
61. Silva Vieira to Jozé Gregorio Pegado. Lugar de Galvão, Timor, January 8, 1846. AHU: ACL/SEMU/DGU, 005, Cx. 15. 1847.
62. Louis Wei, "L'origine des rapports entre la Belgique et la Chine, 1842–1845," *Revue Belge de philologie et d'histoire* 37, no. 2 (1959): 394–407.
63. Snow to John Forsyth. Canton, May 22, 1839. NARA: Despatches from U.S. Consuls in Canton, China, 1790–1906. Volume 2 (May 13, 1839–December 22, 1849). See also E. W. Ellsworth, W. C. Hunter, J. L. Cranmer-Byng, and Lindsay T. Ride, "Journal of Occurrences at Canton: During the Cessation of Trade at Canton 1839," *Journal of the Hong Kong Branch of the Royal Asiatic Society* 4 (1964): 9–41.
64. Balestier to Forsyth. Consulate of the United States, Singapore, April 1, 1839. NARA: Despatches from U.S. Consuls in Singapore, Straits Settlements, 1833–1906. Volume 1 (October 31, 1833–December 4, 1846).
65. Ronald Spector, "The American Image of Southeast Asia, 1790–1865: A Preliminary Assessment," *Journal of Southeast Asian Studies* 3, no. 2 (1972): 299–305.
66. Perry to James C. Dobbin. On board English Mail Steamer *Hindoostan*, at sea, Indian Ocean, October 7, 1854. Perry, *Narrative of the Expedition of an American Squadron*, vol. 2, 196–197.
67. Mario E. Cosenza, ed., *The Complete Journals of Townsend Harris* (New York: Doubleday, Doran, 1930): 157.
68. C. Nathan Kwan, " 'Barbarian Ships Sail Freely about the Seas': Qing Reactions to the British Suppression of Piracy in South China, 1841–1856," *Asian Review of World Histories* 8 (2020): 84.
69. Pottinger to Parker. Government House, Hong Kong, March 8, 1843. TNA: Admiralty, 125/145.
70. Cochrane to Davis. HMS *Agincourt*, at Hong Kong, July 28, 1844. TNA: Admiralty, 125/145.
71. Davis to Keying. Victoria, Hong Kong, December 6, 1844. TNA: Colonial Office, 129/7.
72. Davis to Keying. Victoria, Hong Kong, December 6, 1844. TNA: Colonial Office, 129/7.
73. Keying to Davis. Taoukwang, December 30, 1844. TNA: Colonial Office, 129/7.
74. Keying to Davis. Taoukwang, December 30, 1844. TNA: Colonial Office, 129/7.
75. Davis to Cochrane. Government House, Victoria, January 25, 1845. TNA: Colonial Office, 129/7.
76. Davis to Cochrane. Government House, Victoria, January 25, 1845. TNA: Colonial Office, 129/7.

77. Cochrane to Davis. HMS *Agincourt*, at Hong Kong, January 27, 1845. TNA: Colonial Office, 129/7.
78. T. Wade to Bonham. Chinese Secretary's Office. February 19, 1852. TNA: Colonial Office, 129/39.
79. Jervois to the Duke of Newcastle. Victoria, Hong Kong, April 18, 1853. TNA: Colonial Office, 129/42.
80. Mercer to the Duke of Newcastle. Government Offices, Victoria, Hong Kong, August 8, 1861. TNA: Colonial Office, 129/82. For a recent assessment of the impact of the Treaty of Tientsin (Tianjin) on Sino-British relations, see Kwan, "Barbarian Ships," 99.
81. John Blight to Cleerens. Amboina, September 22, 1846. ANRI: K. 42. Ambon 1264.
82. HCPP: Paper relating to Piracies committed in Indian Archipelago, and the Measures Adopted by the Netherland Government, in the Years 1816 to 1845, for their Repression.
83. Norzagaray to Pahud. Manila, April 28, 1857. AHN: Ultramar, 5172/10.
84. Report by Julio de Tolosa. Manila, July 2, 1862. NAP: Piratas, Leg. 1.
85. Eduardo Carratalá to the [Captain General]. Manila, August 11, 1863. NAP: Piratas, Leg. 1.
86. John Prince to John Anderson. Batavia, November 24, 1827. BL: IOR/F/4/1282.
87. Fullerton to the Jang-de-per-hian of Siak. Singapore, February 7, 1828. BL: IOR/F/4/1282.
88. Vizconde del Pontón to the Minister of the Colonies. Palacio, March 30, 1866. AHN: Ultramar 5202/29.
89. Note by Bonham. Singapore, June 20, 1836. ANM: 2014/0012139. Appendix–to the secret proceedings of the Correspondence for the Suppression of Piracy. 1836.
90. Chads to [Thomas] Bladen. HMS *Andromache*, off Galang, June 29, 1836. BL: IOR/F/4/1724/69433.
91. Chads to Bladen. HMS *Andromache*, off Galang, June 29, 1836. BL: IOR/F/4/1724/69433.
92. Minute by Captain Chads, C.B. since leaving Mr. Bonham. HMS *Andromache*, at sea, October 4, 1836. BL: IOR/F/4/1724/69433.
93. Butterworth to H. M. Elliot. Singapore, June 1, 1848. NAS: R. 15. Governor's Letters to Bengal. January 1847–April 1851.
94. Butterworth to H. M. Elliot. Singapore, June 1, 1848. NAS: R. 15. Governor's Letters to Bengal. January 1847–April 1851.
95. Count Ludolf to Palmerston. London, June 9, 1838; and Ludolf to Palmerston. London, July 31, 1838. HCPP: Papers relative to Piracy in the Adriatic, 1840.
96. Palmerston to Ludolf. London, July 27, 1838. HCPP: Papers relative to Piracy in the Adriatic, 1840.
97. Béchameil to the Minister of the Navy. Orénoque, October 14, 1847. ANOM: Gouvernement Général de l'Algérie, Correspondence Politique Générale 1E, 215.

98. Bernaldez, *Reseña histórica*, 179.
99. Bernaldez, *Reseña histórica*, 180.
100. Clavería to the Secretary of State. Manila, August 6, 1849. NAP: Administración Civil. Leg. 1.
101. Marcaída to the Postmaster General. Manila, February 10, 1841. AHN: Ultramar, 5154/28.
102. Guizot to M. Théodose de Lagrené. Paris, November 9, 1843. In Montero y Vidal, *Historia de la piratería*, 383.
103. Guizot to M. Théodose de Lagrené. Paris, November 9, 1843. In Montero y Vidal, *Historia de la piratería*, 383.
104. H[enry] T[hoby] Prinsep to Bonham. Fort William, July 18, 1838; and Bonham to Prinsep. Singapore, July 2, 1838. BL: IOR/F/4/1841/77129.
105. Wood to Elgin. India Office, London, May 8, 1862. ANM: 2014/0010956.
106. Amirell, *Pirates of Empire*, 48.
107. Torrens to Prinsep. Simla, July 16, 1838. BL: IOR/F/4/1841/77129.
108. Pearn, "Erskine Murray's Fatal Adventure," 20–32.
109. Irwin, *Nineteenth-Century Borneo*, 153.
110. Pearn, "Erskine Murray's Fatal Adventure," 31–32.
111. Chads to Bonham. HMS *Andromache*, at sea, October 4, 1836. BL: IOR/F/4/1724/69433.
112. Note by Bonham. Singapore, June 20, 1836. ANM: 2014/0012139.
113. Balestier to Buchanan. Consulate of the US, Singapore, November 4, 1846. NARA: Despatches from U.S. Consuls in Singapore, Straits Settlements, 1833–1906. Volume 1 (October 31, 1833–December 4, 1846).
114. Manuel Crespo to the Secretary of State. Manila, September 3, 1856. AHN: Ultramar, 5167/27.
115. Manuel Crespo to the Secretary of State. Manila, September 3, 1856. AHN: Ultramar, 5167/27.
116. Urbiztondo to Rochussen. Cartier Général de Zamboanga, March 15, 1851. AHN: Ultramar, 5167/13.
117. Albertus Jacobus Duymaer van Twist to Manuel Crespo. Batavia, August 17, 1855. AHN: Ultramar, 5167/13.
118. The Secretary of State and Overseas to the Secretaries of War and the Navy. Madrid, January 17, 1856. AHN: Ultramar, 5167/13.
119. O'Donnell to Gravestins. Madrid, April 26, 1856. AHN: Ultramar, 5167/13.
120. O'Donnell to Gravestins. Madrid, April 26, 1856. AHN: Ultramar, 5167/13.
121. Norzagaray to the Council of Ministers, Secretary of War and Secretary of State and Overseas. Manila, November 23, 1858. AHN: Ultramar, 5200/22.

122. Coronel Bernardo Ruiz de Lanzarote (Jefe de las fuerzas espanolas expedicionarias a Cochinchina) to Fernando de Norzagaray. Manila, September 1, 1858. AHN: Ultramar, 5200/21.
123. Pottinger to Parker. Government House, Hong Kong, March 8, 1843. TNA: Admiralty, 125/145.
124. Davis to Lord Stanley. Government House, Victoria, Hong Kong, June 21, 1844. TNA: Colonial Office, 129/6.
125. Davis to Lord Aberdeen. Government House, Victoria, Hong Kong, July 5, 1844. TNA: Colonial Office, 129/6.
126. Davis to Aberdeen. Government House, Victoria, Hong Kong, July 5, 1844. TNA: Colonial Office, 129/6.
127. Davis to Keying. Victoria, Hong Kong, December 6, 1844. TNA: Colonial Office, 129/7.
128. Bonham to Lord Palmerston. Victoria, Hong Kong, October 23, 1849. TNA: Colonial Office, 129/30.
129. Bonham to Palmerston. Victoria, Hong Kong, October 23, 1849. TNA: Colonial Office, 129/30.
130. "Correspondance du Maroc," vol. 1, 503–504.
131. Drummond Hay to Clarendon. Tangier, April 27, 1856. TNA: Foreign Office, 99/74.
132. Drummond Hay to Clarendon. Tangier, July 22, 1856. TNA: Foreign Office, 99/81.
133. Drummond Hay to Clarendon. Tangier, July 22, 1856. TNA: Foreign Office, 99/81.
134. Drummond Hay to Lt. General James Ferguson. Tangier, May 30, 1856. TNA: Foreign Office, 99/74.
135. Drummond Hay to Lt. General James Ferguson. Tangier, May 30, 1856. TNA: Foreign Office, 99/74.
136. "L'Archipel des Philippines et la domination Espagnole," *Revue des deux Mondes* 27 (Paris: Bureau de la Revue des Deux Mondes, 1860), 927.
137. Todd, *Velvet Empire*, 19.
138. Chao Phraya Prayurawongse to Chao Phraya Yommarat and Chao Phraya SriPhipat. NLT: JS., 1201/1839.
139. Chao Phraya Prayurawongse to Chao Phraya Yommarat and Chao Phraya SriPhipat. NLT: JS., 1201/1839.
140. Benton, *They Called It Peace*, 13.

Conclusions

1. Antonio Vázquez de Aldana and Valentín González Serrano, *España en la Oceanía (Páginas de la Guerra de Joló)*. (Madrid: Botella y Molina, 1876), 86.
2. Méndez Núñez's report. Anchored in Rio Grande de Mindanao, in front of the cotta de Pagalungan, November 17, 1861. In Vázquez de Aldana and González Serrano, *España en la Oceanía*, 89–90.

3. Vázquez de Aldana and González Serrano, *España en la Oceanía*, 94.
4. Méndez Núñez's report, in *España en la Oceanía*, 90.
5. Vázquez de Aldana and González Serrano, *España en la Oceanía*, 96.
6. Vázquez de Aldana and González Serrano, *España en la Oceanía*, 82.
7. Benton, *They Called It Peace*, 3.
8. Priya Satia, *Empire of Guns*, chapter 6; and *Time's Monster: How History Makes History* (Cambridge, MA: Harvard University Press, 2020), 253.
9. Priyamvada Gopal, *Insurgent Empire: Anticolonial Resistance and British Dissent* (London: Verso, 2019), 60.
10. The most recent article on this topic is Michael Ehis Odijie, "Emancipation in the Gold Coast: The Abolitionist Views of James Hutton Brew," *Slavery & Abolition* 44, no. 1 (2023): 109–130. For some further nuanced views on the subject, see James Walvin, *Questioning Slavery* (London: Routledge, 1996) and Paula E. Dumas, *Proslavery Britain: Fighting for Slavery in an Era of Abolition* (London: Palgrave MacMillan, 2016).
11. Nathan Perl-Rosenthal, "Reading Cargoes: Letters and the Problem of Nationality in the Age of Privateering," in Lauren Benton and Nathan Perl-Rosenthal, eds., *A World at Sea: Maritime Practices and Global History* (Philadelphia: University of Pennsylvania Press, 2020), 78.
12. See, for example, the testimony of Jala Goa in 1838, a native of Balanguingui who confessed to the British of having only turned to piracy after his home in Balanguingui had been "destroyed by a force from Manila" when he was quite young. BL: IOR/F/4/1841/77129.
13. Rudyard Kipling, "The White Men's Burden," *McClure's Magazine* 12, no. 4 (February 1899): 291.
14. Lauren A. Benton, "Pirate Passages in Global History," in Stefan Eklöf Amirell, Hans Hägerdal, and Bruce Buchan, eds., *Piracy in World History* (Amsterdam: Amsterdam University Press, 2021), 279.
15. Benton, "Pirate Passages in Global History."
16. Drayton, "Where Does the World Historian Write From?"

Index